# CHICKEN SOUP FOR THE SINGLE PARENT'S SOUL

## Stories of Hope, Healing and Humor

Jack Canfield
Mark Victor Hansen
Laurie Hartman
Nancy Vogl

Health Communications, Inc.
Deerfield Beach, Florida

*www.hcibooks.com*
*www.chickensoup.com*

We would like to acknowledge the many publishers and individuals who granted us permission to reprint the cited material. (Note: The stories that are in the public domain or that were written by Jack Canfield, Mark Victor Hansen, Laurie Hartman or Nancy Vogl are not included in this listing.)

*Contagious.* Reprinted by permission of Marvin J. Wolf. ©1999 Marvin J. Wolf.

*Come Back Home.* Reprinted by permission of Linda Helen Puckett. ©2003 Linda Helen Puckett.

*A Family Christmas Carol.* Reprinted by permission of Michelle L. Anzelone. ©2001 Michelle L. Anzelone.

*Happy Returns.* Reprinted by permission of Jane Stewart Robertson. ©2002 Jane Stewart Robertson.

*One Cold Winter's Night.* Reprinted by permission of Karen J. Olson. ©2003 Karen J. Olson.

*(Continued on page 343)*

**Library of Congress Cataloging-in-Publication Data**

Chicken soup for the single parent's soul : stories of hope, healing, and humor / Jack Canfield . . . [et al.].
   p. cm.
   Includes bibliographical references.
   ISBN 0-7573-0241-6 (pbk.)
   1. Single parents—Religious life.   2. Parenting—Religious aspects—Christianity.   I. Canfield, Jack, 1944-

BV4438.7.C53 2005
649'.1'0243—dc22

2004062134

©2005 Jack Canfield and Mark Victor Hansen
ISBN 0-7573-0241-6 (trade paper)

Publisher: Health Communications, Inc.
       3201 S.W. 15th Street
       Deerfield Beach, FL 33442-8190

*Cover design by Larissa Hise Henoch*
*Inside formatting by Dawn Von Strolley Grove*

We lovingly dedicate this
book to single mothers and fathers
around the world, and their children.
You're not alone. . . .

# Contents

## 9. JOY AND GRATITUDE

# Acknowledgments

*Chicken Soup for the Single Parent's Soul* was a deeply grati-fying labor of love and a source of great joy for all of us as the book evolved. We are grateful to everyone who offered their support and encouragement and affirmed our belief in this worthy project.

To our friends and families, we couldn't have created this book without you—you have been chicken soup for our souls!

Jack's family: Inga, Travis, Riley, Christopher, Oran and Kyle, for all their love and support.

Mark's family: Patty, Elisabeth and Melanie Hansen, for once again sharing and lovingly supporting us in creating yet another book.

Connor Hartman, son extraordinaire, for your love, end-less support and wonderful sense of humor. Whenever I'm feeling blue, you come along with your big hugs and make everything all right again. I can't imagine life without you, bud. My loving sisters, Julie and Suzie, who I know will always be there, no matter what. My dear father and mother who, even though dealing with a debilitating health problem, have vowed to be the first to buy a copy of this book. Thanks, Mom and Dad. I love you dearly. To my ex-husband and my son's father, Derek Hartman, another single parent, heartfelt thanks for being a wonderful friend and an even better father. Connor and I know that we can always count on you.

With gratitude to my lovely daughters, Heidi Vogl, Monika and Lisa. Thank you for the privilege of being your mother and for hanging in there with me. Though times were often tough, we made it! To Michelle Lawson, my newest daughter, I love you as much as if I had given birth to you! To my grandsons, Tyler and Justin . . . you make my life utterly joyful. To my mother, Sally Randall, for never failing to offer her wisdom and praise; and my father, Don Randall, for teaching me the value of the written word. To my aunt, Patricia Stowell, for the grace she bestowed on me when I needed it most. To Gene Lambert, a wonderful grandpa to Tyler and Justin, for his continued support and guidance. To my dear friends, Larry Reeves and Paul Plamondon, for always being there when needed. And finally, to David Strange, who came along unexpectedly during the completion of this book and swept me off my feet. You've made me believe in love again and that all is possible! Thank you for blessing me with six more beautiful children and four more grandchildren: DeAnne, Dave, Lisa, Angela, Ashley, Cole, Chelsea, Breanna, Noah and Aidan . . . I love all of you.

Our publisher, Peter Vegso, for his vision and commitment to bringing *Chicken Soup for the Soul* to the world.

Patty Aubery and Russ Kalmaski, for being there on every step of the journey, with love, laughter and endless creativity.

Patty Hansen, for her thorough and competent handling of the legal and licensing aspects of the *Chicken Soup for the Soul* books. You are magnificent at the challenge! Thanks also, Patty, for your love and support throughout all the challenges of finishing this book—you were always there when we needed you and with just the right answers.

Veronica Romero, Teresa Esparza, Robin Yerian, Jody Emme, Debbie Lefever, Michelle Adams, Dee Dee Romanello, Shanna Vieyra, Lisa Williams, Brittany Shaw, Dena Jacobson, Tanya Jones and Mary McKay, who support Jack's and Mark's businesses with skill and love.

Gina Romanello, for all your help and support with permissions—a daunting task and one you make look so easy. Thanks, chica!

D'ette Corona for being there to answer any questions along the way.

Barbara Lomonaco, for nourishing us with truly wonderful stories and cartoons.

Nancy Autio, who was there from the beginning with love and endless help whenever we needed it. Houston, we no longer have a problem, thanks to you.

Lisa Drucker, for editing the final manuscript. As always, you are a pleasure to work with.

Bret Witter, Elisabeth Rinaldi, Allison Janse and Kathy Grant, our editors at Health Communications, Inc., for their devotion to excellence.

Terry Burke, Tom Sand, Irena Xanthos, Lori Golden, Kelly Johnson Maragni, Karen Bailiff Ornstein, Randee Feldman, Patricia McConnell, Kim Weiss, Maria Dinoia, Paola Fernandez-Rana, the marketing, sales and PR departments at Health Communications, Inc., for doing such an incredible job supporting our books.

Tom Sand, Claude Choquette and Luc Jutras, who manage year after year to get our books transferred into thirty-six languages around the world.

The Art Department at Health Communications, Inc., for their talent, creativity and unrelenting patience in producing book covers and inside designs that capture the essence of *Chicken Soup:* Larissa Hise Henoch, Lawna Patterson Oldfield, Andrea Perrine Brower, Anthony Clausi and Dawn Von Strolley Grove.

All the *Chicken Soup for the Soul* coauthors, who make it so much of a joy to be part of this *Chicken Soup* family.

Our glorious panel of readers who helped us make the final selections and made invaluable suggestions on how to improve the book: Dale Bendsak, Adam Boyle, Kandace Chapple, Don Chartier, Heidi Vogl Cole, Bobbe Cook, Tracy Cool, Christine Crowley, Cathy Cunningham, Lori Elliott, Kathy Ferguson, Dawn Hagerty, Derek Hartman, Steven Holl, Christine Kurtz, Gene Lambert, Michelle Lawson, Angela Lemieux, Linda Lingaur, Diane Lundin, Claudia McBath, Colleen Moulton, Lori O'Leary, Paul Plamondon, Patrice Popp, Kelly Powell, Sally Randall, Summer Rawlings, Larry Reeves, Joanna Rens, Vicki Rogers, Gina Romanello, David Rose, Brandi Ruediger, Anthony Ryan, Jerry Schy, Lois Sloane, Patricia Stowell, Brenda Thompson, Carla Thurber, Amy Wick and Kerry Winkler.

And, most of all, everyone who submitted their heartfelt stories, poems, quotes and cartoons for possible inclusion in this book. While we were not able to use everything you sent in, we know that each word came from a magical place flourishing within your soul. May the spirit of nature carry you gently toward peace!

Because of the size of this project, we may have left out the names of some people who contributed along the way. If so, we are sorry, but please know that we really do appreciate you very much.

We are truly grateful and love you all!

# Introduction

If you are reading this book, chances are you are a single parent, or you were one . . . or perhaps you grew up in a single-parent family. Amazingly, you are far from alone. With nearly one-third of all American households being single-parent families, there are tens of millions of people affected by single parenting. And the numbers are growing, especially with single-parent fathers. Roughly one-fourth of all single-parent families are now headed up by a single dad.

At some point, society will no longer be able to refer to the two-parent family with children as "traditional."

Single parents are a special breed. We may not always start out this way, but most of us find an uncommon strength and tenacity to survive and thrive. Why? Simply because we have to. We have no choice! We have bills to pay, children to care for, obligations to meet, work schedules and double the household responsibilities. The daily tasks sometimes seem endless, with little time left over for ourselves.

Yet, there is a level of pride we feel because of our role as single parents. Maybe you never would have fixed that leaky sink if you were in a two-parent family. Maybe you never thought you could drive that long-distance trip by yourself with your children. Maybe you managed to purchase that house or open up that business. Maybe you've done lots of things you never knew you could do, but had to because there was no one else to help. You're doing it, and somehow, you're making it.

This book is filled with stories of similar triumphs and challenges from people just like you. Some are sweet and endearing. Others will surely make you shed a tear. Many will make you smile or laugh. And all are uplifting—offering hope, comfort and inspiration. We all have different stories to tell, but we believe you will find a common thread woven throughout this book that other types of families simply won't be able to relate to. But you will.

We are thrilled to share a book that is so close to our hearts. We hope it will resonate with you, too. A wise woman once said that, "As single parents you carry much of the burden, but you also get the majority of the joy." Our wish for you is that *Chicken Soup for the Single Parent's Soul* will bring you a little bit of joy, too.

# Share with Us

We would like to invite you to send us stories you would like to see published in future editions of *Chicken Soup for the Soul.*

We would also love to hear your reactions to the stories in this book. Please let us know what your favorite stories are and how they affected you.

Please send submissions to:

*Chicken Soup for the Soul*
P.O. Box 30880
Santa Barbara, CA 93130
fax: 805-563-2945

You can also visit the *Chicken Soup for the Soul* site at:

*www.chickensoup.com*

We hope you enjoy reading this book as much as we enjoyed compiling, editing and writing it.

# $\overline{\underline{1}}$

# YOU ARE NOT ALONE

*We are never alone.*
*We are all aspects of one great being.*
*No matter how far apart we are, the air*
*links us.*

*Yoko Ono*

# Contagious

*One can never pay in gratitude; one can only pay "in kind" somewhere else in life.*

Anne Morrow Lindbergh

The phone rang, and I clicked off the TV sound, wondering who could be calling so late on a Sunday night.

"It's your favorite daughter," said the voice in my ear.

This is our private joke; Laura is my only child.

"Busy, Pops?"

"Watching a rerun," I replied. "It'll be over soon."

"Should I call back?"

"I know how it turns out. Something wrong, kiddo?" I asked.

"Everything's fine. Pops, I want to ask you something."

"Go ahead."

"When I was fourteen, fifteen, sixteen—was I *really* a lot of trouble? A big jerk?"

I suppressed a sigh. Laura came into my life when she was a year old. When she was five, my wife and I divorced, and Laura moved to another state with her mother. At thirteen, however, she returned to live with me and stayed past her twenty-fifth birthday, when she took her own apartment. This is all of a mile away—close enough to check the efficiency of my clothes washer or to sample my leftovers, privileges she invoked frequently . . . and still does.

"Big jerk doesn't begin to cover it," I replied, expecting a laugh, then thinking through her silence. Even before the divorce, I'd wanted to tell my daughter that she was adopted, but my ex-wife, wary about this, had put me off, and I didn't feel right doing it unilaterally. Then, during an ugly mother-daughter argument, it had slipped out. From then on, relations between them grew tense; if her mother rebuked her, Laura countered, "You're not even my real mom!" One day she phoned, begging to move in with me.

Become a father again? After so many years alone? What would this do to my lifestyle? My privacy? Could I afford to support a teenager? How would I find time to do all the things that good parents do for their kids? At first, I found even the idea overwhelming. Then I started to think. Had I become her father in the usual way, even accidentally, I would be bound to parenthood for life. Instead, I had gone to great lengths to adopt her. I'd sworn an oath to two governments to support her, to *parent* her. When I began to think of it that way, my duty was clear: I had made a commitment even stronger than that of a natural father.

"You were quite a stinker," I said. "A few times, I almost wanted to throttle you."

Laura tested me from the moment I picked her up at the airport. She arrived in white pancake makeup with black lipstick and nail polish. Out of my sight, she smoked cigarettes, drank beer, ditched school and hung out with a mangy flock of ill-mannered delinquents, some of whom abused drugs. She secretly dated a twenty-something until his arrest for burglary, then ran up huge phone bills accepting his collect calls from jail. Tossed out of high school, she enrolled in continuation school, but didn't mend her ways. After ditching whole days, she was soon down to her last warning: the next step was an institution with barred windows—reform school.

"You mean the time I disappeared?" she asked.

"Among others." One day Laura hadn't returned from school. I phoned her friends, cruised the neighborhood, checked with hospitals and finally called the police. After two sleepless nights, she turned up at six in the morning, refusing to say where she'd been, or even to discuss the matter. "I want to go to sleep," was all she said. I lost it. For the first and only time, I hit her. Then, realizing that I was wrong, I apologized.

"How did you ever put up with me?" she asked now.

I hadn't thought about this in years. After I notified the police that my daughter had returned safely, a pair of detectives came to interview her. I think this was Laura's first inkling of how much her disappearance had frightened me, of how much I cared.

"Because no matter how badly you behaved," I said now, "you're my daughter. I didn't bring you into the world, but I *chose* to take responsibility for your upbringing. So even when you make me mad as hell, I love you. That's what parents *do*. They love their children."

"Did I ever thank you for that?" she asked, and I heard her voice catch.

After her disappearance, I made some changes. We went house hunting in a city fifty miles away, and bought the home that Laura preferred; she understood that this was to be *our* house. She enrolled in a school where only the guidance counselor knew of her previous difficulties. I changed professions, from photographer to writer, so that I no longer traveled. Little by little, almost miraculously,

Laura pulled herself together. She made up her failed classes and was elected to the student council during her senior year.

"You thanked me by earning a high-school diploma," I replied.

"That's not enough," she said. "Thank you, Pops. Thank you for loving me unconditionally. Thank you for my life."

I felt my eyes grow moist. "What brought this on?" I asked, and learned that one of her coworkers, a single mom struggling to raise a seventeen-year-old, "gave up on her."

"What do you mean, *gave up*?" I asked.

"Kicked her out of the house," explained Laura.

"That's pretty drastic," I said.

"My friend comes to work every day crying over her daughter."

"Do you want me to talk to her?" I asked.

"Better if *I* do it," replied my daughter.

After a few days, that conversation began to fade. Then, one morning, I returned from shopping to find Laura doing her laundry. We went out to lunch, and while waiting for a table, I wondered aloud about her friend's daughter.

"I fibbed to you," said Laura. "I was really talking about Mom and my sister."

Laura's sister is my ex-wife's daughter from another marriage.

"What's going on?"

"She's moving in with me," she said. "She needs another chance, and I'm going to give it to her. Will you help me with the paperwork to get her enrolled in school?"

"Of course. But that's a big responsibility you're taking on," I replied. "It's going to really change your lifestyle. And can you afford to feed her, buy her clothes?"

"I know all the problems," she said. "But if you love someone, and they're in trouble, you do whatever it takes to save them. You taught me that."

Funny thing about this love stuff: It's contagious.

*Marvin J. Wolf*

"What do you say we give their father sole custody?"

# Come Back Home

*All of us, at certain moments of our lives, need to take advice and receive help from other people.*

Alexis Carrel

Finally, I had to admit to myself that I wasn't making it on my own as a single parent with a four-year-old son and a thirteen-month-old daughter. Reluctantly, I had written my parents asking if I could move in with them until I could find a teaching position and manage on my own. I knew it would not be an easy decision for them to make. Living in a small town, my mother had always worried about "what people would think."

Her response came more quickly than I had expected. As I held her unopened letter, I wondered if the rapid reply was good news or bad. With careful concern, I tore open the end of the envelope. Her typewritten letter was folded in the formal standard she had learned as a secretary after graduating from high school. It read:

*Dear Linda,*

*You must quit beating up on yourself and feeling so ashamed over needing to move back home with the children because of your divorce. I want you to know that you are not the first woman in our family to be a single parent and fall on hard times. I hope you will find courage and take pride in the woman I am going to tell you about.*

*Your great-great-grandmother, Hannah Lappin, headed west in a prairie schooner with her farmer husband and three small children: a boy, six; a girl, two, and an infant son. They settled in a secluded section of Missouri. After five years of her husband's tremendous effort clearing timber, rumors circulated that land, including their claim, was in litigation. Days of anxiety followed, and her husband's health began to fail. He was diagnosed with tuberculosis, and his strength diminished steadily. They lost their farm. They made the difficult decision to make the four-hundred-mile trip back to southern Illinois to her family. There was nothing about this trip that held any attraction for a woman with three children and an invalid husband in the early spring of 1876. On many days, he was too sick to travel. At night, he would sleep outside under the wagon. Inevitably he died, and left his family among strangers in the hill country of Missouri.*

*He was buried along the trail under a pile of stones. Their eleven-year-old son took the reins of the wagon and skillfully drove the team through the ten-mile-wide city of St. Louis and across the big river, still a hundred miles from their family.*

*Hannah's problems were further complicated by her failing eyesight and the awareness that she was several months pregnant. Shortly after arriving at her Uncle David's home, she gave birth to twin boys. Refusing charity from the state, she took in washing. Making light of her blindness, she promised people, "The stains may still be in the clothes, but I will get the stink out." Her great poverty and lack of comfort was felt by her orphaned children, but it was no match for her unwavering faith in God and her ability to give thanks in all things. The three youngest sons became ministers. The oldest son returned to the West to build railroads across Kansas to Denver. Ida, her daughter, after ten years of wedded life, was left a widow with four small children. The example of her mother's faith and determination inspired her, knowing her mother's burden had been a hundred times heavier.*

*Linda, did you not realize that World War II made me a single parent while Daddy was overseas for two years? I had to go back to live with my parents on their farm, miles from town and friends. But it was such a blessing in disguise because Grandma was willing to rock you when you had constant earaches, and I was able to help her with her household chores. Your daddy sent us ration books, so I could get sugar and shoes and gasoline to supplement my folks' needs.*

*Now that you understand that you were not the first woman in our family to be a single parent, please come back home knowing that your parents, grandparents, aunts, uncles, sisters and cousins are here to be family for you. With the rich heritage of women who have found a way to give their children a wonderful future, in spite of hardships, you will be in very good company.*

*Come back home as soon as possible.*

*Love always,*
*Mother*

*Linda H. Puckett*

# A Family Christmas Carol

*We all live with the objective of being happy; our lives are all different and yet the same.*

Anne Frank

It had been snowing since two o'clock that afternoon, and the transmission on my car had been locked into "sled" since I had pulled out of the office parking lot. Time was slipping away, and as I watched the giant flakes tumble out of the sky onto my windshield, I really began to wonder if I was going to make it on time. Of course I would make it. There was no option.

For weeks now, all my daughter, Alexandra, had talked about was the Christmas concert and the usual third-grade scuttlebutt that surrounded it. "Mom, Rachel was supposed to do a solo, but guess what? She's not! Lindsay gets to do it instead." "Mom, I get to stand next to Tyler for the whole concert!" "Mom, you won't believe it, but Lexie's whole family is coming to the concert, even from another state!" This last comment was the one she dwelled on most—making a pilgrimage all the way from out of state to see third-graders sing Christmas carols was a pretty big deal. (It had to have been, to eclipse the excitement of standing next to Tyler.)

As I sat in traffic I thought about all the school events I had attended—alone. Alexandra never mentioned it, but I wondered how she felt about me being the only one who ever came to her events. My own family lived out of town, and her father and his family never quite managed to fit those things into their schedules. I wondered if it bothered her.

The concert was scheduled to begin at seven o'clock sharp. With only a minute to spare, I found myself running: first, through the snow-drifted parking lot, then through the school corridor, with my wet scarf flapping behind me. I entered the crowded auditorium and spied a lone seat near the front. From her place onstage, Alexandra saw me dash for the chair, and she smiled. I was close enough to hear the loud, prepageant chatter of the children onstage.

"Look, Alexandra, there is my aunt and my cousin. They came all the way from West Virginia. I can't believe my whole family is here!"

Alex smiled at Lexie and said, "My whole family is here, too! Look, there she is!" Alex gave me a big smile and an enthusiastic wave. I waved back at her, never once noticing the melting snow dripping off my head.

*Michelle Anzelone*

# Divine Order

*God grant me the serenity to accept the things I cannot change, the courage to change the things I can, and the wisdom to know the difference.*
Reinhold Niebuhr

I answered the phone at my office. It was my oldest daughter, Heidi. "Mom, can you meet me at Barbara's this afternoon?"

Barbara was a counselor my girls and I had seen periodically over the years, often to deal with our individual issues over the conflicts between their father and me—we had divorced years earlier. So when Heidi requested a visit to Barbara's office, I didn't think anything of it.

When I arrived, Heidi was already seated on the couch. Barbara sat in her chair opposite Heidi, and I parked myself in a chair next to the couch.

Barbara delved right in and asked Heidi, "Why are we here today?"

I looked over at Heidi. Her face reddened, she choked up and a single tear glided down her cheek. "I have something to tell my mother, and I'm too afraid to do it alone."

In that instant, I knew. I was about to hear the one thing many parents fear when raising a teenage daughter. I slid next to her on the couch, and asked, "Are you pregnant?"

Heidi was born on New Year's Eve, the only baby girl in the nursery. She was a born performer and loved to sing, dance and act—anything that involved entertaining. A personable, beautiful girl, she had many friends growing up, excelled in her classes and had big dreams of becoming an actress.

As she approached her seventeenth year, Heidi started skipping school, abandoned the friends she had and began to hang around a crowd of kids I didn't approve of. My bright and charming little girl became distant, depressed and unmotivated. I became distraught over this sudden change, and found it increasingly difficult to deal with. As a single mother, it was hard enough raising three beautiful daughters, but this new phase of Heidi's life proved more than challenging. When a new boy showed up in her life, I sensed trouble. And when I sat in the counselor's office that afternoon, I knew I had milliseconds to say and do the right thing to get my daughter back.

Heidi burst into tears, nodding yes when I asked her if she was pregnant. Putting my arm around her, I looked her square in the eyes and pronounced, "I'll do whatever you need me to do . . . that's what I'm here for."

Since Heidi was only nineteen years old, we mutually agreed it might be best to put the baby up for adoption, so he could be raised by two loving parents. It was a tough decision, but it seemed right at the time.

A thousand miles away, a lovely couple wanted to adopt Heidi's unborn baby boy. In Heidi's seventh month, she moved to be near the adoptive family. My heart was torn apart over losing my first grandchild and my daughter being so far away.

Weeks later, after a doctor's appointment, Heidi called to say she could go into labor at any time and wanted me with her. I hopped on a plane, and the next day met the adoptive family. They seemed very nice, and their little girl was darling. Yet something seemed amiss. I couldn't put my finger on it, but an uneasiness washed over me after meeting them.

The next morning, the phone rang. Heidi answered it; suddenly, all the color drained from her face. She hung up and flung herself on the bed, uncontrollable sobs drenching the long strands of hair that covered her face.

In the final hour, the adoptive family had backed out. Perhaps they sensed my breaking heart, and felt I might interfere with their rights as parents. Perhaps they were overwhelmed with taking on another child. We will never know the reason.

Brushing the hair away from her face, I asked Heidi what she wanted to do. Through long, drawn-out tears, Heidi said, "Mom, I never really wanted to give up my baby. I love him. But I can't afford to keep him!"

Sometimes, life has an amazing way of restoring divine order. Suddenly, all the times I toiled to keep a roof over my little family's head, make sure the bills were paid and still provide things like camp, dance lessons and birthday parties . . . all the struggle of raising my girls alone seemed inconsequential to what really mattered: love. Simple as that. And I knew right then and there that this new turn of events was meant to be.

Putting my hands on my hips, I firmly stated, "Heidi, I raised you and your two sisters on practically nothing. We made it, and so will you. Get your butt off that bed! We're going out to buy some baby clothes!"

Heidi has proven to be a wonderful mother. She went back to school and is now pursuing an acting career. Tyler, the absolute light of my life, is adored by his aunts and loved by our many friends. He has brought more blessings to us than we ever could have imagined. He is bright, fun and funny—a born performer, just like his mother.

He is oh so wise, too. One day, when he was about four, I was having a particularly tough afternoon. Tyler walked into my office, glanced up at me and said, "What's wrong, Grandma?"

I replied, "Grandma is a little sad today, honey. I wish I were happier."

Just like the day I slid next to his mother in the counselor's office, trying to find the right words to say, Tyler put his arms around me, looked me square in the eyes and pronounced, "Well, that's what I'm here for!"

*Nancy Vogl*

# Happy Returns

*Each day offers us the gift of being a special occasion if we can simply learn that as well as giving, it is blessed to receive with grace and a grateful heart.*

Sarah Ban Breathnach

"Happy birthday, Jane!"

Inwardly, I groaned. Couldn't our too-efficient receptionist have forgotten to consult her calendar just this once?

"Thanks, Carol." I tried to inject enthusiasm into my tone as I zoomed into my office. The less said about this momentous occasion, the better.

However, by leaning forward at her desk, Carol could look through the open doorway right toward my desk. She did this, beaming a huge smile at me. "Lordy, lordy, look who's forty! Planning a big celebration tonight?"

"Nah. Just family."

My mother would probably bring over a cake, and my sole hope for the day was that it would be her heavenly chocolate, full of fruit and nuts and spices. My daughter,

Kathy, had the night off from the movie theater where she worked part-time—"shoveling popcorn," as she put it—and my son, Stewart, would have finished his paper route long before I got home. We would sit down together to something quick and simple, maybe the tacos the kids liked. No romantic candlelit dinners for this birthday girl.

Carol's smile widened, if that was possible. "It's nice with just family."

Faker that I was, I agreed. Then I grabbed my coffee mug and scurried off. Unfortunately, to get to the kitchen, I had to pass through the art department. One of the designers looked up and chortled, "Over the hill now, huh, Jane?"

"Rub it in, Bill," I grumbled. Still on the sunny side of thirty, Bill just grinned.

Another designer, Dottie, was a little more perceptive, and with good reason. At about forty-five, she was even more shopworn than I was.

"You know what the French say, don't you?" She peered up at me slyly through her auburn bangs. "They don't think a woman is even worth noticing till she's forty."

I grimaced. "I don't know any Frenchmen."

She just gave me a throaty chuckle and went back to her work. I filled my coffee mug and skulked back to my office. My desk was turned so that my back was to the raw January day outside, but I seemed more than capable of making my own gloom.

Bill was right; I was over the hill. And I hadn't exactly reached much of a pinnacle on the way, either. As I slurped coffee, I summarized in my head: I had achieved no real career, just a low-paying job as a small-time copywriter. I had salted away no savings. I had provided my children with none of the things they assured me all their friends had: VCR, microwave, answering machine, vacations. Worst of all, for one who had spent her childhood playing Cinderella, I had failed—both in my marriage and during the three years since it had ended—to find true love.

Even so, the minutes were ticking away, as quickly as they had for four decades, and the billing sheet in front of me was waiting for entries. So I applied myself to the task of writing a brochure for seed corn.

Seated as I was just five or six feet from the receptionist's desk, I had learned to tune out the opening of the front door, especially when I was under such enchantment as "yield per acre." Therefore, I was a little startled when I heard an unfamiliar voice speak my name in a questioning tone.

I looked up. "Yes?" A man was standing in my doorway holding some sort of huge, shapeless mass covered in tissue paper.

"Flowers for you."

He stepped forward, deposited what he claimed to be flowers on the corner of my desk and disappeared.

Carol took his place in the doorway and demanded, "Did somebody send you flowers?"

"I guess so," I replied, dazed.

"Some secret admirer you forgot to tell me about?"

I tried a shaky laugh. "I doubt that."

"Well, aren't you going to look at them?"

"Well . . . yeah." As I ripped away the tissue, I wondered if Carol could possibly be right. Had I somehow impressed one of the few men who had taken me out? My rational side butted in to remind me that wasn't likely. Maybe the people in the office or a kind client had taken pity on me.

The bouquet that emerged from the tissue paper was an enormous sheaf of spring flowers: irises, daisies, carnations—quite a contrast with the scene outside my window. I was stunned.

"Well, see who they're from," practical Carol ordered.

I fumbled for the card. The tiny envelope bore my name in the unfamiliar handwriting of someone at a florist shop. I pulled out the card.

"Dear Mom." I smiled as I recognized the self-conscious, curlicue letters I had watched develop for a dozen years. "Today, life begins—right? Love, Me."

My eyes stung. Of course. Who else could it have been but Kathy? Kathy, who had lent me her favorite top because she thought I had nothing suitable to wear to a party. Who had once found me sitting alone in the dark and whispered, "Mom, what's wrong?" Who had offered to split weekend nights out with me so someone would always be home with Stewart.

I reached out and started touching petals. Each festive pastel made a memory spring forth, and I thought with tender dismay that my hardworking daughter could ill afford such an extravagant gesture.

Dottie appeared next to Carol. "Oooh, flowers! Who from?"

I blinked against my tears and said proudly, "My daughter."

"Aaaw," Carol cooed. "That's so sweet."

I could tell it was more of an effort for Dottie. "That's very nice."

My only answer was the radiant smile a woman is supposed to wear on her birthday. I just couldn't hide the fact that I had found true love.

*Jane Robertson*

"I'd like to get married again, but I'm afraid
I won't be able to get the 'Single Parent and Proud of It'
bumper stickers off my car."

# One Cold Winter's Night

*The healthy and strong individual is the one who asks for help when he needs it, whether he's got an abscess on his knee or in his soul.*

Rona Barrett

My son Ryan wanted a dog—desperately. He was a preschooler and had just lost his favorite person in the world, his grandpa. I wanted to say no. I was a single parent working full-time. Ryan had special needs. When did I have time for a dog?

Nonetheless, I called the Humane Society and described our lifestyle and Ryan's disabilities to the woman on the other end of the line. She told me that all their puppies had been adopted but a mother dog was available. The woman insisted that Ginger was just what we needed. The dog was half border collie and half sheltie. I went down to the shelter, paid my twenty-five dollars, signed a document that said we would have her spayed and left with our new dog.

Immediately, Ginger became Ryan's best friend and protector. She slept in his room at the foot of his bed.

Oftentimes, I would find them sleeping together, heads side by side on the pillow, bodies under the colorful quilt. Ryan held her ears with one hand as he sucked the thumb on his other. He told her stories, gave her supporting roles in plays where he was the hero and dressed her in capes and hats. When he was learning to latch the hook on her leash, a task difficult for his hands affected by cerebral palsy, it could sometimes take five to ten minutes. She sat through it all, calmly and patiently, waiting for him to get it right. She looked mournful when he was upset, and consoled him by letting him bury his little face in her fur and cry when other children wouldn't play with him. She knew what her job was, and she made it her vocation. She never abandoned him.

She was a teacher for Ryan and a respite provider for me. When Ryan played with Ginger I knew he was relatively safe—after all, she had bloodlines from two major herding breeds. If Ryan tried to leave the house on his own, Ginger sat in front of the door and yipped to alert me. If Ryan jumped on the bed she "rode" on the bed, too. She taught him laughter, friendship and silliness. She taught him loyalty and trust.

One winter, I came down with a severe case of strep throat. My symptoms had gotten progressively worse, until one evening, my fever had risen so high, I was truly a little out of my head. I wanted to go to the hospital emergency room, but it was twenty degrees below zero outside. My car was old. I didn't want to take a chance that it would break down, exposing Ryan or me to those temperatures for even a short amount of time. Everyone I knew was out of town, busy or had small children of their own. I decided to "tough it out" until my appointment at the clinic the following day.

Ginger must have kept Ryan busy most of the evening while I faded in and out. I don't even remember giving him dinner. I know he ate because I found cookie crumbs, chips and cheese slice wrappers on the kitchen counter the next day. I had set the oven timer to ring every hour that evening, so that if I did doze off I could wake up and check on Ryan. But the oven timer wasn't waking me up; the dog was. Every time I dozed off, Ginger barked or pulled at me to wake me. She sat with Ryan, eyeing me anxiously. The third time I went to set the oven timer, I gave up on it. I looked at Ginger, and I swear we had a telepathic moment. I knew that she would continue waking me and keep an eye on Ryan as sure as I knew that my eyes are brown. This knowledge flooded me with relief.

About ten o'clock that night, after Ryan was in bed, his "blankie" in one hand and Ginger's fur in the other, I had a moment of lucidity and realized that I had not taken the dog out since seven o'clock that morning. I motioned for her to go out and she came to the door, looking at me dubiously. I slipped my arms into my coat, hooked up her leash and led her out. As we reached the stairs on the deck, she whined and turned to go back into the house, all the while watching me.

With a wind chill factor of thirty-five degrees below zero, what dog wouldn't whine? I think she might have saved my life that night because I am not sure that I would have made it back into the house. I remember feeling suddenly very confused and wondering what I was doing outside. I do not remember going back into the house; I believe she herded me back inside. That night, she slept in the hall between the bedrooms instead of her usual spot on Ryan's bed.

The next morning when I woke, I was still sick, but my fever had abated. My son was still sleeping. I went to fill Ginger's food dish and water bowl. I stared at them in amazement. Both dishes were full. She had not eaten or drank anything the day before. Ryan knew that he was not supposed to give her table food, so I doubt if she had even snacked with him. All I know for sure was that my baby was safe because a little brown dog named Ginger had kept him safe, and had kept me from harm.

After I went to the doctor, got my antibiotics and started to feel better, I cooked Ginger a hamburger—a great big one with gravy, changing the table-food rule a bit!

The whole experience taught me a valuable lesson. I had been so busy trying to be supermom that I had inadvertently isolated myself. In a time of crisis, I found myself with a limited number of people I could count on for help. I needed to get out more and allow myself to be a person, not just Ryan's mom. I needed to meet more single parents and more parents of disabled children so that I would have more support and resources when I needed them. I joined parent support groups and reestablished contacts with friends. I made new friends who were in similar situations. I reduced my work hours and still managed to pay the bills. My life became more balanced than it had been. We were happier.

Ginger is no longer with us, but each year we hang an ornament on the Christmas tree for her. After Ryan goes to bed I look at the tree and remember the little brown dog and that cold winter night. Our new dog, a retriever mix named Poppie, sleeps in the hall outside Ryan's room.

*Karen J. Olson*

"I take it this is a single-parent home?"

# It Takes One to Help One

*Help your brother's boat across and your own will reach the shore.*

Hindu Proverb

I've been a single mother for nearly seven years and have a terrific twelve-year-old son, Connor. Divorce forced me back into the working world, a world I had left far behind with the birth of my first and only child. I had always intended to go back to work at some point, but had also thought the choice would be mine as to when that point would be. Angry, disappointed and unable to return to my former high-paying graphics position because of the technology jump during my "hiatus," I realized I would have to start over at the age of thirty-six. I had attended college off and on over the years, but never finished my degree, now much to my dismay. I had never thought I'd need a college degree to raise happy, beautiful children, or to cook sumptuous meals for my husband and friends, or to attend every "Mommy & Me" class I could find, in search of other lucky mothers like myself to befriend.

Well, all that came to a screeching halt as my son entered elementary school and my rocky marriage gave way to an avalanche of accusations and arguments, finally ending in divorce. I knew it was for the best, but it still hurt. We would remain friends and raise our son together, both of which have miraculously happened with much more ease than trying to stay together "for the sake of the child." I often wondered if getting a divorce made me a "quitter," but have since decided it definitely did not. I can honestly say I tried my very best to make that marriage work—it just didn't.

When I put on work clothes for the first time in years, I also realized I would have to put on a façade, too—a façade that I was a capable, hardworking, enthusiastic woman who just couldn't wait to come to work every day, leaving my little boy to ride that big bus to school every morning for forty-five minutes, then be cared for by others until I could pick him up after a long workday. Gone would be the lazy afternoons of playing Candyland, watching cartoons or building Lego airplanes, while he munched carefully carved apple slices and homemade cookies.

Through a friend, I heard about a secretarial position in the hospital where she worked. It was entry-level and the pay was less than half the salary I was making when I left the workforce. My shock gave way to dismay when I was told there were many applicants for the position, mostly from within the hospital itself. Still, I faxed over my freshly redone résumé (briefly dreading the six-year lapse in employment) and was scheduled for an interview with Robin, who would be my boss if I could somehow manage to make her see that this soon-to-retire "domestic goddess" was just what she needed! Not an easy task for a woman who hadn't spoken in complete sentences for years.

Since my wardrobe at that time consisted mainly of jeans and more jeans, I borrowed a suit from my sister and nervously drove to the interview. Taking a deep breath, I walked into the office, an office of women, two to be exact, both well dressed and obviously younger than me. My hopes sank as I faced a consummate career woman who surely wouldn't understand why I hadn't worked in many years, not to mention the fact that as her assistant I would be several years her senior.

However, I liked her immediately—she was warm and obviously very intelligent. She asked me all the right questions, taking note of my lack of certain computer skills, yet kindly saying, should I be hired, there were in-house courses offered that would bring me up to speed quickly. Then she dropped the bomb. She asked if I had any children. At the time, I did not know that this question is a big "no-no" on an employer's part. (Even so, I would have answered honestly, anyway.) But I thought that surely this would end my chances of getting this position—I had seen her type before (heck, I'd been one), and I figured she'd have no interest in hiring a soon-to-be-divorced mom when she could have her pick of qualified candidates already working for the hospital. My heart sank, but I told her proudly about my wonderful son and the fact that I was returning to work a "little earlier than planned," so that I could take care of him on my own.

I sat across from Robin, in front of her big mahogany desk, while she studied me briefly, certain she was trying to find a nice way to say, "Thanks, but no thanks." Instead, she reached for a large framed photo on her desk and turned it around for me to see. There, smiling from the picture were a brother and sister, both younger than my son, who looked exactly like their mother. My eyes quickly looked to her left hand—it was ringless. I looked around the desk for other photos of the family—there were none. Robin smiled at me and said, "When can you start?"

That was the beginning of my life as a working single parent, and I will always be grateful to the other working single parent who gave me a chance when she clearly might have had a better choice, at least based on what she read on a résumé. I will never forget her, and when she left to pursue other career opportunities, I cried and thanked her again. Sometimes, it takes one to help one.

*Laurie Hartman*

# Single Mothers Unite

*Every problem contains the seeds of its own solution.*

Stanley Arnold

Life can be eerie sometimes, but for me, in the months immediately after divorce, it felt downright scary. It was like watching the world pass by with the sound turned down. Society clearly went about its business, but I didn't, not really. Yes, I was functional: I brushed my teeth, did the laundry, did the grocery shopping, but I was never aware of doing any of these things while I was doing them. Sometimes I'd reach into the fridge for milk and wonder how it got there. Or, I'd suddenly notice that I was miles out on the freeway and had forgotten where I was going. Looking back, I wonder how my post-divorce blues were perceived by my young son, Cooper. He was only seven at the time, but what did he make of Mama sleepwalking through her daily life?

The cold reality of economics soon chased away my paralysis. After seventeen years in a happy, prosperous marriage, I suddenly found myself plagued by worry and doubt. How on earth was I going to support this little boy on my own? Fear gripped me by the throat—a deep, relentless sense of doom pervaded everything I did or felt. And it wasn't just about money. It was the loneliness. It was not understanding my place in the world anymore, not knowing where I belonged. For the first time in my adult life, I felt utterly powerless and alone.

I would wait for Cooper to fall asleep at night and then, curled up in a fetal position, I would let myself cry. To make things worse, I couldn't even curl up in my own comfy bed in my own, beautiful house; it had to be on a strange bed, in a small room I was forced to rent upon relocating to Los Angeles after the divorce. For a while, I allowed the fear to take over. The worry about where I could go and what I could do infected my every waking moment. The sensation became so gut-wrenching that I retreated into meditation—a practice I had always nurtured for pleasure now became a place of escape.

It was in a prolonged meditation that I had a realization—a warm, peaceful feeling filled my body and mind. A clear, intuitive thought pierced through the fog. It was filled with peace and joy, but mostly with pure intention. It told me to "find another single mother to share with."

Bolstered by this clear message I went in search of a house big enough for two families. When I found the house, I posted a notice: "Single mom seeks same to pool resources and share a house with a garden. Let's work together to create a safe environment for our children." I received eighteen responses. At first, I felt that this good thing happening was all about me. But as I started to have conversations with the moms who responded to my notice, it became clear that this was bigger than me. This was about all of these women looking for a way to connect, and not just for house sharing, but as single mothers who needed to reach out to someone who understood what they were going through. But I only had one house, what could I say to the other seventeen? After chatting with several of the moms over coffee, it struck me that some might have more in common with each other than they had with me. Two had three-year-old boys. One mother had a sixteen-year-old girl and lived close by another who had a fourteen-year-old girl. It made perfect sense to put them in contact with each other. And so I did. And they were grateful.

If eighteen single moms were looking to share with another single mom in my small neighborhood, how many hundreds must there be in the greater Los Angeles area? How many thousands in California? How many millions in the United States? I did some research and found that there was no forum where single moms could find each other to house share. That familiar intuitive feeling came over me: *why not me?* Why not take the initiative and create my own vision of a place where single moms could connect; a place for us, by us, where we could pool resources to build healthier, happier, more secure home environments. So I founded *www.co-abode.org*, a Web site designed exclusively to connect single moms for house sharing and friendships. It took a lot of time and an incredible amount of effort, but within a year I had a full-service Web site up and running. Today, we have 16,000 members, many of whom are sharing homes all over the United States.

Only another single parent truly understands how lonely and sometimes frightening it is to face every single day raising your children alone, which is just one of the reasons that single parents make ideal roommates for each other. And the messages I receive from the single moms who've connected through Co-abode is so heartening. They rejoice in doing half the shopping, half the cooking, half the cleaning, and getting twice the house they could have afforded alone. Recently divorced women tell me how they've been able to hold on to the family home by bringing in another single mom to help share the financial burden. And instead of dwelling in a sad and lonely place, they now have a friend to laugh with, or a shoulder to cry on when the bad memories creep in. But more inspiring than all of this is what they say they've achieved for their children. I hear about warm kitchens full of children's laughter, two-year-old boys who assume they are brothers, and teenage girls who share the bus to school with new surrogate sisters, knowing that they have so much more to return home to than they ever had before.

It may take a village to raise a productive member of society, but we can make a great start with single moms who unite in their devotion to their children and their willingness to help themselves. By doing so, the world is just a little bit better.

*Carmel Sullivan-Boss*

# The Family in My Heart

*The bond that links your true family is not one of blood, but of respect and joy in each other's life. Rarely do members of one family grow up under the same roof.*

Richard Bach

One Labor Day weekend I was enjoying a peaceful bike ride with my family on spectacular Mackinac Island in northern Michigan. My two-year-old son, Justin, was napping behind me when I heard, "Aunt Shelly, I have a question for you!" Without a second thought I replied, "I have an answer!" I was expecting six-year-old Tyler, who was trailing behind me on his two-wheeler, to ask if I was up for an ice-cream cone and a break from the long ride. Boy, was I wrong.

"Why is it that Justin's my brother and you are his mom, but my mom is my mom and you and Justin live in a different house than me?"

Somehow, I managed to appease Tyler with a simple response and successfully change the subject. The complicated answer is that he and Justin share a father, something

Tyler knew, but obviously didn't understand. I spent the rest of the ride reflecting on the amazing twist of events that had occurred in my life over the previous three years.

In April 2000, as a single mother, I gave birth to my beautiful son. Before my baby was born I had learned that Justin's father also had another son with a young woman named Heidi.

When Justin was eight months old and a full two months had passed without a word from his father, I decided to contact Heidi. We had known each other from a distance, and although we had had some minor confrontations in the past, it didn't feel awkward to connect with her as I knew she was the one person who could understand what I was feeling. I was new at being a single mother and valued her experience. We began talking and e-mailing every day, nonstop. The funny thing is, we found out we were alike in so many ways!

Shortly after our initial conversation we decided to bite the bullet and meet with the boys. I'll never forget that night. Tyler, who was four at the time, presented me with a rose, and Heidi had a cake decorated that said, "I love you, Justin." Everything was perfect. By the end of the evening, Justin had taken his first steps toward Heidi. With those first steps, we both knew it was the beginning of something very special for all of us.

From that evening on, Heidi and I have become practically inseparable. Even today, it truly feels like a miracle. We are now in our fourth year of sharing the ups and downs of parenting. Where others might let jealousy, anger and resentment get in the way, we have chosen a decidedly different path. We are single mothers joined together by fate, and we have chosen to see this as a great blessing.

Tyler, now eight, loves the fact that he has another aunt, and in turn, I have fallen head over heels for him. Heidi is known as Aunt "Didi" to my rambunctious, now four-year-old Justin, and the two brothers horse around and get into all kinds of mischief, as brothers typically do. When I look at the two of them, Tyler and Justin side by side, both with caramel-colored skin, curly hair and soulful brown eyes—and both with dimples so deep you could sink quarters into them—I know that we were meant to become a family. Heidi and I have vowed to raise our two children together as much as possible. It really is a testament to the love we both share for our children and for each other.

As for me, I've learned two very important lessons: first, your "family" is who you choose to hold in your heart, not necessarily those who share your bloodlines. Not only did I gain a nephew in Tyler and a sister in Heidi, but also Heidi's mother, Nancy, has "adopted" me as her own and Justin as her grandson. Heidi's two sisters, Monika and Lisa, have embraced us as well. I am very blessed to have become a part of such a wonderful family.

The second very important lesson I've learned is to never tell Tyler that I have the answer before I know the question. I'll let Heidi answer the tough ones.

*Michelle Lawson*

# The Cost of Hope

*The service we render others is the rent we pay
for our room on Earth.*

Wilfred Grenfell

Danielle sat down with a sigh, discouraged and exhausted. The day had proven frustrating. With only forty dollars left in her wallet, she desperately needed to find a bank to cash her paycheck. She was living in a new city with no local bank of her own—and the banks were not eager to help her. For more than two weeks, she made attempt after attempt—to no avail. With her cash supply dwindling fast, she had no other resources. How could she continue to support herself and her two children? She wondered just how much longer she and her children could get by on the little money they had left.

Taking a break from her struggles, Danielle decided to attend a meeting at the local women's resource center. The women there had been a strong source of encouragement since she fled her home in fear for her safety. Her thoughts were far away as she settled into a chair in the meeting room. In deep despair, she longed for renewed hope that she could make it as a single mom.

"Good afternoon, everyone," a voice said, breaking Danielle's thoughts. It was the leader of her women's group. "Does anyone want to start?"

Sitting next to Danielle, Amy cleared her throat. "I would," she said. Amy began to share the details of her desperate situation. She had run into severe personal struggles and was just days away from losing her home and her car. Her phone and electric services were both scheduled for disconnection. Her husband had gambled away their money. What little she had tried to squirrel away, he had used to support his drug habit. Their relationship had deteriorated to the point where she feared for her very safety. The last of the money she managed to tuck away allowed her to buy food for her children and diapers for her baby. She had nothing left. Nothing.

As Amy described the extent of the situation, Danielle heard God's soft whisper in her heart: "After the meeting, give Amy twenty dollars." Danielle immediately thought, *But I can't. I only have forty dollars.* She heard the order again. It was unmistakably clear. Danielle knew she needed to comply. When the meeting concluded, she reached into her purse and quietly slipped twenty dollars to Amy. Knowing Danielle's situation, Amy was reluctant to accept it at first. But as a crowd of women came to give Amy hugs of support, Danielle told her that God wanted her to have it. Then Danielle left.

As Danielle unlocked the door to her car, she heard someone call her name. She turned to find Amy walking toward her. Tears filled Amy's eyes as she began to speak. "How could you have known?" she asked. A large tear rolled down her cheek and dropped onto her shoulder as she reached into her purse. She pulled out a small amber prescription bottle. "I took the last one yesterday." She pointed to the bottom of the label. "I'm a medication-dependent diabetic. I need this medication every day. I had no idea what I was going to do." Another tear rolled down her cheek as she pointed to the refill cost printed clearly on the label: $20.00.

It was at that moment that Danielle was renewed with a sense of hope and peace. She told Amy that she did not know, but God did. While Amy's situation seemed to be a mountain before her, God alone could help her navigate every step and meet every need to move beyond that mountain, one step at a time. The words of hope that Danielle spoke to Amy that day were the very words of hope she herself needed.

Now with just twenty dollars left in her wallet, Danielle decided to try cashing her paycheck at just one more bank before heading home. While she anticipated the rejection she had received at so many other banks, she was somehow filled with renewed confidence and optimism. With hope in hand, she walked into the bank adjacent to the women's center. Moments later, the bank cashed her paycheck with no questions asked.

Beaming, Danielle returned home. While she knew there would be days ahead that would certainly hold challenges, her newfound hope inspired her. She never did see Amy again, but she continues to rest confidently that God is still looking out for her and is meeting her daily needs, just as he continues to look out for Danielle and her two children. As for Danielle, it has been three years since that day. While she realizes true hope has no price tag, she continues to be thankful for the lifetime supply that she received for the price of just twenty dollars.

*Susan Hamilton*

# Not Alone

*W*hen *a thing is funny, search it for a hidden truth.*

George Bernard Shaw

Christmas was only two weeks away. I usually loved the Christmas season and all the joy it brings, but this year any joy I exhibited would be forced. It was the first Christmas for my small daughters and me since my husband had announced he was not happy and had moved away. It was our first Christmas without him.

"Since the divorce . . ." everything seemed to be referenced by this event. I never wanted to be a single parent, but that is what I had recently become. The responsibility of caring for my two little girls was sobering. As their only safety net, I felt vulnerable. Rampaging through my mind were questions such as: *What if I get sick? What if I cannot find a teaching job? Who will take care of the girls if they become ill, and I am at work? What if I make the wrong financial decisions?* I was fearful of how I would possibly handle all these challenges alone. And somehow, this first Christmas without my husband made my aloneness even more pronounced.

The girls' father left us for what he called "a better life." It was not better for us. I was frantically taking twenty-one hours of college courses, including student teaching, in an attempt to finish my degree in one semester. I had put off obtaining this teaching certification to have the girls, but now I desperately needed it before I could even seek employment in my field. And until I finished, I was forced to live in a city far away from family and friends. I could not afford to spread it out over another semester; so despite the heavy load, I pushed forward.

The fall semester had been exhausting. I tried not to leave my young daughters with the sitter more than was absolutely necessary, and I felt it my duty to be cheerful and ready for interaction when I picked them up. That meant I did no studying or assignments until after they were in bed for the night. I lost considerable weight and was truly just running on fumes during that last week of the semester. There was little time to eat or sleep. The stress and sadness I felt were almost unbearable, and with all my family in another state, I felt I was facing it all alone.

The few hours of sleep I had each night were so welcome that it was difficult to even stir when my alarm blasted me awake each morning. Yet this night, a strange sound startled me out of my deep sleep. I had heard a loud *thump.* As I tried to shake off the effects of sleep, I heard the familiar sound of the heater coming on, but now something else penetrated my groggy state. A muffled voice was speaking, and it was coming from the direction of my bedroom closet. The closet door was closed, but I could still hear someone talking, asking a question that I couldn't quite make out. All my senses came alive, heightened by fear. My eyes widened, trying unsuccessfully to pierce the darkness and make sense of the situation. I strained to hear. It clearly was not the voice of either of my little daughters. As the grogginess left, I realized with increasing alarm that there was a stranger's voice in my walk-in closet!

I lay very still, too terrified to move. I was like a rabbit that freezes, almost without breathing, in the hope he is camouflaged and the hunter cannot see him. I did not want to move, but then I remembered that I was no camouflaged rabbit. I was a mother—a mother with two little girls to protect. There was no one else in the house to help. Those sweet babies were my sole responsibility, and I was not going to let some intruder get to them. I had to think clearly and act quickly. I renewed my efforts to analyze the muffled voice. My heart was still pounding, but I decided the voice did not seem to be coming any closer to the bed, nor did it seem quite so ominous. However, it did have an eerie singsong cadence.

Since the divorce, I was down to one phone, which was in the kitchen on the other side of the house. A run there would leave my sleeping babies in the adjacent bedroom unprotected. I ruled out a plan to make a run for the phone, but something had to be done, and it was up to me to do it. I decided to confront this intruder myself. That decision caused a trusted old habit to kick in. I sent an arrow prayer to God: "God, I'm in trouble. Please help me."

With my heart pounding, I inched my way across my bed, dropped to the floor, pulled out the gun I had purchased for protection from the bedside table and crept toward the closet door. It was time to find out who was having this conversation in my closet. Fortunately, the closet light switch was outside the door. I flipped on the light. With lightning speed and far too much force, I flung the door open. Still wearing my short nightgown, I spread my legs and took a bold "gun stance," much like you might see on a *Charlie's Angels* movie poster, and pointed my gun in the direction of the voice.

That's when I saw it.

Lying on the carpeted floor was an overturned, brightly wrapped Christmas present. Now I could clearly hear the repetitive message it was emitting: "Hello. I'm Mickey Mouse. Do you want to play?"

Again. "Hello. I'm Mickey Mouse. Do you want to play?"

Reality hit that I was pointing a gun at my daughter's wrapped Christmas gift, a prerecorded Disney talking telephone. A week before, I had installed the battery, wrapped the phone and hidden it on the highest closet shelf until it was time to put it under the tree. Somehow it had slipped off the shelf, flipped over and activated a button that produced this one-sided conversation from Mickey.

Mickey's muffled voice droned on.

"Hello. I'm Mickey Mouse. Do you want to play?"

Stepping into the closet, I lowered the gun and slid my back down the wall until I was sitting on the floor. The overturned talking package was directly in front of me. The crisis was over, and as relief flooded over me, I found myself crying and laughing at the same time. Crying in relief that the exaggerated fear I had conjured in my mind was unfounded, and laughing at the ridiculousness of the situation. I had terrified myself over a toy!

Sitting on that closet floor, God reminded me in a most humorous way that I was not alone—never had been and never would be. Through this noisy toy still talking away, he let me know that with him by my side, I had the courage to face the *thumps* in the night and any other challenge life would bring my daughters' or my way. I had feared being alone, but this night's experience taught me a precious truth about that fear: God is my refuge and he would never leave me. No matter my situation in life, I was not alone, and the spirit of Christmas could fill my home.

I reached over and righted my daughter's toppled Christmas gift. This released the depressed button and finally Mickey was silenced. And so were my fears.

*Jennifer Clark Vihel*

# 2

# A FRESH PERSPECTIVE

*Life is an eternal dance. The movements of the dance are choreographed through your awareness. Every movement is part of the dance; therefore, every space-time event is meaningful and necessary. It is the order within the chaos.*

Deepak Chopra

# My Daughter, Once Removed

*You know quite well deep within you, that there is only a single magic, a single power, a single salvation . . . and that is called loving.*

Herman Hesse

Aiesha is the first thing I think about when I wake up each morning. I haven't spoken to her in a month, but all her messages are still saved on my answering machine. A T-shirt lies in the exact spot where she left it during her last visit three months ago. I still tell her that she is my favorite person. Aiesha is eight, spoiling for nine. She is my daughter, once removed.

In my wide-eyed youth, I subscribed to such naive notions as "love makes you a parent," and "twenty-three chromosomes don't make you a daddy." Now I believe that fatherhood is created every morning at six, when you creak out of bed to crack eggs, rattle pans and let yourself be hustled into granting your kid ten more minutes of sleep. I still believe that genes don't make the parent, but now I ask, "What does a voided wedding vow make me?"

I know Aiesha because her mother, Shana, was my college girlfriend. She was wild and beautiful; her ways the complete opposite of my self-conscious, bookish ones. I broke up with her and then, years later, found myself wishing for her again. We were only together again for less than six months, but we did stay in touch after our breakup. Five years later, I moved to New York for graduate school. When we threw a surprise party for my mother's fiftieth birthday, I invited Shana. She showed up with a buoyant two-year-old who had impossibly round cheeks and whose favorite response was "No!"—even to things like, "You are adorable."

Soon Shana and I were hanging out again, back to our old routines. At some point in those first months of being reunited, I realized that I loved Shana and that Aiesha had already chosen me as her father. Shana and I got married.

I think men secretly want to raise their daughters to be the kind of women who were out of their league when they were young. And so it was with Aiesha. But really, it was about the words, teaching her the words to old classics like "Ain't No Sunshine" and giggling through the part where Bill Withers sings, "And I know, I know, I know, I know, I know. . . ." Kids love repetition. She turned out volumes of poems, plays, songs and stories that were duly typed up and e-mailed to all my friends, co-workers and distant relatives as evidence of her burgeoning literary genius.

There were signs early on, now that I think of it, that the marriage was headed south. I saw in gradual degrees that my wife was less and less interested in our relationship and knew that I was at the point where many a man would have bailed. I chose to work harder. When the newspapers ranked Aiesha's public school at the bottom half of those in the city, I reduced my grad classes and worked part-time to send her to a private school. When Shana was stuck at work a few hours before her women's group meeting was to be held in our apartment, I came home early and surprised her by cleaning up and preparing the food. I was like an outfielder who knows that the ball is headed for the bleachers, but smashes face first into the wall trying to catch it anyway. In my world, there was no such thing as a warning track.

Here is a marital cliché: You're in the kitchen cooking dinner when your spouse returns home from a hard day at the office and announces it's over. Just like that. When she told Aiesha that I was leaving, Aiesha asked, "Does this mean I don't have a father anymore?"

Friends, mostly female, tell me, "Once a father, always a father." But experience tells me differently: I could just as easily be evicted again; Shana could remarry and leave me a parental second-string player. Experience has taught me that ex-stepfather does not exist as a census category; I no longer qualify for a Father's Day card.

I know that I deeply and profoundly love that little girl. I understand the weight of the bond between parent and child. I also know that I was trying to single-handedly undo the mythology of black men, that I wanted a family that would laugh past the bleak statistics and indictments of black male irresponsibility. When I married Shana, Aiesha had not seen her biological father in more than a year. As far as I know, she has not seen him since. I saw tragedy in her growing up as yet another fatherless black girl, another child whose father abandoned her in favor of emptier pursuits. I wanted to be like my old man, quietly heroic in raising my brother and sister, and never once letting on that they were not his biological kin. I wanted to be a keeper.

These days, I know that my relationship with Aiesha is unwieldy, sagging beneath the weight of its own ambiguity. Fatherhood is all about watching the daily changes, whether it is hearing the new word she learned or noticing that now she doesn't have to stand on a stool to reach her toothbrush. But I know that in a year or two, my work may require that I move to Texas or California or Alaska, and it's possible that I'll fade from her memory.

Christmas is a hard, bright day, and I wake up alone with my head heavy. Aiesha has left me a message saying that she has a gift for me, and could I please come today so she can give it to me. Her mother and I have lived apart for six months, and I don't know Aiesha as well as I did in June. In another six months, she'll be a different child altogether.

When I see her outside, riding her bike in the parking lot of her building, I think about how she has grown tall and slender as a reed. I bought her a watch, yellow and red, but with no cartoon characters because Aiesha fancies herself a sophisticate. The note says:

*Dear Aiesha,*

*My father once told me that keeping track of time is the first step to becoming an adult. I hope you think of me when you wear this.*

She gives me a gift card. Written in her best eight-year-old scrawl, it says simply, "I love you." She's telling me the plot points to her latest story, the one she wants to publish when she's twelve. A moment later, she wants me to toss her into the air. "One more time!" she pleads, again and again, until my deltoids are burning.

She still remembers most of the words to "Ain't No Sunshine."

Today, she's my daughter. Today.

*William Jelani Cobb*

# Chasing a Rainbow

*People only see what they are prepared to see.*

Ralph Waldo Emerson

The year I got divorced was one of the hardest I've ever faced. An accident, just two weeks after my initial separation from my husband, kept me hospitalized for more than two months, and recuperation lasted another two months. Finally on my feet and back at work, I found myself faced with the responsibilities of finding a home, caring for my two children and adjusting to a new job—all while coping with constant pain.

"I just have to do this one thing," I'd tell the children each time they approached me to read to them, help with homework or just talk. Lost in my own maze of coping, I was unable to reach out to them in their pain and suffering. Adding guilt to my other burdens only made the stress increase.

Then I became very ill. A combination of a very bad case of flu and infections put me in bed for a week. Each morning the children got up on their own and went to school. They came home and made their own meals. I vaguely recall being awakened and fed canned chicken soup. I drifted in a land between sleep and unconsciousness. When I was able to move from the bed and walk through the house, I discovered it in shambles. Dirty laundry and dishes; messes everywhere I looked. I didn't think I would ever be able to catch up with the housework again. The checkbook, too, had suffered. I had no paid sick leave, and the burden of managing finances without regular child-support payments forced me to return to work before I had fully recovered.

The children began calling me at work. "I'm sick; I don't feel good, come and get me; I've missed the bus—honest, Mama, I didn't hear them call my bus number!" All were a bid for the time and attention I didn't feel I could spare them. And each call meant missed work, missed pay.

The day came when they both called within five minutes. Neither child had managed to make their bus home that afternoon. Could I come pick them up? As I hurried from work it began to rain heavily. I was crying as I stopped at each school. This was all too hard, and I didn't want to do it anymore. There was no end in sight, no hope of a better life.

As we turned toward home, the clouds broke and sunshine poured onto the wet streets. A huge rainbow gleamed in the sky above us, colors brilliant and clear. It was the most beautiful rainbow I'd ever seen in my life, and my children were in awe.

"Is there really gold at the end of the rainbow?" my youngest asked.

I told him honestly I'd never seen the end of a rainbow.

"How do they know?" he asked.

"I don't know," I replied.

"Well, it looks like it ends just over that bridge," he said. "Can't we go look, Mama?"

I thought of the hundred things I needed to do. There

was work to finish; there were chores and laundry to be done. I opened my mouth to say no, but when I started to speak, out came a "yes." The children shrieked with excitement. The end wasn't just over the bridge, or across the railroad, or in the field beyond that. We drove for more than thirty miles, sometimes seeing the end just ahead of us, the colors shimmering and shining, the light dancing through them. I looked at my children, their eyes shining, and at the rainbow ahead of us and kept on driving.

We laughed and talked—really talked—for the first time in months. We talked about my accident, the divorce, their fears, their schools, their dreams. We planned future rides and projects. I felt my shoulders relax and my grip loosening on the steering wheel. My children's eyes were free of worry.

We decided to stop the chase an hour after it began. We turned to head for home. We'd found something wonderful while chasing that rainbow, something even better than that coveted pot of gold. We'd found ourselves a family again; we'd rediscovered the value of our relationship to each other. We'd remembered what it felt like to have fun. And we'd started making plans for a future that felt hopeful and full of promise.

Several years have passed, and my two children are grown. But when we are together, there is a bond between us. One of us will smile and ask, "Remember when we chased the rainbow?"

We do. It was the day we found hope again.

*Terri Cheney*

# Mommy's Moon

*The eyes of my eyes are opened.*

e. e. cummings

I was twenty years old when my wife died, leaving behind only a sparkling memory of her touch and a beautiful baby girl named Aurora. We called her Rory for short, because I always liked the name Rory, and through constant use, I had gotten my way.

Rory grew quickly, and like all bright-eyed children, she led me through a range of emotions that parents often experience with these beautiful, frustrating little bundles of tears and wonder. But something was coming, and I wasn't sure I could deal with it.

"She's going to ask questions." I heard over and over again from my well-meaning friends. It was usually backed up with either, "It's going to be hard," or "I wouldn't want to have to answer them."

Rory was stumbling on unsure baby legs toward that fateful day, and I was dreading every moment of it. When she was asleep or off at a garage sale with her grandparents, I would sit in my room and plan strategies, writing down the things I wanted to say to her. Every carefully worded speech I prepared ended up at the bottom of the wastebasket, or shredded on the floor, as I became more convinced with each passing day that I would blow it and say something stupid.

We were sitting on the front porch one brisk summer night, watching the cars whiz past the house, and I was telling Rory about how interesting it was that every car that went past contained people with a different story to tell. Rory was drinking from her juice cup and not really listening, a skill she'd developed from my constant need to talk to her.

She turned on my lap then, and asked a question.

"Daddy, where is my mommy?"

I stalled. My heart was pounding, and I began to fumble. I was at a loss for words. *What do I say? How do I make this one better?* I couldn't think. My mouth was dry; I felt like I was chewing on cotton balls.

"She's in heaven," I said stupidly. I'm not a religious man, but it was the only thing I could think of.

Rory thought this over for a moment. "Is that in Canada?"

I almost smiled. We had been discussing Santa Claus earlier, and I was informing her of his Canadian nationality, as the North Pole was in Canadian territory. As far as Rory knew, everything was in Canada.

"No, honey," I said, holding her close to me. "I think it's way up in the sky, past all the stars, even beyond outer space."

Rory looked up at the night sky, and her eyes gravitated toward the big yellow moon hanging in front of us. Suddenly, her eyes brightened.

"The moon!" she squealed.

"Yup. A big old yellow moon," I said. "Rory, did you know that those dark spots are mountains and valleys?" Ever the educator. Like I said, Rory learned how to ignore me out of necessity.

"Mommy's moon," she said, still smiling.

"What was that?" I asked, confused.

"Mommy's on the moon, where she can see me," Rory replied. I gasped. Her logic amazed me sometimes.

"What is she doing up there?" I asked.

"Fixing my broken toys. I hope she comes back someday."

And that was that. Leaving me speechless, she went back to her juice cup.

I like to tell myself that I am responsible for my daughter's imagination. I also like to tell myself that my little girl will always be a little girl. Somehow, I don't really think either is true. I do believe, however, that adults complicate things that don't need to be so complicated. For me, it was coming to terms with mortality and loss. For Rory, it was as easy as looking up into the night sky.

*J. W. Schnarr*

# I Love You Double

*Accept the pain, cherish the joys, resolve the regrets; then can come the best of benedictions— "If I had my life to live over, I'd do it all the same."*

Joan McIntosh

Taking a big bite of his pancake at our favorite breakfast haunt, out of the clear blue, with syrup dripping out of the corner of his mouth, my five-year-old grandson, Tyler, said, "How come I don't have a dad?"

The inevitable question had been asked, and I was the one left to answer it. *Think! What do I say?* In an important moment such as this one, when you need to think quickly and come up with the best possible response, it's amazing how much can run through your head in a flash.

Tyler's inquisitive face caused me to dredge up a lot of old memories—how challenging it had been raising my own three daughters alone. Countless times the girls would lament over not having a "normal" family, and I would go overboard trying to make up for their "lot in life" as children of a single parent. Adding to that, my relationship with the girls' father was always strained, we never had enough money, and we were four girls trying to grow up together at the same time (yes, me included). Just trying to survive wreaked havoc on the kind of home life I wanted to provide for my little family. All of it amounted to some pretty tough times—emotionally, mentally and physically. Through the years, guilt was an emotion I often struggled with: from taking the initiative to leave the girls' father to not being able to provide for them financially in a single-parent home as well as they might have been provided for in a two-parent home. I ached for them daily, knowing none of us had it easy.

Snapping back to the present and looking at the beautiful child sitting across from me, I relished the gift of his being. Tyler was the best of all bonuses bequeathed me for all the years I struggled as a single mom. Knowing the legacy of single motherhood that had been passed on to my oldest child, I desperately wanted my daughter and grandson to have more stability and freedom from the challenges of being in a single-parent family than I had.

Tyler had posed a serious question, and I had to find the right answer for him, right then and there. Telling him that some children simply don't have a mom or dad just wasn't adequate, nor was it true in his case. Five-year-olds demand the truth. But should I tell him that his father is in prison? That Tyler's presence here on Earth goes back to a time when my daughter was having a tough time in her own life? Would that imply he was a mistake? No, no child is ever "a mistake," *never, ever*, regardless of the circumstances. But how do you explain any of this to a little boy? And what would his mother want me to say in this instance?

Then I realized what Tyler really was asking: *Am I complete? Do I matter? Am I loved?* And then the words came to me. "Tyler, you don't have a dad in your life right now, but you do have a mom who loves you double." I repeated and emphasized, "Double," adding, "and with Grandma loving you as much as I do, make that triple!"

Reflecting on my seemingly brilliant reply, it suddenly hit me that the guilt I had immersed myself in for years and years had been useless. I realized I did the best I could given my circumstances, and that, in my case, the girls fared far better with just a mom than they ever would have in a two-parent family fraught with constant fighting, turmoil and unhappiness. I loved them double, too.

Responding to my answer, Tyler looked at me with a face full of satisfaction and replied, "Well, I guess that makes me pretty lucky then, doesn't it, Grandma?"

*Nancy Vogl*

# The Missing Branch

*In every winter's heart lies a quivering spring,
and behind the veil of night waits a smiling dawn.*
                                        Kahlil Gibran

I grew up in a Tinkertoy family, one that was irregularly taken apart and put together in new ways. My parents divorced when I was six. By the time I was a freshman in college, I'd had five parents and stepparents, had attended nine schools, and had nine siblings with five different combinations of parents.

I met some of my brothers and sisters, not when they were born, but years later. Once I was introduced to a group of six or seven children, two of whom, I learned the following day, were to become my siblings. It took me a few hours to figure out who was who. Some people have a family tree. I have a family forest.

After growing up like that, I wanted, oh so much, for my children to have a stable family. When I married (with two of my stepsisters meeting for the first time at my wedding) and later had two daughters, I was sure that my wife and I would never divorce.

My wish was granted: my wife and I were never divorced. But it turned out that, like a character in one of the children's stories I read to our daughters, I had made the wrong wish. One day, when our youngest child was still nursing, my wife found a lump in her breast. It was cancer. We tried every treatment New York City had to offer, but nothing worked. I buried my wife in a Queens graveyard on August 11, 1995, two years to the day of the diagnosis. Our daughters were three and five.

I did the things for my kids that you do in that situation. I hugged my daughters when they cried—between attending school events, taking them to bereavement groups and setting up playdates. I listened to them, so they would know someone cared about their feelings.

Fortunately, New York offers lots of help to kids who have lost a parent. My daughters benefited from Motherless Daughters' Day events (celebrated the day before Mother's Day) and bereavement camp. They loved the attention they received when speaking at training sessions for those dealing with bereaved children.

I also tried to fill my daughters' days with fun, so they will understand that life can be good. In this too, it helps to be in New York. Though the prejudice against single-parent families may survive elsewhere, it is long gone here. I have heard of parents in other places saying "no" to playdates at the homes of single fathers, but we have more playdate offers than we can accommodate. And when it comes to little girls sleeping over at our place, there's only one parent who hesitates—me. I'm sleep-deprived enough, thank you.

Most parents who invite one of my daughters to a birthday party invite the other without being asked. When my girls, who like to act, are in shows, sometimes more than twenty friends and relatives watch them perform.

Perhaps in part because we are in a city where unusual

families are the norm, things are going well for my daughters. To be sure, they have their moments of pain. Once my younger girl, still too young to read and write, asked me to scrawl a message to her mommy on a balloon: "You'll always be in my heart." Then she let go of the balloon, and we watched it sail into the sky over the East River. Her older sister longs for a mother more than anything else in the world.

But most of their lives are filled with joy. My older girl once told a classmate's mother, "Every morning I wake up happy because I know I'm going to do something fun and exciting." Her sister's assessment: "I think things are going well. Even though Mommy's dead, things are working out."

Perhaps my greatest victory appears in my older daughter's journal from first grade. One day she had written in it that her life was very hard. When her teacher wrote back, "Why?"—I suppose anticipating the obvious answer—she replied that her sister whined a lot.

In the end, I could not prevent the fate I had hoped to spare my daughters: the Tinkertoy aspect of their lives. Our little family is not broken, but a piece of it is gone. Maybe someday I will bring someone home to my daughters to join us—not to replace their mother, but certainly to be an important part of our family in her own right. But whether or not that happens, well, I'll still have two wonderful children to raise to adulthood. Two children who must never ever feel like Tinkertoys.

New York is helping in that endeavor. In this city, no one looks twice at a man reading to kids on the subway, shopping for girls' underwear or joining his daughters in a Maypole dance. If you have to be in our situation, New York turns out to be a pretty good place for it.

*Jeff Sovern*

# The Grass Is Always Greener . . . Isn't It?

*What makes us discontented with our condition is the absurdly exaggerated idea we have of the happiness of others.*

Anonymous

My daughter, Sara, and I had been on our own for about a year, and our lives had settled into a pleasant routine, even though her father no longer lived in our home. Fortunately, he continued to be the best dad he could, despite the restraints of our separation and impending divorce. There were times, however, when my mind drifted to "what could have been" had our marriage endured.

At the end of most summer days, Sara and I would eat a frozen treat and "porch stoop," relax on the front steps just watching the world go by, before heading in for the night. Early one evening, I spotted our neighbors across the street leaving their house. As the front door opened, their giggling school-age daughters eagerly scampered down the steps to the car, with their parents in happy pursuit. All four of them wore that summertime-sweet "everything is right with the world" expression as they waved to us in hearty greeting. Since my neighbor held a quilt in her arms, I presumed they were heading for the local park for some fun and ice cream. A Norman Rockwell, *Mayberry, R.F.D.* snapshot of the ideal and conventional family. The image of their "intact family" created a momentary melancholy in my consciousness; our "broken family" would no longer enjoy the spontaneity of that picture-perfect family repast. One more image to file away as "nevermore."

The next day, their eight-year-old daughter joined Sara for an afternoon of play, and while taking a snack break, I casually mentioned her family's previous evening of fun at the park. Her face belied no awareness of what I mentioned, so I prompted her further. "You know. When you and your family took the blanket to the park last night to play and relax?"

Still she expressed no outward comprehension. "Huh?"

"Well, what did you do last night after supper?"

"Oh. Last night my mom and I went to the Laundromat to wash my blanket, and my sister and my dad went to the barber so he could get a haircut. Then we came home. I wish I coulda' stayed with you to sit outside on the steps."

Out of the mouths of babes. Normal, intact and desirable are in the eye of the beholder, regardless of the shape or size of your family. We weren't broken after all. In another's eyes, our grass was greener. Thereafter, I've rarely entertained speculation of what the future would, or could, have held. Instead, my energy has been focused on new family snapshots, and like families everywhere, the tapestry of our lives included the mundane along with the special. While contentedly "porch stooping" that night, the summer lightning bugs flickered just a little bit brighter, the cicada chirped more melodiously and our frozen treats never tasted more mouthwatering and satisfying.

*Carol A. Kopacz*

"It's embarrassing, Dad! I'm the only kid in the neighborhood living with *both* parents!"

# Where Are You Paddling?

*Row, row, row your boat, gently down the stream. Merrily, merrily, merrily, merrily, life is but a dream.*

Unknown

I'm a single dad, raising my daughter as her custodial parent (her mother lives in Canada), so these times we share together are especially memorable. My daughter, Kelcie, was in kindergarten when she taught me my biggest lesson about navigating through life. It happened when our YMCA father-daughter "Indian Princess" tribe went on a campout, and we shared our first canoeing experience. Kelcie gleefully ran to the lakeshore, climbed in front with her paddle, and I settled into the stern with mine. Five other father-daughter canoe teams pushed off at the same time.

The others paddled in different directions with varying degrees of swiftness toward the neighboring camp on the far shore, the intriguing inlet to the south or north toward a lakeshore cabin. Kelcie and I barely made any headway at all.

As a professional speaker who is always eager to edu-cate, I presented Kelcie with a highly customized fatherly seminar on the theory of canoe physics. While stroking with my own paddle to balance her tentative strokes, all of which were on the right side of the boat, I patiently explained how one *should* paddle.

"Stop paddling, Dad! I want to do it myself."

"But honey, you're only paddling on the right side, and that's why we're curving to the left and hardly making any progress. Look how fast Jeff and Jessica are moving. They're paddling on both sides of their boat and they're already halfway to the cove. Now I'll paddle on the left back here to balance your strokes on the right. You see?"

"No! I want to do it my way."

"Sweetheart, if we don't paddle together and you just stroke on the right, we'll go in one big circle and we'll never get to the cove or the inlet or the boat wreck or any-where. You do want to get somewhere, don't you? We're already way behind the others."

"I don't care. I want to do all the paddling myself."

I, the expert on all things, saw Dave and Susie's canoe already nearing the distant inlet, and Jeff and Jessica had almost reached the cove. Their wakes showed that their courses were mostly straight and true. When my daughter wasn't looking, I furtively stroked my paddle on the left side to straighten our course.

Kelcie caught me. She whipped around and shot me a defiant look: "Dad, stop it! I want to paddle on my own."

My instant seminar had not impressed her. No hint of applause. "You'll see. We'll be far behind all the other canoes. They'll be having fun at the cove, and we will have gone nowhere but in one big circle." I sat back sullenly, annoyed that my child was ignoring my excellent, wise advice. I abandoned my "let's get somewhere" strategy and let Kelcie paddle her own way. Sure enough, we slowly arced in one big lazy circle. And, as I leaned back in the stern with the paddle in my lap, I realized I was enjoying the view much more than if we had been making straight, swift progress toward a destination. Kelcie was happy, and I was, too.

That's how she taught me that the goal of father-daughter canoeing is not to reach a destination swiftly; it's to enjoy being together and to relish where you are while respecting others' wishes and learning a little something. And isn't that also the goal of life?

The lesson in the canoe helped me to determine the direction for my own life. Giving a thousand talks, making X million dollars or being featured on some TV show is not really that important in the scheme of things. My uppermost goal is to raise a loving, happy child with whom I enjoy life. Here's how I pull it off: When I first became a single parent, I closed my big impressive downtown office and added office space to my home. I get up very early, between four and five, and work in my home office until seven. From seven until nine, I'm on dad duty with Kelcie. After breakfast and schoolwork together, I walk my daughter to the bus stop and chat with the other parents and kids. When the bus pulls away, I return to my office. At 3:44 P.M., I walk to the bus stop and welcome my child home. I don't work in the evening; I parent.

My days are now more balanced, and I know I can spend more time on work later in my career. I'm content to have a comfortable life; I don't want a yacht or a mansion. Because of my priorities, my clients can count on having a happy, healthy, sane person show up in front of their audiences. And most important of all, my daughter and I both benefit from having a satisfying, loving relationship.

Knowing where I'm paddling makes the journey all the more joyful.

*George Walther*

# My Eyes Are Red

*A brook would lose its song if God removed the rocks.*

Ancient Proverb

"My eyes are green, Mommy," my three-year-old daughter, Maddison, tells me, making the sign for "green" with her small fingers, as we lie in her bed.

"Very good, honey! You're getting really good at your signs. I'm so proud of you! What color are Mommy's eyes?"

Maddison stares intently into my eyes, a puzzled look on her face. "Um, your eyes are red," she says, twisting her fingers around each other and dragging them down her lips, the sign for "red."

"Red!? My eyes are red?"

"Uh-huh." She nods her head enthusiastically as young children do, and points her finger to my eye. "They have red . . ." Unable to adequately describe my eyes with her preschool vocabulary, she makes a squiggly motion with her hand, indicating to me that I have red lines on my eyes. "And a little bit of green."

"Only a little bit of green?"

She squishes her pudgy forefinger and thumb together and smiles, "Only a little bit." She pauses as her face grows serious. "Mommy? Why do you have red eyes?"

I have to think about the answer to this. My daughter has reached the wondrous age of questioning everything, and simply telling her that my eyes are tired would not be a sufficient answer for her. I go over a mental checklist of all the reasons that my eyes are tired, trying to find one that is suitable to share with Maddison.

I can't tell my innocent young child that my eyes are red and tired because every day over the past two-and-a-half years since her father left us I have had no rest. That I have to get up every morning and remind myself to be patient while trying to deal with the distractions of a child with ADHD. That at the end of every day I repeat to myself, "I will not put my child on medication to make it easier on me," or that it bothers me that I cannot understand my own child's speech and have had to wait a year to get her into speech therapy.

I can't tell my sweet little girl that my eyes are red and tired because I worry that we don't have enough money. That I have had to choose which bill goes unpaid this month so that we can eat and have a roof over our heads. That I cannot afford to buy her a new lunchbox for preschool, even though yogurt spilled in her old one and I can't get the rancid smell out of the cheap vinyl. That I'm upset because I can't provide her with all the little things her heart desires.

I can't tell my precious angel that my eyes are red and tired because I have too much work to do, and fear that I don't give her enough of my time. That I spend hours every day trying to complete my high-school graduation requirements so I can get a good-paying job. That I spend four hours a day cooking and cleaning and picking up children's size-ten socks. That I spend a minimum of two hours a day trying to get my writing career going, and countless hours a week researching prospective jobs and trying to figure out if I can make it as a writer. That I find it difficult to make time for myself, and my emotional well-being is suffering because of it. Or that every night I collapse in my bed three hours later than I should have, and that I am physically and emotionally exhausted.

I look at my little girl, whose tiny face mirrors my own, and I have an overwhelming urge to shield her from the cruelties of life. I could not bear the guilt of burdening her with the reasons that my eyes are red and tired all the time. Moments have passed, and Maddison is still waiting for an answer from me.

"Excuse me, Mommy," she says. I have been trying to teach her to excuse herself when she needs to interrupt somebody. I know that I have done a good job, because she is interrupting my thoughts, and not my speech, which is what I had been focusing on. Her intelligence astounds me.

"I asked you why your eyes are red."

"I know, sweetheart. Mommy's just trying to think of the answer."

"Okay, Mommy. I'll be quiet so you can think." She plops herself back down on her pillow and patiently awaits my reasons.

I still had not come up with an answer that was appropriate, so I had to ask myself why I go through so much every day. I deal with her ADHD without giving her drugs because I don't want to stifle her brilliant personality, which Ritalin seems to do. I patiently teach her sign language as I learn it myself because it helps her to communicate without the frustration she feels about her speech difficulties. We suffer financially because I choose to be home with my daughter, instead of working forty hours a week. I work hard trying to get an education, so that some-day we can have more money without my being away from home and her.

I finally had my answer.

"Sweetheart, Mommy's eyes are red because I love you more than anything else in the world."

"Okay, Mommy."

My answer seems to have satisfied her curiosity, and we settle in to read a bedtime story and sing a verse of "You Are My Sunshine."

"Mommy? Why am I your sunshine? I'm not sunshine, I'm Maddison! And skies aren't gray, they're blue, Mommy."

I laugh and wonder if all three-year-olds are this logical. And why did she ever have to learn the meaning of "why" anyway?

*Trina Wray*

# 3

# SPECIAL MOMENTS AND MIRACLES

*There are only two ways to live your life.*
*One is as though nothing is a miracle.*
*The other is as if everything is.*

*Albert Einstein*

# Happy Father's Day!

*A child is the root of the heart.*

Carolina María de Jesús

While Mrs. Berry stood at the front of the class talking about an assignment, Elizabeth stared dreamily out the window. With fewer than two weeks left in the school year, she couldn't seem to concentrate. Visions of swimming, trips to the beach and endless days of pure fun filled her head. *Would Mom make us go to that awful camp again this year? Even worse, would she have Mrs. Pulowski, who always smelled of garlic, babysit us again?* Elizabeth wrinkled her nose at the thought.

Mrs. Berry's voice interrupted her daydreaming. "Elizabeth! Perhaps you would care to join the rest of the class?"

Elizabeth snapped to attention and tried to stay focused while Mrs. Berry described the Father's Day cards they were supposed to make. Although Elizabeth's mom said that most holidays were made up by greeting-card companies so they could sell more cards, Elizabeth thought they were more fun than ordinary days.

Mrs. Berry passed out construction paper and pieces of fabric that had been cut into the shape of neckties. They were supposed to fold the paper in half to make a card, then paste the necktie to the front. She wrote the message that was supposed to go inside on the blackboard. Dutifully, Elizabeth folded her yellow piece of paper in half, but stopped and frowned at the blue necktie-shaped fabric she had been given. Taking her scissors out of her desk, she began to cut the fabric. It was hard because the scissors were dull, so she struggled for a few minutes, trying to get the right shape. By the time the rest of the class was writing their message on the inside of the cards, Elizabeth was still working on the front of hers, but she didn't mind. She was almost always among the last to finish. Mrs. Berry said it was because she spent so much time daydreaming.

When Elizabeth finally did look at the message on the board, she noticed something else written next to it. She felt her face grow warm—she hadn't heard Mrs. Berry's explanation that anyone who didn't have a father could make a card for a grandfather or an uncle. She had messed up again. Mrs. Berry was going to be upset.

As her teacher walked up the aisle, Elizabeth tried covering her card with her arm, but Mrs. Berry gently lifted it so that she could read it. Elizabeth sat very still, waiting for her to say something, but when she looked up she saw a tear roll down Mrs. Berry's face. That's when she knew she had *really* messed up. She had never made Mrs. Berry so upset that she cried.

When the class was dismissed for the day, Elizabeth waited until all the other kids left so that she could apologize.

"I'm sorry for not listening," Elizabeth said. "I'll make another card if you want. I'll do it at home and bring it in tomorrow. I promise."

"What are you talking about?" asked Mrs. Berry.

"My Father's Day card. I know you're upset because I didn't do it right."

"Elizabeth, that was the best card in the whole class. It was so sweet it made me cry."

"You cried because it was sweet? You really think it was the best one?"

Mrs. Berry just nodded.

Elizabeth was so happy that she ran out of the classroom.

When her mom came home from work that night, Elizabeth decided it would be okay to give her the card early, since it was the best one in the class.

On the front of the card was a drawing of Elizabeth's mom, with the blue piece of fabric cut to look like a bow in her hair. Inside the card she had written:

*Dear Mom,*

*I know you work really hard to be both a mommy and a daddy. I want to thank you and wish you a happy Father's Day!*

*Love,*
*Elizabeth*

When her mom read the card she started crying, just like Mrs. Berry had.

"Are you crying because it's sweet?" asked Elizabeth.

Her mom just hugged her and cried some more.

*Hazel Holmes*

# I Love You, Daddy

*And now these three things remain: Faith, hope and love. But the greatest of these is love.*

1 Corinthians 13:13

How could any of us possibly know what is going to happen from day to day? Certainly the entire world was unprepared for what happened on the bright, autumn day of September 11, 2001. As for my world and the world of those I love most, life was forever altered on that fateful Tuesday morning.

My wife, Shelley, and I took separate cars to work on September 11. We usually drove in together, the two of us and our two children, Drake and Chandler, but Shelley's office was preparing to move to the other side of the Pentagon in two days, so she would be staying late. I wasn't very pleased about this, and I told her so the night before, but she was proud of the confidence that her supervisors had placed in her and wanted to set an example—I couldn't argue with that.

She left for work before I did that morning. I had the kids in my car, and when I stopped at Burger King to get them some breakfast (a treat for being good while I was alone with them in the car), the attendant told me that Shelley had just been there. She stayed ahead of me the whole way into town, and I didn't see her again until I brought the kids into the Pentagon day care. She was standing at one of the windows looking into a classroom when I saw her. I'll never forget the moment she saw us: She was wearing navy blue chinos, a blue oxford-cloth shirt and her beautiful smile. The kids ran to her as soon as they saw her, and we took them to their respective classrooms.

After we dropped the kids off, Shelley followed me to my car where she gave me an air kiss so she wouldn't get any lipstick on my cheek. Then I drove off to my office a few miles away. I talked to her again, at about 9:30, when she called me about the World Trade Center attacks.

Ten minutes later, my beautiful, gracious, kind, passionate wife—devoted mother to our beautiful children, a woman who loved all children and life itself—was gone.

Words can't begin to describe the loss.

Shelley remains a part of my life and the kids' lives in little miraculous ways. I've struggled to find the right way to keep her memory alive daily, and I think I'm succeeding. I'm still working on me, on going on without her physical presence next to me, but I've come to the point where I know she is with me, all around me, whenever I need her. She has let me know in many ways that she is watching over us, and knowing how much she loved us, I can honestly say that I'm not surprised.

At the end of September, the kids and I left Washington and moved to my parents' house in Morgantown, West Virginia. They live in the country, their nearest neighbor about a quarter-mile away, so we had lots of sunshine and peace and quiet, just when we needed it. Chandler was twenty months old at the time, and just beginning to put two or three words together to form rudimentary sentences. One day in early October, I was standing under a tree with Chandler in my arms. Holding her, I found myself crying because the child psychologists had told me that Chandler probably was too young to retain any of her own memories of Shelley into adulthood—that Chandler's memories of her mother would be composites, pieced together from the recollections of those who knew her mother. Reflecting on how much Shelley loved her children, the unfairness of it all overwhelmed me, and I wept quietly.

The child psychologists also told me not to hide my feelings from the kids, but to explain them, so they would know it's okay to grieve. So I looked at Chandler with tears in my eyes and said, "Daddy's crying because he misses Mommy."

Chandler looked up at me with her innocent blue eyes and said: "I love you, Daddy."

Given the simple two- or three-word sentences she had put together up until that point, I was surprised that she had put these words together so cohesively. I had never heard her say the word *love* before. Over the next two weeks, whenever I told Chandler that I missed Mommy, Chandler would reply with: "I love you, Daddy."

One day in mid-October we were standing under the same tree. Again, I told Chandler that I missed Mommy. Again, Chandler said, "I love you, Daddy."

I was suddenly curious, so I asked her, "Who taught you to say that?"

Without a moment's hesitation, Chandler replied, "Mommy."

Several months after September 11, one night when I was feeling particularly down, I decided to do a little house-cleaning to take my mind off my sadness. I came across a piece of paper on which Shelley had typed her notes for the reading that she gave at her brother's wedding in July 2001.

The reading was from Corinthians, and as my eyes raced across the words, they came to rest on the last line: "Love never ends."

I stand in awe of Shelley's never-ending love for our children and for me.

*Donn Marshall*

# Your Friend, Mommy

*The toughest part of motherhood is the inner worrying and not showing it.*

Audrey Hepburn

I gave birth to Whitney in the spring of my teenage years. From the outside, this could have looked like a logistical nightmare. Indeed, sometimes it was. Diaper changes interrupted studying, and she had to be put to bed before I went off to my school dances. I was filling out elementary-school registration forms for her while trying to meet college financial-aid applications for myself. Now that she's fifteen, it feels like she has always been a part of my life. We've shared important moments. She was there when I learned how to drive, graduated high school and got accepted to college—Harvard, no less! We've been doing our homework together for years.

Whitney and I used to go over her homework in the evenings. We were often so tired (and irritable) by the time we sat down that these sessions could be tense—sometimes ending in tears or bruised emotions. Our evening meetings often came at the close of long days; days that

Whitney and I had likely spent starved for each other's affection. Otherwise, we shared rushed exchanges: *Do you need lunch money?* Yes. *Don't miss the bus!* I won't. *Grandma will be here when you come home.* Okay. *I have a class tonight and I'll come in to say good night when I come in.* All right. *Did you eat?* Not yet. *I love you.* I love you, too.

When we sat down, our hearts ached with questions that we didn't ask: *Are you as famished for my attention as I am for yours? Am I special to you? Are you okay? Am I doing okay? Are you happy that I am yours, and you are mine? Are we going to make it? We made it by the skin of our teeth today, but can we pull it off tomorrow, next week . . . next month, next year?* We looked for answers to these unspoken questions in every touch, glance and remark. We scrutinized each other's tone of voice and facial expressions for affirmation. A curt response or innocent correction could be mistaken for disapproval. I knew I had to be careful not to communicate anything that could be taken the wrong way. I tried to exude excitement. Most of the time, I fell short, holding exhaustion at bay just long enough to muscle some neutrality.

One evening, Whitney was finishing a homework assignment in which she was instructed to draw a grid and place the people that she knew into the correct categories: friends, family, neighbors and so on. I checked it over for mistakes. Everything was in order, except that she had drawn a picture of me in the "friends" box.

"Whitney," I said, "this picture of me is supposed to be in the 'family' category."

She looked at me, her big brown eyes wide and charitable. "You're my friend, too," she said. She was not defensive or offended. She spoke as if she were reminding me of an eternal truth that I had only momentarily forgotten—the same way she would remind me that two plus two equals four.

"Oh," I said quietly. I was embarrassed, but delighted to be reminded of all of the special roles that we filled in each other's lives.

That evening I went to bed assured of the answers to our unuttered questions. *Yes, you are special to me. No, I wouldn't want to belong to anyone else in the world. Absolutely, we are going to make it. We are okay.*

*Patricia J. Lesesne*

# Spilled Coffee

*Always be nice to your children because they are the ones who will choose your rest home.*

Phyllis Diller

The sun streams in through the small, dusty kitchen window, casting a dull reflection over the creamy brown pool that's forming on the tabletop littered with bits and pieces of glazed ceramic. I can't help but laugh over the spilled coffee and broken cup.

It wasn't always this way.

My two boys, William and Leslie, were eleven and thirteen respectively, when their mother died of a brain aneurysm, and I was left to raise them alone. I was working full-time at a local auto-parts factory, and we had moved into a smaller house to make the expenses more manageable. The house was old and heated by an oil furnace that shot fire out of its rusted frame every time the flame kicked in. In the living room, there was a wood-burning stove, an old relic from when the house was first constructed in the early twentieth century.

I was always tired and constantly behind in my

responsibilities. I worked long, eight-hour shifts on a hot, stifling factory floor, then came home to two squabbling youngsters ever ready to explode in hormonal frustration.

"Dad! Les hit me!"

"He broke my model car!"

Every day, I shuffled in the house, half awake, to hear some variation on this story—details of the punching, shoving and name-calling that had been taking place for the past hour and a half, when the boys were left unattended after school. I would handle the diplomatic role of fatherhood as best as I could, while simultaneously trying to cook something resembling a wholesome meal and get Will and Les to do their homework.

I thought I had reached my breaking point one cold January night. The boys were watching a video in the living room while I was stooped over the dining-room table trying to figure out a way to pay the bills and fix a steadily worsening transmission problem in my car.

"Dad, I'm bored." Will came to stand next to the table, shuffling back and forth in the way that was typical of his impatient, hyperactive personality. I barely gave him a glance before responding.

"Go wash the dishes, then."

"But Daaaad . . . ," he whined, stamping his foot pleadingly.

I shot him a stern look, allowing him to see that I meant business, and said, "Go watch the movie with your brother, then."

"Les turned it off. He's watching football."

I didn't pay much attention to this comment, as I was just now noticing that my son was bundled up with sweatpants, socks, a sweater and a blanket draped over his shoulders. I thought about asking him why—my sons seemed most comfortable (particularly when company was over) running around the house with nothing on but their underwear, socks and a mischievous glint in their eyes—but I realized why immediately: the house was freezing. I hadn't noticed it before because I still had my coat on from poking around in the garage, but I almost saw my own breath exit my lips in wispy trails of vapor.

I hollered, "Les! Turn that movie back on or go to bed!" as I walked over to check the thermostat. It was a shade over forty degrees in the house, yet the temperature was set to sixty-five. Worried, I went outside into the yard.

It took me a while to find a stick and get the cap off of the metal pipe that stuck up out of the snow in our backyard, but I soon discovered what I had feared most: We were completely out of fuel oil.

I cursed and kicked at the snow for a moment, completely lost as to what I should do. I walked back toward the garage to find an ax so I could chop some firewood from the loose brush in the tree line by the edge of the property. I never made it, as I heard Will's wailing sobs from the side of the house.

When I walked back into the house, it was like a war zone. Will was squealing and sobbing with horror in his eyes, blood covering his small hands as he clutched at his bloodied nose. Les was sulking in the corner, staring at the television, which had been knocked off its stand and now lay half-broken on the floor.

"Les hit me!"

"He said I couldn't watch television, and you said I had to go to bed!"

Somehow, by some divine force I imagine, I didn't lose it. I cleaned up William, gave them both a good long lecture and postponed their punishment until the next day, then sent them both to bed. I spent the rest of the night gathering up blankets for the boys, cleaning up and getting a fire started in the stove. Every hour or so, I had to put another heap of small branches in it so the fire would stay lit, but it kept the house pretty warm.

The next day, I worked my shift after only an hour or two of sleep, all the while worrying about how I could afford more fuel oil to heat the house.

Always tired and always behind, stress, anxiety and exhaustion were constants in my life. Somehow I managed.

Times were never really easy, but there were a lot of moments I remember fondly. All that hard work paid off in the end, for now I can sit comfortably in my house with my dog and talk with my grown sons, two men I am proud of and with whom I share both friendship and love.

Will is home for a week from the state university, an hour and a half away. Les is also visiting for the day, driving in from Chicago where he is a graphic designer. We were sitting around the table, drinking coffee and just catching up.

Les said, "Oh, Dad! I have to show you the new magazine layout I'm working on." He reached under the table for his briefcase, and at the same time, collided with Will, who was returning to the table with a freshly poured cup of coffee, which dropped and shattered on the table.

We all jumped, startled. William groaned, then teased, "Da-a-a-ad! Les spilled my coffee!"

Les replied in an equally mocking fashion, "Nuh-uh! Will started it!"

I laughed so hard, I nearly spilled my own.

*Richard Parker*

# The Sandbox Revelation

*The greatest part of our happiness depends on our dispositions, not our circumstances.*

Martha Washington

I spent all morning cleaning the house because my mother was coming over for dinner that night. When I was through, I decided to take my four-year-old out so that no new messes would accumulate before my mother arrived.

We were sitting at the park having a snack when I noticed that he was watching a father and son playing in the sandbox together. I asked him what he was looking at. Gazing up at me, he said, "Why don't I have a daddy?" I was so shocked by the question that I couldn't think of a thing to say. Noticing my confused expression, he stood up and gave me a big hug. With his arms still around me, he looked me in the eye and said, "It's okay, Mommy. We don't need anyone else making a mess in our house, anyway."

*Christine E. Penny*

"What stuff under my bed?"

# The Day I Became a Mother

*This is the miracle that happens every time to those who really love; the more they give, the more they possess.*

Rainer Maria Rilke

"You'd understand what I'm saying if you were really a mother," my friend said that morning in Sunday school. There it was, out in the open, what she and the others thought.

It was Mother's Day, and our church always recognized the mothers present by having them stand. I had watched this happen year after year as a single woman with no children. I had always sat and clapped along with the rest of the congregation. But this year was different. I was still single, but I was now a foster parent.

I had been thinking of that day as my own first Mother's Day, and now it had been ruined. I looked down at the two little girls sitting next to me. *Was I a mother? Did I have the right to be recognized? What dues had I paid to become a member of that elite group? What was a mother, anyway? I wasn't even "Momma" to the kids who passed through my home. I was "Aunt Dorothy."*

When the time came to recognize all mothers, I bent down to speak to the child nearest me. I pretended I wasn't aware of what was going on until it was too late. "Darn, I missed it," I whispered aloud as the mothers sat back down. "There's always next year." Who was I fooling?

Foster children came and went that year, each with their own set of problems. I wiped their noses and doctored their scrapes and cuts. I refereed their disagreements and took away privileges when necessary. I was there to wake them up and take them to school, and I was there to tuck them in at night. I comforted those whose sleep was interrupted by nightmares. And when they left my care, I cried.

Shortly before Mother's Day the following year, one of the girls in my care was going through a particularly difficult period. Dealing with her anxiety attacks, coupled with the day-to-day problems of the other three girls in our home, along with my duties as a school librarian and teacher, began to take a toll on me.

I didn't have a husband to share the problems with or to say, "Hey, it's your turn. You deal with it this time." Yes, there was the social worker, but it wasn't the same. I was alone as a parent. *Why was I putting myself through this? I wasn't their mother. I was just "Aunt Dorothy," and not really that. What was the use?*

One morning when I was feeling very frustrated, I made a decision. I would call my caseworker that afternoon and tell her that I quit. That was when I heard a voice call me by name. "Dorothy, remember all those years ago when I told you that I had a special job for you? Well, these children are it."

Being a mother is a calling. Most mothers have their children delivered by doctors; a few lucky ones, like me, have ours delivered by social workers (and sometimes a deputy or two). Either way, being a mother is far more than giving birth. It's being there through the bad times as well as the good. That was the day I became a real mother.

On Mother's Day, I sat with my four girls in church. When they asked for all mothers to stand, I quickly got to my feet. There was no doubt in my mind as I looked at each of the girls: I was their mother for right now, and they deserved—and were going to get—all the love and attention I could give them.

A few years later, the other mothers in my church were lucky when it was decided not to recognize the mother with the most children. As a single mother whose household now included three adopted daughters, two foster children, two former foster children who had come back to the roost, and one foreign-exchange student, I had them beat by a country mile.

*Dorothy Hill*

# Love and Cheeseburgers

*Each day comes bearing its own gifts. Untie the ribbons.*

Ruth Ann Schabacker

Things have been hard for a friend of mine. She and her six-year-old son have just moved into their own apartment, a break they needed to get out of a difficult situation. The responsibilities of having their own home puts pressure on her while she tries to support her son, and once in a while, it gets the best of her.

The little guy is a typical six-year-old: mischievous, energetic and curious. His questions deluge her daily as he discovers the world around him. Most of the time, she takes it all in stride, amazed at how easy it is to please him. The promise of a simple cheeseburger from his favorite restaurant is enough for him to be on his best behavior for an entire weekend. His mom is grateful she can give him what he wants, at least for now.

One evening at the end of a very long day at work, the demands of the day were heavy on her mind. After picking up her son at after-school care, the two of them went home for dinner. While going through the motions of preparing his food and looking over his first-grade school papers, the tasks of being a single mom overwhelmed her. Once she had him bathed and tucked into bed, she sat down in the living room and cried. Everything hit her suddenly and without warning. The recent loss of her beloved grandmother, combined with the responsibilities of single-parenting, was just too much. Wiping tears from her eyes, she looked up to see her son peeking into the living room from the hallway.

"Mommy, are you okay?"

"Yes, honey," she replied. "I'm just a little sad."

He walked over to her and wrapped his small arms around her neck. Though she tried to hold them back, her tears fell even more freely, and her son reassured her that everything would be all right. Hurrying back to his bedroom, he returned quickly, handing his mom a small piece of paper folded into a crumpled square.

She opened it and read its message: "I love you, Mom."

She would have reached out at that moment and held him for eternity, but he had gone into the kitchen and was busy making her his special dish. It's the only thing he can cook, and it took him quite a while to prepare it.

Finally, he came into the living room with a plate of buttered toast. It was all he had to give, that and the note.

While he sat there proudly, she ate every bite, even though the butter was in a huge clump in the middle.

"That's what love is all about," she later told me. "He gave me all he had, wrote the words he best knew how to spell, prepared the only food he knew how to prepare. I'm not nearly as alone as I was feeling that evening. I have a wonderful son who loves me."

Sometimes, when you least expect it, a blessing from God shines through your darkest moment. For my friend, that blessing is with her all the time, in tennis shoes and tiny blue jeans.

I asked her what in the world a parent could do when a child has given his all.

She smiled and replied, "The next day, I took him out for a cheeseburger."

*Kathy Bohannon*

# Oh, to Be Rich!

*Not what we have, but what we use, not what
we see, but what we choose—these are the things
that mar or bless human happiness.*

Joseph Fort Newton

I lay on my bed, legs propped up against the white
cinder-block wall, desperately wishing my mother would
call. But I remembered the last time I'd seen her, right
before the train for Providence pulled out of the station,
"You know how expensive it is to call," she said, then
squeezed me tight and said good-bye.

This was my first birthday away from home, and I
missed my mom, missed my sister, and most certainly
missed the special pound cake my mother always made
for my birthday. Since getting to college that year, I would
watch jealously as the other freshmen received care packages from their parents on their birthdays—and even on
ordinary days. Big boxes containing summer slacks and
blouses, brownies and packages of M&M's and Snickers,
things they needed and things they didn't. Instead of feeling thrilled about my upcoming eighteenth birthday, I felt

empty. I wished my mom would send me something, too, but I knew that she couldn't afford presents or the postage. She had done her best with my sister and me—raising us by herself. The simple truth was, there just was never enough money.

But that didn't stop her from filling us with dreams. "You can be anything you want to be," she would tell us. "Politicians, dancers, writers—you just have to work for it, you have to get an education."

For a long time, because of my mother's resourcefulness, I didn't realize that we were poor. She did so much with so little. She owned and took care of our house, practically nursing the forty-year-old pipes and oil furnace to keep us warm throughout the cold winters. She clothed and fed us. She found ways to get us scholarships so that we could take violin, piano and viola lessons from some of the best teachers in Philadelphia. She never missed an opportunity to have a tête-à-tête with our schoolteachers, and she attended all our plays and musical performances. My mother had high hopes for my sister and me. She saw the way out of poverty for us was education. We didn't play with the other children on the street, didn't jump double-dutch or stay out late on the porch laughing and talking with our neighbors. We were inside doing our homework and reading books. She sat with us while we did our work and taught us how to learn what she didn't know by plowing through the *World Book Encyclopedia* or visiting the library. And she did it all on eight hundred dollars a month.

I have vivid memories of Mom sitting with us on the concrete steps out back, under the far-reaching branches of the sycamore tree. Her voice would float up as she recited, "I think that I shall never see, a poem as lovely as a tree," or "We are climbing Jacob's ladder." Then she would hug us. I can still feel the sense of safety that washed over me like warm water. I felt my chest expand with joy as I listened to her voice close to my ear saying how she yearned us into being: "I told your dad, 'Rosie, I've already got sons, now I need girls.' And within five years, he gave me not one, but both of you."

But what a struggle it was for her.

"Please, Mom, can we go to the movies?" we'd beg.

"No, we can watch a movie at home," she'd say, turning to channel 10.

"Can't we get nicer pants than these ugly green things?" we'd say as we went through the black plastic bag filled with hand-me-downs from our cousins.

"These will do you fine for now," Mom would say.

"Why can't I have money to buy french fries after school?" I would plead, my nostrils full with the remembered smell of sizzling grease and freshly salted potatoes.

"No, you don't need that mess. Besides, I've made split-pea soup with carrots and potatoes."

She never bought anything that she could make herself, and only for emergencies did she tap the spotless credit she maintained at Sears and at Strawbridge & Clothier, a Philadelphia, family-run business based in Center City.

I felt our lack most deeply after Christmas, when the other kids talked about the new games and expensive outfits they had found tucked under their live Christmas trees. I didn't mention our silver tree that we unpacked and repacked every year, or that there were only a couple of items for me under the tree: some books, socks, maybe a pair of shoes that I needed. And because my dad wasn't around, Mom pressed me into service—I would wrap my younger sister's gifts so that she could wake up excited, believing that Santa had left goodies for her on the floor beneath the tree.

Thanks to my mom's sacrifices and big dreams, I'd made it to the Ivy League: Brown University in Providence, Rhode

Island. Yet I was afraid that I wouldn't measure up to the other students. They seemed to exude confidence and the smell of money. I felt so lost, so far away, as if my mom had said, "Well, if you're old enough to go six hours away, you're old enough to take care of yourself."

My roommate joined me on the bed. "Hey. After we study, we'll go to Campus Center and get ice cream and cake." I nodded, closed my eyes and imagined the cake my mom would have made. She would take out her stand-up mixer and the chrome bowl, then add the butter that she'd let sit out until it was soft. She would pour in the sharp sugar grains in a narrow stream. *Mmm.* I could see the golden yellow of each of the twelve eggs, swallowed under the rapid blur of the spinning beaters, and I could almost smell the vanilla and nutmeg filling the house while the cake baked.

As I daydreamed, there was a knock on the door. My roommate opened it to find a deliveryman asking for me. He handed her a large rectangular box, which she carefully placed on the desk near my bed. "Open it." I did, and inside was a vanilla cake with chocolate frosting. In icing were the words: *Happy Birthday, Sande! Love, Mom and Rosalind.* My skin tingled with excitement, as if my mom were right there hugging me close. How had she managed to afford it? I felt as if I were back on the steps with her, safe and secure while she sang and told me how much she loved having me in her life. I ran out to the hall and knocked on my dorm mates' doors. "Birthday cake," I called. As I cut cake for the ten students gathered in my room, then watched their faces as they ate, I didn't need to eat to feel both full and rich inside.

*Sande Smith*

# Watching Over You

*Every experience, every thought, every word, every person in your life is a part of a larger picture of your growth.*

Macrina Wiederkehr

I was a single parent, divorced eleven years and raising my thirteen-year-old son, Michael, alone. Michael had recently taken up skiing at the nearby ski hill. Late one afternoon, I took him and his friend Joe to ski. Given all the trouble teens get into these days, I was always very careful about where they went and who would be there. The community ski facility was quite nice, with an area for food and drinks in the upper loft.

Most parents would drop their kids off and would come back hours later, but before I could feel comfortable about leaving, I had to be sure they were safe and having a good time. I told the boys that I would stay in the loft and watch them ski for a while (even though in the evening with the lights on the hill, you could rarely tell who anyone was as they came skiing down). Hour after hour, I stood there watching each little figure go up in the lift, then ski downward. A couple of times, the boys came in for some food and hot chocolate. They laughed, sharing their triumphs and defeats on the hill, got warmed up and off they went again.

After nearly four hours had gone by, I found myself standing at the window, feeling a bit lonely and sorry for myself—I was tired and weepy. I allowed my thoughts to wander about how my ex-husband was probably out having a great time, with no responsibilities to tie him down. How great it would be to just be able to go clothes shopping or have some fun, something just for *me* for a change.

Suddenly, a voice broke through my self-pitying mood.

A young man, whom I had never met, said, "Hi, excuse me, but I noticed you've been standing there for hours. You're watching your kids ski, right?"

Rather taken aback, I responded, "Yes, that's right."

He replied, "Well, I just wanted to tell you, if there were more parents in the world like you, it would be a better place." And then he pushed the door open and left, as suddenly as he had come.

My mood lifted, and a smile spread across my face. I recalled the passage from the Bible: "Don't forget to entertain strangers, for by so doing some have entertained angels unawares" (Heb. 13:1).

The young man's words brought me a very strange but comfortable feeling. I felt God had sent him, this angel, to remind me of what was really important in life. I knew in my heart that there was nothing else I'd rather be doing at that moment, and nowhere else I'd rather be.

*Linda Ferris*

# Coloring On

*Things turn out best for people who make the best of the way things turn out.*

Anonymous

Welcome to my life. An average day for this single parent: trying to juggle a three-year-old, a full-time job and all the errands in between. Lately, I had been *beyond* stressed. My shifts at work were getting cut; less hours meant less money, and as a single mom who hadn't received a dime in child support, the pressure was mounting. I hate to admit it, but there are times when I suddenly stop what I'm doing and indulge in a brief moment or two of feeling sorry for myself. I never wallow for too long, because there are other things that need tending to, but on occasion, I allow myself to stop and shed a few tears, or just a weary sigh. Then I regain my composure and carry on. Even when it seems like the world is falling apart, you have to find a way to piece things back together.

One afternoon after work, I picked up my daughter, Stella, at the babysitter's and we headed for the grocery store. While shopping, she asked me to purchase an overpriced, cartoon-decorated snack item. I told her no (three-year-olds don't understand what a budget is), and she started whining. I was tempted to give in as she persisted, but managed to hold my ground. After a few minutes of pleading, she realized I wasn't negotiating, so she gave up.

After we arrived home, Stella approached me as I was unloading the groceries. "I'm sorry for being mean to you at the store, Mommy."

I knelt down and gave her a hug. "It's okay, but you have to understand that whining won't get you anywhere." I sighed. "It's hard being a single mom sometimes." I still don't know why I said that out loud. How could her little mind comprehend that statement? I kissed her on the cheek, and we both went back to what we were doing.

Later on that night, Stella was coloring a picture. She seemed frustrated that it wasn't coming out the way she intended. She stopped her coloring and looked up at me. "Mommy? It's hard being a Stella." Then she looked down again and went back to coloring. For one of the first times that day I smiled, even chuckled to myself. For that brief moment, I felt a bit of clarity. She was beginning to understand that, for all of us, for different reasons, life is hard at times. And sometimes, all you can really do is stop for a moment, sigh and go back to coloring. I sat down and picked up a crayon to join her.

*Sierra Sky Brocius*

"This is a 'Single Parent' patch. It helps you do the job of two parents at the same time."

# Finding Change

*It is the nature of grace always to fill the spaces that have been empty.*

Goethe

A banging from the kitchen woke me up. Getting out of bed, I glanced at the clock on the nightstand: 2:30 A.M. The rest of the house was quiet; the children were still asleep. With trepidation, I headed down the short hall to the source of the noise. As I flipped on the light, I noticed a small mound of snow on the kitchen floor just inside the door. "What in the world?" I muttered.

It was then that I became conscious of the keening wind outside. Now, more out of curiosity than fear, I opened the back door. The wind had blown the storm door open, and there was a good foot of snow wedged tight against the outside of the kitchen door. We were in the midst of a full-fledged February blizzard. Taking broom in hand, I quickly cleared the threshold of the snow, grabbed the banging storm door and latched it tight. Taking the small rug in front of the sink, I rolled it up, pressed it tight against the inside of the storm door for insulation, then shut the kitchen door.

Realizing there would be no school the following day for any of us, I decided to wake the children. They had to see this. I climbed to the large bedroom on the upper floor of our small Cape Cod to wake my sons, David, fourteen, and Christopher, twelve. "Wake up and come downstairs. We're having a blizzard!" Next to my bedroom, on the first floor, was Cathy and Julie's room. In spite of all the commotion, they were still asleep. Julie, the eight-year-old, was easier to rouse than her ten-year-old sister.

Within minutes, the five of us were gathered in front of the picture window in the living room. When we had gone to bed that night, the weather had been a rainy, and almost balmy, fifty-five. Now, the ferocious wind was driving snow horizontally, and there were drifts up to two feet in height. While the children watched, I turned on the radio. During the night, the temperature had dropped forty degrees, and it continued to plummet. Twelve inches of snow had already fallen, with six to ten inches more expected. All the rain that had fallen the day before was now frozen into a thick sheet of ice beneath the snow. The roads were closed to all but essential personnel. All schools closed until further notice. Upon hearing that last item, the four children began to cheer. Me, too. It was my first year of teaching, and I looked forward to snow days just as much as the kids. Fifteen minutes later, everyone was back in bed, looking forward to sleeping in and a few days of freedom.

That morning, worry woke me early. I did a quick inventory of the refrigerator and pantry and felt we would be okay. My ex-husband's meager support check always went just for groceries, and most times, never far enough. My teaching job was with a county program for severely retarded children. I loved my job, but I was bringing home about half of what a teacher in regular education earned. Money was always tight. But I was a good cook who could do wonders with a pound of pasta, a bag of beans or a small piece of meat. With the children home all day, I knew they would eat more than usual, but I still felt we would be okay. No luxuries, but plenty of staples. I had $1.25 in my billfold to buy milk later in the week. That was all.

The next two days turned out to be a lot of fun. We played games and cards, made cookies, popcorn, and homemade bread and pizza. We read a lot. The neighborhood kids cleared off a large area in the middle of our street, and all the kids went ice-skating on the "rink" that had formed from the frozen rain. A good time was had by all—until the doughnut crisis hit.

It seemed small at first, then grew to monstrous proportions. After eating a breakfast of cereal and toast, Cathy asked for doughnuts. The other three then took up the mantra. David said that since the roads were still closed, he and Christopher would gladly walk the two blocks to the doughnut shop to pick some up. I said no. They pleaded some more. I again said no, this time a little more emphatically. That held them for about fifteen minutes. But they had doughnuts on their minds and soon started over again. After my third no, David asked a simple question: "Why not, Mom?"

I could feel my tears start, and rather than let them see me cry, I brushed away the tears and decided to confront them with the truth. "We can't afford to get any doughnuts. I just don't have any extra money for something like that. Not until next week. So that has to be the end of it."

*Great job, Mom!* I thought, as I looked at their unhappy faces. I didn't need to share this burden with them.

They started to turn away, then David said, "Hey, I bet I have some loose change in my drawers, or in some of my pockets. I'm gonna go look."

"Me, too," the other three chimed in, as they ran to their rooms. I watched them go.

"Me, too," I whispered to myself, as I went off to search among my things.

Looking through my bedroom, I remembered the drawer where I kept my purses. I always kept at least a quarter in each one for an emergency phone call. I found a dollar bill in one, and three quarters in the others. I went to the kitchen and put my money on the table. Soon, everyone else came running back, clutching an assortment of coins in their hands.

"You first, Julie," David said. The youngest triumphantly lay down twelve pennies, three nickels and two dimes. Then Cathy, grinning, added fifteen pennies, a dime and a quarter. With a flourish, David and Christopher put their coins down at the same time—a collection of eighteen pennies, four dimes and three quarters.

I was amazed. We had more than enough for a dozen doughnuts. "Okay, bundle up, then. Off with you two," I said to the boys. "I'll start the hot chocolate."

Fifteen minutes later, cold but happy, they returned with a box of a dozen doughnuts. Then David put another bag on the table. "What's that?" I asked.

David answered with a huge smile. "The owner said because of all the snow, business was slow, so he gave us six more doughnuts! Free!" This time I didn't try to stop my tears.

A minute later, with napkins passed around and hot chocolate poured, we were eating our doughnuts. Our wonderful, delicious, mouthwatering doughnuts. And to this day, nothing has ever tasted as good as those doughnuts eaten in our tiny kitchen, warm against the freezing snow outside.

*Rosemary Heise*

# Toast Means Love

*Happiness does not depend on outward things, but on the way we see them.*

Leo Tolstoy

Without a doubt, my favorite food is toast. Not just any toast; it has to be slathered with butter and placed under the broiler until it's just right. I love it when it is perfectly browned and a small circle of melted butter gathers in the center. Toast reminds me of love.

When I was a little girl, we would all cuddle up in my mother's bed and eat toast together. We sat there under the blankets—my mother, my sister, my brother and me—munching our hot, crispy squares and telling why we loved each other. Not big things, just little everyday things: cute dimples, funny laugh, wavy hair.

When I was in college, my friends teased me about my love for toast. I decided to find out why I loved toast so much. I called my brother and asked him if he loved toast as much as I did. He laughed and said that we all ate toast back then because we were poor. He doesn't eat toast anymore. So I called my sister. She said that when we were little, since we didn't have any other food to eat, we ate toast. She despises toast.

Finally, I called my mother. As I began to quiz her about my toast obsession, she interrupted. She said, "Honey, we ate toast because I was twenty-three years old at the time. Your father left us, and I didn't have a job. I went to the welfare office, and the social worker that I talked to said, 'The country didn't give you those babies.' I got mad and walked out of there, and I got myself a job. Sometimes, all we had was bread, but I wanted to make it nice. I needed to have you three nearby me because I was scared back then, and I needed your comfort and your love. I'm sorry."

"But Mom," I wailed, "I thought toast meant love!"

She was silent for a moment, then said quietly, "It does, sweetie. It does."

*Toni Hall*

# 4

# OVERCOMING OBSTACLES

*The marvelous richness of human experience would lose something of rewarding joy if there were no limitations to overcome. The hilltop hour would not be half so wonderful if there were no dark valleys to traverse.*

*Helen Keller*

# Arms of Love

*Love is a force more formidable than any other. It is invisible—it cannot be seen or measured, yet it is powerful enough to transform you in a moment, and offer you more joy than any material possession could.*

Barbara de Angelis

I sat looking out the window, seeing new life growing in the early dawn of spring. The more I stared at the scenery, the more my sight blurred: I felt a warm drop—my own tear falling—as I wondered how life could be so cruel to me. What had I done to anger God so much that he would allow everything I ever loved to be taken away, one by one, piece by piece? I had made many poor choices in life, but God had always forgiven me. Where was he now? Why didn't I feel his mighty arms wrapped around me like I did when I was a kid?

Two years ago, I met a woman and saw life in a way I had not experienced before. Simplicity. Friendship. Communication. Love. I did all the things I knew to do: brought flowers, made home-cooked dinners, read books with her, watched the mist from a waterfall we'd spent all day hiking to, prayed together while holding hands.

What happened? What did I miss? What didn't I hear? I lived life to the fullest with her, and we gave God our best, inspired to live a wholesome life under his eyes. But, in our humanness, we made a choice. One that God would not overlook this time. I would be a great poster child for "it only takes once."

For the next nine months my baby's mother vanished. It affected my work, my eating, my sleeping; anger and bitterness consumed my time and thoughts.

Then, domestic relations called to inform me that I had a son, and papers were on their way for wage attachments. Why didn't she tell me? What was his name? Did he look like me? Why, God, why?

I prayed I would find the right legal help and be able to create the income needed for funding a campaign to have my son in my life. I was able to find two attorneys and had the help of family and friends to encourage me throughout the whole mess.

Finally, eight weeks after that first call, I met my son for the first time. One look at him and love like I had never felt before overwhelmed me, accompanied by the pain of seeing his mother for the first time since the fateful evening of his creation.

The next year was spent in the courtroom. I exhausted my entire savings, sold my home, let the car go back to the bank and now rely on private funding and donations for the food on my table and the house I currently live in.

His name is Noah. He looks like his daddy. He acts like his daddy. He lives with me half the time, but we love each other all the time. I sit and stare at him for hours and watch him while he sleeps. I listen to his breath in the night while he lies next to me, asleep and snuggled against my chest. I help him count the toes he has recently discovered, as he wonders why they move by themselves.

As I sit here, I look out the window at the springtime of new life. But the more I stare out the window, the more my sight blurs. I feel a warm drop—my own tear falling— as I sit wondering how life could be so good to me. What have I done to please God so much that he would allow everything I have loved to be given to me, little by little, one day at a time? I have made many poor choices in my life, but God has always forgiven me. I feel his mighty arms of love wrapped around me like I did when I was a kid. His name is Noah. He is my son.

*Jeff Gemberling*

# A Bit of Mom in All of Us

Six wooden orange crates in our living room were our table and chairs. My brother Barney, age six, and I, age nine, got them for our unfurnished apartment at the grocery store a block away. Mom thanked us for bringing them and said, "They're not pretty, but they'll do just fine." Each night, by swinging the closet door open and lowering the Murphy bed for Barney and me, our living room became a bedroom. Mom slept on the sofa that had been shipped along with dishes and other necessities on the same train that brought us to San Francisco in early 1930. Our front yard was the sidewalk on busy Franklin Street two flights down. Our backyard was the tiny space barely large enough for the apartment house trash cans.

Mom and Dad had divorced, when divorces were rare except in movies, and the Great Depression was at its worst. With no alimony checks arriving, no work she could find and being unwilling to live off our grandparents, who were barely surviving themselves, Mom had come to San Francisco from Denver with Barney and me. At the time, neither of us had any idea why we were moving, nor did we know about the divorce.

In this vast city, Mom knew no one. The only employment

she found during our first several months was occasional part-time work packing bacon. The thirty-dollar monthly rent was soon in arrears, despite our walking almost everywhere to save the nickel streetcar fare, stuffing card-board in our holey-soled shoes and managing to survive with precious little to eat.

Barney and I were among the earliest latchkey kids. The nearest park, six blocks away, was where many of the homeless and the vagrants spent time, so Mom wouldn't let us go there. Except for walking to and from the grocery store a block away, to and from school a mile away, and to meet Mom on Saturdays after work once she got a steady job, we were cooped up in the apartment, even during school vacations. Although Mom walked to and from work, where she was on her feet ten hours a day, six days a week, she'd take us through Golden Gate Park and along the beach on Sundays. We enjoyed those treks immensely, and they cost nothing but shoe leather. Our penalty for not obeying or failing to complete a task, either of which happened only on rare occasions, was the deprivation of our Sunday outing. She was a "tough love" mom. Once her punishments were decided, they were irrevocable, no matter how many tears we shed or how much we pleaded.

I recall only one time when I thought the dreaded pun-ishment was deserved, but it was not meted out. While at the store, with Mom's grocery list in hand, Barney and I bought a pack of two Hostess cupcakes. After we bought it, we felt devastatingly ashamed to have spent an extra nickel when money was so scarce for important food. When we told Mom about it, she just got tears in her eyes and said, "It's okay. I understand."

One day, Mom only had fifty cents left to last the three days until her next paycheck. A panhandler approached her with a plea for food money. Mom gave him a quarter. Later that day from our front window, we saw him drinking wine by a billboard across the street. I asked Mom how she could have been so generous. She replied, "If we do our best to help people in need, no matter how they use our gifts, God will take care of us." The next day, a check came in the mail from a friend who had sold some of Mom's best furniture. That got us by and paid the over-due rent.

At last, Mom got a temporary Christmas job at a down-town department store, but the first check wouldn't arrive until after the holiday. On Christmas Eve, we ate a meager supper and only had a can of spaghetti and a quart of milk left to eat on Christmas Day. Mom was dead broke. Barney and I were putting on an entertainment we had prepared for days as her Christmas gift: poems, songs and hymns we had learned at school. It was interrupted midway by a knock at the apartment door. There stood a man with a basket of canned foods, fresh fruit and a small turkey for us as a gift from the department-store associa-tion that had learned we were in need. We thanked him, and he left. I never knew until then that happiness can make people cry. Mom hugged us, and our tears gushed out. Then we knelt as Mom said a prayer thanking God for his goodness and asking him to bless the good people who were his hands, providing much nourishment for us on the birthday of his son, Jesus Christ. We thanked God again at church on Christmas morning, then what a deli-cious feast we had—and we had enough food left until Mom got her paycheck!

Soon after that, Mom found steady, full-time employ-ment at the department store. As soon as her bills were paid, she bought a real table and chairs, and even a five-dollar radio, so Barney and I could listen to programs like *Black and Blue: The Detectives, Chon Du the Magician* and *Jack Armstrong: The All-American Boy*, as well as the Notre Dame football games on Saturdays—all after doing homework and chores, of course. And we all enjoyed evening programs like *One Man's Family, Mert and Marge, Jack Benny* and *Inner Sanctum.*

Those were important early years for two brothers, who were loved, protected and guided by a 100-pound mother with a 100-ton heart, determined that her sons would survive and become well-educated, God-loving citizens. Mom died at ninety-three. Barney has seven children, twenty grandchildren and three great-grandchildren. My wife and I have eight children and nine grandchildren. Both Barney's and my own are close-knit, hardworking, loving, caring families, all trusting in God, living life fully and doing our best to make this troubled world better for future generations. A bit of Mom is in all of us.

Life would have been different and perhaps easier if Barney and I had been raised by both our parents. We might have learned how to fish and swim, swing a hammer, use a wrench and a saw, and how to play sports at younger ages. But I doubt that we could have become as industrious and caring as we are, or as grateful for the blessing of life's great adventure, were it not for the indomitable spirit of that very dear, independent, single parent we called Mom.

*James W. McLaughlin*

# Divorce—Cut and Dried

*It takes two to speak the truth—one to speak, and another to hear.*

Henry David Thoreau

My divorce was already looming on the horizon by the time I realized my fourteen-year-old firstborn had been carving deep gashes in her milky forearms, using a clean but unforgiving X-acto knife. I had been temporarily blinded—my perceptions dulled by my own worries and sixteen-hour workdays.

I truly believed my top priority as a soon-to-be single mother and freelance writer was to boost my solitary income to something above the poverty level, before we (my oldest, her seven-year-old sister and I) were officially on our own. My oldest's quest was to escape from emotional bankruptcy through a dramatic expression of her fears and a pain so great it had paralyzed her heart.

Our struggles intersected one quiet Colorado summer evening when I collapsed after midnight on the sofa beside her. My priorities instantly shifted when she lovingly leaned against me, squeezed my hand and forgot to cover the battle scars that now covered her arms.

"I love you, Mommy," she whispered as her fingers laced between mine. I opened my strained eyes, lifted my head from the cushions of the couch where it had landed, raised her fingers to my lips and found myself suddenly mute.

"Baby," I finally managed in little more than a whisper, "what has happened to your arms?" I will never forget the dirty-brown color of dried blood—the angry, silent swelling that flanked the heartbreaking crust.

Her eyes widened, she broke her finger's grip on mine and rushed to pull her long sleeves back over the marks. It was too late. Pandora's box had been opened. The secret would never be secret again.

"Hon?" I said, as I gently nudged the sleeve back and ran my fingers along the wounds. "Did you do this to yourself?"

"You wouldn't understand," she answered. "It's not about suicide or cutting my wrists."

There must have been a goddess of single motherhood watching over me that night, and she must have been astonishingly kind. I'm not sure how, but I somehow found the courage to resist panicking and stepped inside my daughter's troubled mind.

"I will understand," I promised, "if you'll help me. And neither one of us is moving from this sofa until I do."

For the next three hours, we talked and cried together about the terror she had been shouldering alone. She mapped out her feelings with remarkable clarity and wisdom. And I had the good sense to let her talk.

All her life, my daughter had watched two people fight to save a relationship that was never meant to survive. For fourteen years she'd locked herself away in her room to escape her father's high-volume anger and her mother's esteem-shattering acceptance of the verbal abuse. She wasn't afraid of the thought of her father leaving us. She was afraid

I would launch an emotional retreat, and in the end, beg him to stay.

It wasn't such a far-fetched scenario. Years before, her father and I had separated for a seven-month stretch. I'd started college classes to get my teaching degree. He'd found a new girlfriend with kids of her own. But before any divorce papers were filed, his girlfriend had had enough of him. With "for better or worse" echoing through my head, I'd reluctantly submitted when he asked me to come back home. Vanessa's conception guaranteed the temporary success of our reconciliation. But nothing, other than our census standing, had really changed.

"Every time I got my hopes up," my baby tearfully explained that night, "every time I thought we'd finally have a little peace, you guys up and changed your minds." Stress and turmoil silently tore at my teenage daughter, but she didn't know how to tell me. So she went numb as a self-preservation alternative. Her only release from that numbness was the selective carving of her delicate arms. "That momentary sting," she said, "helped me hide from the pain of being afraid."

As the sun came up over the Rocky Mountains, I made her a promise and exacted one from her in return. "This won't be another false start," I swore to her. "It'll be a fresh one—no turning back this time." She believed me, and agreed to talk to me the next time she ached for the feel of the blade.

It's been five years since my daughter and I traded midnight true confessions. Five years since I filed for, and finally got, my divorce. Five years since she has made a cut in her arms. We haven't lived in the lap of luxury, but I've managed to earn enough to pay for the sanctuary my family deserves.

Seven books and twelve hundred articles later, strangers and acquaintances assume my greatest accomplishment

has been finding success as a professional freelance writer—
supporting two daughters as a single mother. My family
knows better: I won the fight of my life the night I was
smart enough to listen to my baby. Helping to heal her
secret wounds is the success story that will always matter
to me most.

*Kelly McLane*

# Lighting the Way

*Hope is the thing with feathers
That perches in the soul . . .*

Emily Dickinson

Jillian and I wept in the July heat of my attic bedroom. I had raised my baby girl to graduate from high school and be accepted into six good colleges only to miss our biggest deadline of all. By June, as Jillian's friends were selecting their favorite schools, we had run out of money.

"Mom, in a few more weeks, everyone is going away but me. I feel like I'll be all alone." What I felt was beaten. After working four jobs simultaneously and attending night classes for sixteen years, I now faced an impasse any courageous single mom would battle all odds to avoid.

"It's okay. Something will work out in a totally unexpected way," I said. That's what we always said. This time, it sounded feeble. I rocked her in my arms as I smoothed the golden strands of her hair, heavy from our tears. Still hugging her, I closed my eyes, searching the past for answers.

This capable young woman had exhibited the guts to partner with me since 1978 when I brought my newborn home. With no job, no money, no car, no husband and no education, it was no easy path, but Jillian got the pep talks early on: "Look, we're two women alone in the world, but we're gonna make it. You'll see. We're gonna shine! And we're both going to go to college." Then I would smile, whispering, "I'm going to graduate before you!" She loved that part. Maybe it was because of the twinkle in my eyes. She'd flash a dazzler back at me that would light up my face.

As it was, only God could have sent that July phone call from Sister Louise that spelled relief. Sister Louise, our darling guidance counselor at Immaculate Heart Academy, said Jillian had been nominated for a couple of scholarships. I gasped. "Call the college," she kept repeating.

Suddenly we were being "sent" to Manhattan College, Mayor Giuliani's own. Jillian was trusting my instinct to jump headlong into a thirty-foot wave as we filled out the sea of papers for the loans. As I waded through the paperwork, I couldn't help but remember her at age three, scrambling toward a swing set to hug an abandoned screaming child. Where does the time keep going? And what will we find there?

In her senior year at Manhattan, Jillian came home one weekend joyfully announcing her assignment as practice teacher for kindergarten in a lovely Riverdale school in the Bronx. "Influence them while they're little, or it's too late," she informed me.

Monday morning she called me in a panic. "Mom, I didn't get the school I expected. Worse yet, I got fifth graders in a rough neighborhood."

"Be their light," I told my most precious treasure on Earth. "Go in there and be their light."

Armed with that, she marched forward into her darkness. What they learned from her was how she loved them. What she got from those fifth-graders in the Bronx was how they celebrated her, how they cried with love for her when she had to leave them.

The children of single parents are wise beyond their years. She saw me cramming for the endless exams as we witnessed with awe that my education was catching up to my talents. I was always being summoned by the unfinished messages in my paintings, or my children's book for adults or the multitude of other projects that waited while the larger work of my masterpiece transformed herself before me.

There's a new picture now in my office: Jillian with her class of sixth-graders. Oh, the brilliance of her smile, the beauty of their diverse faces, the flash of wonder over what they could be that is special. To the untrained heart, it might seem an ordinary group photo. To me, it is the most extraordinary landscape, life's classroom filled with living, breathing "hopes for tomorrow" just waiting to happen—like she did.

Jillian, having grown up on hugs and benign neglect under the grace of a quilt, seems to feel she has lacked nothing. For me, her trust was my lantern when the lightbulbs blew, when the heater stopped at midnight or the car went dead on a dark highway. Earning our college degrees tested every belief regarding the appearance of sudden glimmers, the kind that intervene against the impossible. To my bliss, her unwritten agreement with life knew Love is the highest law. Her trust taught me how we keep lighting the way for one another.

*Patty M. Kearns*

# Traditions

*Every new beginning comes from some other beginning's end.*

Semisonic

Holiday traditions have always had great importance in my home. My children love Christmas and all the rituals associated with this special time of year.

My husband died suddenly, and at the age of thirty-eight, I was a widow. One week later, I gave birth to our third child and only son, whom I named after his father.

When the first holiday season without David rolled around, I was determined, for the children, to keep all the Christmas traditions that my late husband and I had established. Every year on Thanksgiving morning, our home was transformed into Christmas City, with beautiful ceramic churches, rinks with free-moving skaters and musical houses we collected at the annual holiday craft fair. Beautiful lights wound together with greenery adorned the staircase and fireplace of our home. My husband would set up the tree with lights and the angel on the top, and the children and I would place the ornaments and tinsel on it. When it was completely decorated, our daughters, Nicole and Amanda, would turn on the angel light. It was magical for them, and we always looked forward to the coming of Christmas.

That first Christmas season somehow came and went effortlessly. With the help of friends, we managed to get the tree in just the right spot and decorate it. Everything went off without a hitch.

By the second year, I was feeling confident that I could do all the Christmas preparations by myself. Through the year, I had asked for help from many friends who graciously lent a hand with whatever I needed, and I was incredibly grateful. However, it was painfully apparent that all my friends had plenty to do at their own homes, so I worked on being more independent. Raising a seven-year-old, a five-year-old and a one-year-old is challenging in and of itself, but adding a traditional holiday season with everyday activities? Brutal! Despite my good intentions, Thanksgiving Day came and went without the traditional decoration ceremony. Time flew by, and before I knew it, I realized it was only a few days before Christmas! There were no presents and no decorations whatsoever.

I was discouraged and overwhelmed. The only present I wanted was the looks of joy on my children's faces as they opened their presents on Christmas morning. I had to pull it together for them. That night, once the children were in bed, I ran up and down the attic stairs carrying boxes, ceramic decorations and the tree, which was so heavy that I could only carry it down one flight of stairs. So I set it up in the family room on that level. I worked until two in the morning decorating the house. The children were delighted with the result when they awakened, but I was spent.

The night before Christmas Eve, I managed to get a sitter so I could go Christmas shopping. I went from one store to another canvassing the mall for presents for my children, friends and family. I call it "power-shopping," and luckily, I'm great at it.

Christmas Eve was a blur of visits to family and friends and attendance at Christmas Eve mass. We got home at nine, and I managed to get the children settled down and tucked into bed. That's when the fun began. I had some serious wrapping to do. By 4:30 that morning, my entire body was shaking with exhaustion, but everything was wrapped, assembled and ready for a joyful day.

My daughter Nicole was in my bedroom, one inch from my haggard face at 5:45 sharp. Bubbling over with excitement, she asked to open the family room door to see if Santa had arrived. I told her to wait for her sister, and then come and get me. At least it's what I said in my head—to this day I'm not sure what came from my lips, because at 7:00, I heard the sound of rustling paper coming from David's crib. I bolted out of bed to find him buried beneath a heap of Christmas wrap, chewing on an empty Barbie doll box.

I ran from his room to the family room to find every gift opened and strewn everywhere. Not even the stocking presents were left. Nicole looked at me sheepishly, knowing that she might have made a wrong move, and Amanda ran to me, dressed in her sister's oversized hat and mittens, holding a Tonka truck meant for David, joyfully exclaiming, "Look what Santa gave me!" The heat that rose from my feet to my head could have melted steel! I shrieked at my girls, sending them to their room to sit on their beds. They immediately began to cry as I stormed out of the room ranting and raving all the way downstairs. I had missed Christmas! The only part of all the traditions that I was looking forward to was seeing them open their gifts, and it was gone. Suddenly, I caught myself and realized what had really happened, and despair hit me like a boulder. I had ruined Christmas for my beautiful children.

I burst into uncontrollable tears and ran up the stairs to

my daughters' bedroom. They were waiting, little angels with tears in their eyes, ready to offer apologies to me. I stopped them, hugging them close to me, sobbing. "This is not what Christmas is about. It's not the presents; it's the birth of baby Jesus!" I cried. "I need to ask *you* to forgive *me.*" With smiles on their faces, Nicole and Amanda replied, "Okay, Mama! Let's go look at what Santa brought us."

Children are awesome with forgiveness. They forgive as God does, unconditionally. I felt so humbled by their love. I took them into David's room, and we pulled the papers from his fists and teeth, wiped the wrapper ink from his lips, redistributed the toys and played with their gifts.

I had tried so hard to keep everything the same with our family, but it wasn't the same. As a single mother, I was not capable of keeping up all our old traditions. In the frenzy that was the holiday season, I didn't see that the children never noticed the absence of our old rituals. They just wanted to be with me. I was now a single parent with limited time and energy, and that energy needed to be reserved for nurturing my babies. I let go of the traditions that were too much for me, kept the simple ones that meant so much and created new ones. Traditions are only important because they bring families closer. It is repetitive togetherness with a theme.

Nicole is now eleven, Amanda is nine and David is five. As a single mother, I've now learned to shop early. I wrap early. I go to bed early. I ask for help from my dear friends. The tree goes where it lands. When I feel that frenzy coming on and the pace gets hectic, I'm reminded to let go and be present to the meaning of Christmas. Our home is filled with family and friends, filled with laughs and love. We express our gratitude as a family. These are the traditions we'll never let go of.

*Suzanne Aiken*

# Single Mother by Choice

*In the darkest hour the soul is replenished and given strength to continue and endure.*

Heart Warrior Chosa

*Single mother by choice.* I think I winced the first time I heard that phrase. Who would actually choose to be a single mother? I desperately wanted the wedding band promised me by my firstborn's father. That wasn't meant to be. On October 8, 1997, my twenty-third birthday, my oldest daughter came into the world screaming at the top of her fluid-filled lungs. When I found out about my second, I entered into a marriage just so I would no longer be a single mother. But the union ended even before I gave birth.

The night after I gave birth to my second baby, after our visitors were gone and little Averie was sleeping, I cried. I cried so hard that her exit wound began to hurt. So much so that the morphine given to me did nothing to dull the pain. The pain I was feeling wasn't merely physical. What had I done? I was barely making it with one child. And I had the sheer audacity to bring another life into the world? What was I thinking? I was a single mother again—not just of one, but two.

Years went by in a blur of long days and even longer nights. Even though I was living with my parents, there were still bills that piled up. I couldn't seem to get ahead. And child support was a nonissue. I didn't want the help if it wasn't given freely. Sleep was an old friend I had somehow lost contact with, but how I longed for a reunion. My frustration began to manifest in ways that I wished it wouldn't have. I was so tired that if I was idle for more than a minute, I crashed. Hard. Whether at work or being up with my youngest, who never seemed to sleep, it never failed. And I began to wonder why I even bothered. My mother was such a doting grandmother that I was sure that my girls would be better off with her. I contemplated leaving them. Being a single mother was more than I could bear.

One night, after dealing with the stress of my job for six days straight, I slumped through the front door. I was nearly in tears. I didn't know which end was up and felt like I was truly losing my mind. I was a complete failure at being a mother. I prayed for God to show me that he had some reason for choosing me to be these precious girls' mother. But while looking at the pile of dishes that needed washing and the laundry that needed to be done, and yet again no sleep in sight, I couldn't see a reason.

Bath time, which usually was one of my favorite times with the girls, held no joy for me that night. I had resigned myself to leaving. They deserved a better mother than one who couldn't take care of her bills or help keep the house immaculate, and was basically too tired to enjoy them. Couldn't they see what a failure I was? Mothers were supposed to be strong. Single mothers were supposed to be invincible. And I was about to crack.

As I was washing the dishes, Kara, my oldest, came up to me and asked for some bubbles. I scooped up a handful and placed the suds in her little hands. She looked up at me with those brown eyes, so like her father's, and grinned as if I had given her diamonds. Then she closed her eyes and said the words that stopped my heart: "I want my mommy to be a princess."

My chest constricted. I couldn't breathe. And I watched her in awe as she puckered her little pink lips and blew the suds away. She wanted me to be a princess. I looked toward heaven and wondered if that was his sign. My baby, who really wasn't a baby anymore, wanted me to be a princess. Ten minutes later, little Averie, who hadn't been within earshot when Kara made her wish, called me Princess Mommy. In that instant, I realized that no matter how badly I thought I was doing, and no matter how badly I wanted them to have a father, I was enough. God thought I was enough. Kara and Averie thought I was enough. And regardless of what anyone else might have thought, that was all that mattered.

*Single mother by choice.* I now feel a great sense of pride when I think of it, because it wasn't a choice that I made. God chose me to be a mother. Their mother. Their *single* mother.

*Brandi N. Rainey*

# Bad Day, Good Life

*This, too, shall pass.*

William Shakespeare

When I awoke at o'dark early, I never would have guessed, as I watched the falling snow, that that would be the day that changed my life—a day that would become a yardstick by which I would gauge any hard day thereafter.

The kids awoke, washed, dressed and had breakfast, and we set out for the school/workday with about six heavy, wet inches of snow already on the ground. I don't even think I realized my daughter was still wearing her tiger slippers, I was so concerned with driving on the winter country roads, but I'm sure her first-grade teacher understood the harried life of a working mom.

I dropped the kids off at elementary school and headed on to work. It wasn't long before a car on the road ahead of me skidded sideways and another car, avoiding her, pushed my car into a guardrail. With a smashed fender, I trudged on to the lab. The company I worked for had been dumping chemicals into the sink, and hence the sewer, and since I knew this would kill the aerobic bacteria in the treatment plant for the town, I complained to my boss that it would be cost-effective to bulk the waste and sell it for "potpourri"—a tank load of mixture that could be refined, and not only settle the problem of dumping, but also make a few bucks for the company.

My idea didn't go over well, and I was instructed to do the dumping myself! Oh, dear. What to do? I spoke to a friend who suggested I call the health department and put a stop to this dangerous practice. Unfortunately, when I made the call, I had no idea the company recorded all incoming and outgoing telephone traffic. By the early afternoon, I was called into the personnel department and summarily fired. No severance, no consideration, no job!

I was so embarrassed about being let go, the first time this had ever happened to me, I went out with my tail between my legs, consumed with worry for my family's welfare. I drove the damaged car to the babysitter where the kids went after school, who informed me she no longer wanted to work at home and I would have to find someone else to care for my children. With the kids in the car, the snow now piled up to a good twelve inches, I drove home in the afternoon made dark by the blizzard, feeling the worst I had ever felt. What was I going to do?

No job, no babysitter, no income and two little ones to provide for soon had me crying as I drove. Of course, the kids started crying, too. We made it home to the apartment, and when I stopped to pick up the mail, there was an eviction notice in with the bills. The week before, the new landlord, who lived at a distance and had hired an incompetent to care for the property, hadn't bothered to fix the heat in my building or remove the ice from the entrance. My elderly neighbor had taken a spill, and but for one-quarter inch when she landed, would have hit her eye on the corner of the cement step. I had taken it upon myself to call and complain. He assured me he would "take care of it." Little did I know he meant removing the complainant rather than fixing the problems.

I was completely disheartened. Now, not only did I lack a job and a sitter who would watch my children while I looked for another one, but we also faced having to look for another place to live, which could likely mean another school. As we stepped out of the car, my daughter said, "Look, Mommy!" She pointed to the hood of the car, from which black smoke was pouring forth at an alarming rate. It was at this moment of my life that my attitude and entire way of being changed. I began to laugh. Then the kids began to laugh, and we stood there, in the still-falling snow laughing until it hurt.

I'm not sure what made me laugh, but I had come to the point where crying was no longer a solution and laughing at the sheer absurdity of the day was my last resort. It was at this point that we all learned the lesson of adversity: we arrived at the end of our despair and clicked over to the sheer epiphany that nothing else could go wrong, and things would just have to begin to go right.

Needless to say, we found another home, another school, another job and another sitter, one who lived right next door and became a good friend. But from that day on, every time things became difficult in the extreme, they never were more difficult than that day. I knew in my heart that if we could get through that day, we could make it in life. That one day, when I thought my world had fallen apart, became the barometer by which I measured all hard days. No matter what happened, I would immediately think back and know: if I could get through that, I could get through this and through anything else that came my way. Together we persevered and made it through life as a single mom with two kids.

*Barbara Stanley*

# About the Doubt

He cried for the first time at eleven o'clock one February morning. It would not be the last time, but it would be the best time. I had given birth to my soul and did not even know it.

An enthusiastic young nurse, not yet used to the arrival of new life, grinned at me and said from beneath her garishly flowered surgical cap, "You have a beautiful baby boy! Do you want to see him?" "No," was my flat reply. She giggled and brought him to me from behind the drapery.

"Oh . . . he's so ugly," I said. And he was—bald except for a fringe of shoulder-length, stringy brown hair, and covered in blood and some sort of let's-not-talk-about-what-it-is goo. I was drugged, but I remember asking myself, *What's the matter with you? You aren't supposed to think or act like this!*

That was Thursday. By the following Thursday, we were home, and I was waiting for that "mother love" thing to kick in. I nursed him, I held him, I changed him, I bathed him, I this'ed him and I that'ed him . . . and I waited.

So I can't tell you if it was while I was winding the swing or cleaning up something better left to the imagination, but there it was—a moment when my heart felt as though it were stuck on the upside of a beat so powerful that had it burst free from my chest it would certainly have ended up orbiting Venus.

The years passed. I had some doubts about this love that felt so powerful. Doubts as profound as the love I had for my son colored every moment of the next twenty years. His childhood was destined to be fraught with struggle. There was never enough money. There would be no Prince Charming to come along and save us from the poverty I fought to overcome. Positive male role models for my son were nonexistent. The men I attracted were not interested in signing up for the family plan, and any less than that was simply not an option.

Try as I might, underemployment became my principal career. I went back to school with dreams of becoming an educator. When day care was not available, I dragged Matt to class with me, where he sat through long lectures without complaint. Four hundred and sixty-four dollars a month meant tough choices on a regular basis, and we visited the food banks more than once, not just for food but clothing as well. Many a meal consisted of nothing more than boiled potatoes. My meager credit rating deteriorated to horrendous as rent took precedence over luxuries like a telephone and credit cards. I finally got my bachelor's degree, but my dream would not be realized because graduate school proved too great a challenge for this single mother.

I had failed.

What kind of role model was I? Should I have kept him? Should I have given him up to a family who would have provided for him much better than I ever could? These doubts recurred with every layoff and corporate downsizing to which I fell victim.

One doubt that I never had was my love for and responsibility to him. He inspired me when there was no inspiration to be found. I watched him grow and his dreams grew right along with him. We rarely traded a cross word. He grew up long before he should have. When worry consumed me, he comforted *me,* soothing away the tears that flowed, despite my efforts to control them. This loving, wonderful child deserved so much better. By being his mother, I could not let go of the feeling that I had done him some great disservice.

Yes, I doubted myself, but never doubted for a moment this one mission in my life. We spoke openly of anything about which he was curious. I answered his questions to the best of my ability and admitted my limitations when I simply did not know. But this I did know: he was never bad, just sometimes did things that were not good. It was my belief that love without condition was not love without responsibility. On the few occasions when he got into trouble, he was expected to face the consequences of his actions; but I was, and always will be, there.

In spite of the challenges, we persevered, and we laughed far more often than we cried. Matt and I were a team.

Disruption and upheaval were regular parts of his existence. Money issues dictated that we move a lot. He attended no fewer than seven different elementary schools. Every move was either an attempt to improve our situation or simply save us from homelessness. There were only two constants in those days: our love and my doubts. By the time he got to middle school, it was clear he was someone special. Repeated displacement had robbed him of opportunities he would surely have been offered under more stable circumstances. Yet Matt had shone like a beacon in every school that he attended. His hard work, resultant scholarships and financial aid made it possible for him to go to college.

We continued to speak regularly about anything and everything that was going on in his life. Memorial Day weekend of his sophomore year he came home for a visit. I can't recall how the conversation started, but he talked about one of his roommates whose father was the CEO of a major international corporation. John had grown up not wanting for anything but had told Matt that he would trade it all for the kind of relationship that Matt had with me.

Then Matt said to me, "Mom, I want you to know that despite being dirt poor and never knowing where the next meal was coming from, my childhood was the happiest time of my life. I would not trade having had you for a mother for anything in the world. You gave me a sense of self that tells me that I can accomplish anything if I set my mind to it. You taught me values that I cannot find fault with, and I learned by your example what true love is. I could not have created a better parent if I had been able to custom order you. I feel incredibly lucky to have had you for my mother. Thank you for giving me life." With those words, my choice was finally vindicated.

Matt graduated from college with honors. He managed to study abroad for a year and is now in California pursuing an acting career. I don't worry anymore about whether I did the right thing. His life, his courage and his determination reassure me daily that he is the best person he can be, and I take pride in the fact that I had a hand in that.

*Wanda Simpson*

# Water on Tadpoles

*Seeds of faith are always within us; sometimes it takes a crisis to nourish and encourage their growth.*

Susan Taylor

In the late 1970s, unmarried women with children were not called "single mothers." A mother who had never been married was a thing of scorn, to be shipped off to relatives or an unwed mothers' home. My mother was a *divorcée*, only slightly more honorable. It was a loaded word, spoken with portent and the undertone of sexual looseness, preceded by "hot-to-trot" or followed by a knowing wink. It was the year I saved the tadpoles or they saved me.

We had a hard time finding a place to live. In Georgia, the bosom of the Bible Belt, they treated my mother like Jezebel. A woman without a man was sin waiting to happen, a threat to good women, a temptation to their weak husbands. "We don't rent to divorcées," a heavyset landlady would say. "We've heard all about you people, the wild parties and dope and carrying on. This trailer park is for decent folk." They always put emphasis on the word *decent,* they'd tilt their heads back, jaws set, noses slightly in the air, feeling superior and finding it delicious.

We finally found a near-vacant trailer park that would tolerate us heathens, the divorcée and her redheaded tomboy. It had one dirt road that formed a loop, five trailers spread out like tin petals on a half-plucked flower. The trailer park was wooded with oaks dripping moss. I had hoped to find other children in the park, but there were none. Our new neighbors were mostly elderly folk who eyed my mother with salacious interest, hoping to witness firsthand some of those wild dope parties they'd heard about. My hardworking mother would prove a great disappointment to them.

I was a latchkey kid before the phrase was coined; working mothers were still rare. For several hours each afternoon, I was free to do as I pleased. Indoors, I played the radio; I danced and sang, plundered my mother's makeup and ate sugar right out of the bowl. Outdoors, I would ride my bike or go on safari in our park, hunting lizards and daddy longlegs.

Later in life, I have come to find great comfort in solitude. But when I was seven, freedom and loneliness were bound together, impossible to feel one without the other. I ached for my mother, for the company of other children, for friendship of any kind.

At the other trailer park, where we had lived when Mom and Dad were still married—when we were still *decent*—I could walk to school. There were lots of kids there; the park had a playground with a swing set. Our neighbor let me eat scuppernongs off her fence. My dad had coaxed a squirrel into eating cereal out of his hand. But that trailer park was for military families only. When my parents divorced, Mom and I had to leave.

This new home was farther from the school; I met the bus at a corner about two blocks from the park. Walking to and from the bus stop, I could feel the cool metal of my house key dangling from a string against my chest—always underneath my shirt, never on top of it, Mom taught me.

That spring brought heavy rains to our park; puddles turned to small ponds. One afternoon on safari, hoping to find a snake, I found something far greater—a frog's eggs in one of the puddles. Each day after that, I hurried home from the bus stop to check on them. I talked to them about school, and told them about all the juicy flies they could have when they got bigger. After a week of scorching Savannah heat, just as the eggs were becoming tadpoles, I noticed the pond was shrinking. The mother had left her babies in a place that seemed safe at the time, but was rapidly turning foul. The tadpoles would surely die.

I found an empty milk bottle underneath our trailer, filled it with water at the spigot around back, hauled the sloshing jug to the pond and dumped the water into the tadpoles' little world, apologizing for the startling cold-ness of it. This became a favorite part of my afternoon, hurrying home from the bus stop to water the tadpoles, kneeling to get a closer look. I checked for any changes—bulging eyes, budding legs—and to chase them through the cool water with my finger.

On my daily walk home from the bus stop, I began to notice, or rather feel, someone watching me. I walked a little faster, clutching the strap of my book bag, feeling like prey. The feeling grew more pronounced with every day; I could feel the weight of eyes on me, eyes as hungry as hands.

I was ready to tell my mother about this, had even re-hearsed what I was going to say, then realized it sounded ridiculous: a bogeyman in broad daylight. I was much too mature for that. Mom and I had so little time together in the evenings, I wanted it to be nice. The last thing she needed was another problem.

I tried to convince myself the feeling was just my

imagination, like monsters under the bed. I told myself to quit being such a chicken, but I could still feel those eyes boring into me. One cloudy afternoon, I stepped off the bus; the air was as heavy as oil. As I walked past an over-grown azalea, a man stepped out from behind it.

"Where'd you git that red hair from?" he drawled. Scared motionless—breathless—I looked up into the man's gaunt face, his eyes pinched close together. He slithered closer. I could feel my feet trying to flee, my house key tapping against my hammering chest. "You sure got a mess of freckles. Why don't you come inside and see my puppy ...?"

I managed to inhale—sharp and sudden—the exhale came out in a scream. "I HAVE TO GO RIGHT NOW! They're expecting me at home!" I flew all the way back to the trailer park, went inside and hid until I was sure he hadn't followed me. When it felt safe, I went out to water the tadpoles.

As soon as Mom got home, I told her about the man. "You did good, Sugar," she said. "Just like I told you—holler loud, run like heck and never let on that your mama's not home." But they had been expecting me at home—a whole puddle full of them. Mom smiled, brushed my hair back from my forehead. "Lord, look at the dirt. Go wash up." The ease in her voice made me believe the cri-sis was over, that I'd taken care of it. "Tell me again now, Sugar, which house was it?" So calm, she was just curious.

Mom made a few phone calls the next morning. I don't know what was said, but that afternoon the school bus began dropping me off right in front of our park; the dri-ver waited and watched until she saw me unlock the door.

And that very night, at last, it rained. A sweet, drench-ing rain, cleansing and cooling. I could hear the thirsty earth gulping, sighing in blessed relief. I slept with the drum-sound of rain on our metal roof.

The tadpoles and I were going to be just fine.

*J. D. Gidley*

# Staying the Course

*Be like a postage stamp—stick to one thing until you get there.*

Josh Billings

Someone once told me that the road to success is always under construction. Helpful advice, as I was one of those individuals who took an early detour in life's journey, and it was some time before I got back on course. Pregnant, married and a mother at sixteen, my second child was born when I was seventeen. I had my third child when I was twenty. As a high-school dropout who had only completed the tenth grade, I was terribly self-conscious, and my self-esteem was virtually nonexistent. I went back to school when I turned twenty-three, thinking I'd feel better about myself if I got my diploma. But that effort only lasted six weeks. Once again, I dropped out of school, flunking algebra for the second time in my life.

I was a two-time high-school dropout with no job skills, trapped in a rapidly deteriorating, abusive marriage. I took in baskets of ironing and cleaned people's homes to make a few extra dollars. I was homebound and lonely, and my husband and I drifted further and further apart. When I was twenty-six, what I both feared and desired happened: my husband walked out on my children and me.

The combination of a low-paying secretarial job and lack of child support put me on the poverty line, and for two-and-a-half years, I struggled, directionless.

Finally I realized that no one was going to rescue me. If my life was going to change, I had to do the changing. I didn't know what I wanted, but I was clear on what I didn't want. I didn't want to be this miserable for the rest of my life.

The first step in getting my life back on track was to finish high school, so I took, and passed, the high school equivalency test, sparking my first feelings of adequacy.

One day, someone casually mentioned to me that there were state-funded programs for "people like you." After several inquiries, I took a big step, recognizing I would have to go backward before I could go forward—just like freeing a car that's been stuck in the mud. My backward step was the choice to go on welfare so I could fulfill the one thing I had dreamed about: a college education. I was now thirty years old.

Reaching the threshold of a goal often presents us with defining moments. For me, the first of my obstacles wasn't tackling the course work. It was the registration process! Three times that first day, I failed to follow directions. Three times, I had to leave the line and go back to a former station where I had neglected to fill out a line on a form or get a compulsory checkmark placed in a box. As I was told once again to go back and rectify yet another error, panic coursed through my body, beginning at my toes and ending in my throat. Embarrassed that I couldn't follow simple directions like everyone else in line (most of whom were nearly half my age), I wanted to run away and never try again.

Fears that had plagued me before began to resurface: *Who are you to think you can go to college anyway? If you can't even register, how do you expect to take a class—and pass it?* I got out of line, desperate and ready to bolt. But then I saw something that made me stop: a young woman, sitting on a bench, in tears. I went over to her and asked what was wrong.

She blurted, "I don't know how to register!"

I blurted back, "Neither do I!"

We laughed in spite of our mutual dilemma and awkwardly helped each other through the process.

Compared to registration, taking the course work became a breeze. I studied hard, and despite my insecurities, achieved honors. Getting my community college degree was a life-transforming experience that taught me many things.

An important lesson gained from going forward was learning I could "learn," and getting an education helped me create a better life for my children and myself. I was forty years old when I earned my bachelor's degree, chipping away at it one class at a time. That, too, was a landmark. For me, the remarkable part of this whole story is that I now make my living helping others learn. The books I write and the seminars I conduct are all about discovering our potential and enhancing this journey called "life."

I also learned that life is full of "construction zones" that sometimes slow us down or cause us to retreat. The important thing is that I eventually traversed the bumps instead of stopping or turning back. Staying the course helped me to graduate through life's rough spots, even though there were many detours.

As single parents, we all face defining moments, and in those moments, whether we forge ahead or turn back determines the direction our lives will ultimately take. By sitting down with that young lady who couldn't fill out her registration form, I ended up helping myself. Helping others and giving to others is as much for us as it is for them. And it seems to me that this is the ultimate lesson of life.

*C. Leslie Charles*

# 5

# INSIGHTS
# AND WISDOM

*Wisdom is meaningless until our own
experience has given it meaning.*

Bergen Evans

# Kitchen Comfort

*To us, family means putting your arms around
each other and being there.*

Barbara Bush

My life is a juggling act. I'm a single mother of two sons;
I've got a busy work schedule and limited resources. But
there is one thing I don't worry about: when I come home
at night, dinner is already started. A typical weeknight at
my house looks like this:

My youngest child is snapping the ends off the green
beans.

My eldest is mixing his secret salad dressing.

The babysitter is working on the shopping list for tomorrow's dinner—the kids want to make lasagna.

I throw on an apron, send the babysitter home and join
my kids in the dinner preparations.

Sounds too far-fetched for your home? It doesn't have
to be. If my family can do it, any family can.

Our meals weren't always such happy group efforts.
Seven years ago, my life was shattered by divorce, leaving me with a six-month-old infant and a very angry

seven-year-old. I had no family nearby and very little money. The burden of rebuilding my career as a food writer and publicist while simultaneously single-parenting my children seemed insurmountable.

While I did my best to work during my youngest's nap times, by day's end I was physically exhausted and emotionally depleted. Typically, I shooed the boys out of the kitchen so I could perform yet another chore: making dinner. When I got the meal on the table, I left them to eat alone so I could have five minutes' peace. Retreating to my bedroom, I collapsed onto my bed and cried. I felt horrible about my family life and helpless to change it.

A year passed, but not much improved. At the end of my rope, one evening I thrust some basil at my youngest, who was then eighteen months old, so he'd leave me alone. Lo and behold, he spent ten minutes happily tearing the basil into little pieces. I was shocked at how he stayed on the task without uttering a peep.

Suddenly, I saw an opportunity. He wanted to help me, and I sure needed help. Why not let him cook with me?

So he and his older brother began doing lots of tasks in the kitchen: peeling vegetables, grating cheese, pushing the blender and food processor buttons, plucking the leaves from herbs, tearing up salad greens, kneading dough, stirring risotto, even helping me make homemade pasta!

It was incredible what they could be persuaded to do—all because I invited them into the process and believed in their ability to really help. Yes, it got messy at times. And at first, I would feel rushed, sabotaging the moment by grabbing something away because they were taking so long. Then I realized I no longer had any reason to be in a hurry. As long as the kids were with me in the kitchen, they were not whining about dinner. They were busy and content. I stopped worrying about the mess or how long it took to cook the meal. And though it was hard to stick to it, I decided to enjoy the process of cooking with my kids and not worry about the meal itself being perfect.

We started to laugh a lot at dinnertime. And my eldest son began to rely on that time of day to share his worries and fears. We would talk about tutors and help for him in school, and over time, his problems lessened. He was getting the quality time he needed.

With this mind-set, you won't make the mistake of getting tense and impatient, grabbing food or tools away from the kids because they're too slow. The kids won't end up running off in tears. You'll just be talking, going along cooking, and soon, you'll realize that new lines of communication and strong bonds are forming.

Family cooking has another tangible reward. After preparing the meal together, you'll actually want to sit at the table and enjoy it together. It may well become your favorite part of the day.

*Lynn Fredericks*

# The Can Opener

*Human beings, by changing the inner attitudes of their minds, can change the outer aspects of their lives.*

William James

My life used to be a movable feast: a dream home, a husband who loved me, two beautiful children. And then suddenly, life was a can of condensed soup. Chopped, boiled-down and vacuum-packed—the bare essence of what life was meant to be. My husband and I were divorced, I was raising the children alone, and I had twenty-five dollars to my name. Our new home was a run-down townhouse with an overwhelmingly musty smell that permeated everything. The dining-room ceiling had a hole in it, the carpet was threadbare, and the walls looked like they'd been sponge painted with grimy fingers.

I was panicky, trapped. How could I get us out of this mess?

I opted for sheer willpower and guts. I would find us a way out of this place and reclaim our former life. I lowered my notoriously hard head and charged—smack into a steel wall. I scrimped enough to fix the dining-room ceiling, and a week later it sprang a new leak. I got the oil changed in the car, and the brakes went out on the way home. I got the extra work shifts, I worked all night, I worked in my sleep, but nothing changed.

Enter the can opener.

For one thing, it reminded me of our divorce: my ex-husband had taken the new electric can opener, leaving me with a rusty handheld model. For another thing, it had this look about it, as if it had been around a lot longer than I had, so it was cleverer. Plus, it was getting me at a disadvantage. I'd been late getting off work, traffic was horrendous, the kids were hungry and grouchy, and I'd broken a brand-new lightbulb when I set my packages on the kitchen counter. And we were having soup for the hundredth meal in a row.

I hooked the opener on the soup can and started turning the key. It made a small slit and stuck. I tried again in another spot. Stuck. I tried again, until I had six little slits in the lid. Was the opener smirking at me? I threw it down and grabbed a butter knife, jamming it into one of the slits. The lid wasn't budging. My face turned the color of tomato soup, and I thought I was going to blow my own lid. I fought down the rising frustration. I was not going to come undone over a lid that wouldn't.

I tried distraction and called my mom.

"Hi, Mom," I said cheerfully.

"Hi!" she said. "What's wrong?"

How could she tell? Suddenly, I cracked. I started sobbing uncontrollably. I could only get out one sentence:

"I . . . can't . . . get . . . this . . . can . . . open!" I gasped. All my efforts to be strong, cut apart by a silly old can opener and stubborn soup-can lid.

My mom didn't say anything for a moment, and then suddenly, we were both laughing. We laughed and cried together till I calmed down.

When I hung up, I picked up my rusty opponent and stared at it. Wasn't it symbolic of my postdivorce life? I was coping by using worn-out techniques—bullheadedness, tunnel vision, distraction—and I wasn't getting anywhere at all. I needed a new tool, a new way of thinking. After all, condensed soup isn't half bad when you add things to it. Maybe I should have concentrated on the good stuff: the spice of trying new things, some meaty family time, the comforting broth of relaxation. In other words, I could show my kids that I savored what I did have instead of hungering for what I didn't.

When my mom sent me a brand-new can opener in the mail a week later, I put it to good use, but I hung on to the old one. It's my rusty reminder that when life hands you a raw deal, you make soup.

*Kathline Collins*

"You have reached the Single Mom's support line."

*Reprinted by permission of Randy Glasbergen.*

# No Greater Love

*A* rich child often sits in a poor mother's lap.

Spanish Proverb

One day, I found a little girl in the street, so I took her to our children's home. We have a nice place and good food there. We gave her clean clothes, and we made her as happy as we could.

After a few hours, the little girl ran away. I looked for her, but couldn't find her anywhere. Then after a few days, I found her again. And again, I brought her to our home and told a sister, "Sister, please follow this child wherever she goes."

The little girl ran away again. But the sister followed her to find out where she was going and why she kept running away.

She followed the girl and discovered that the little one's mother was living under a tree in the street. The mother had placed two stones there and did her cooking under that tree.

The sister sent word to me, and I went there. I found joy on that little girl's face, because she was with her mother who loved her and was making special food for her in that little open place.

I asked the little girl, "How is it that you would not stay with us? You had so many beautiful things in our home."

She answered, "I could not leave without my mother. She loves me." That little girl was happier to have the meager food her mother was cooking in the street than all the things I had given her.

While the child was with us, I could scarcely see a smile on her face. But when I found her there with her mother, in the street, they were smiling.

Why? Because they were family.

*Mother Teresa*

# Emptying the Nest

*All changes, even the most longed for, have their melancholy, for what we leave behind us is a part of ourselves; we must die to one life before we can enter into another.*

Anatole France

I was tired at the end of a five-day business trip in New York, but I still took two subways to Chinatown to get my daughter carryout. It's our tradition: after every trip I take to the Big Apple, I bring Adair the vegetarian roast duck that she can't get in Kansas City. It's made of soy and gluten and arrowroot, alchemically combined to bear an amazing resemblance to its poultry alias.

I took her treat back to the hotel and stuffed it in the crowded minifridge. Then I put Post-it notes as reminders on the alarm clock, the TV and the bathroom mirror: Roast Duck, Roast Duck, Roast Duck. In the morning, I will hand carry the Styrofoam box to La Guardia in two plastic bags (veggie duck is one juicy dish), then through the terminal at O'Hare for the change of planes. There is nothing I would not do for my child.

This child, however, is now sixteen. She drives. She has a job, a checking account and a debit card. She also has wings—small ones, not finished growing. Still, they're her favorite appendage because, with them, she'll fly away to meet her own destiny—and to get her own roast duck.

This young lady who looks like me and thinks like herself has been in my thoughts from the instant I saw that the pregnancy test strip registered positive. She was uppermost in my mind when she was three and clung to me like ivy, and when she was thirteen and walked ahead of me at the mall so no one would think she was with her mom. It didn't matter: nine years of just-the-two-of-us had cemented our bond. After her dad died, Adair and I became a unit, what the sociologists would call a nontraditional family: a mother, a daughter and three cats. We were nontraditional in the way we approached life as well: I worked at home writing articles and books, so I could be present as a mother. We home-schooled, so Adair could travel with me for most of the speaking engagements that helped support us.

Through it all, I have loved her warmly, tenderly, totally—and surprisingly, given the bum rap teenagers get, I love her more now than ever. That's how love works when it's working properly. With a friend or a mate, you're supposed to love more as time passes and grow ever closer. With a child, however, a child you love more than your own life and breath, the bittersweet goal of the relationship is to grow apart.

This will not be a problem for my daughter. Her wings get larger and stronger every day. She is talking about going to college a year early. "Why waste time?" she asks. Well, she doesn't exactly ask. It's more of a statement. "This is my future," Adair tells me. I can hear in her voice that this future is more important, and perhaps more real to her, than the confusing waiting period that is the present. "I want to buy an apartment as soon as I can," she says, "and start putting away some money every month for my retirement."

*Her what?* I'm thinking, as I look fifty in the face and wish I'd thought about my retirement when I was thirty, let alone sixteen. *Old writers don't retire,* I told myself until not long ago. *They just die.* Somehow, even though I held on to the Bohemian sentiments of my own youth for far too long, I have raised a child who is solid and level-headed. The genes for these traits no doubt came from her father; I didn't stand in their way. I am proud of that, but not nearly as proud as I am of her.

With all her maturity and apparent good sense, though, the transition concerns me—the transition from "safe at home" to "at large in the world." Did I put too much emphasis on reading good books and not enough on learning to read people? Will she be able to protect herself, use her wits and avoid the con artists and smooth talkers and risky charmers who flock to attractive young women like bees to clover? She is no doubt wiser than I was at her age, but she has to be. When I was her age, things were simpler. We took *The Brady Bunch* seriously, for heaven's sake. I have other worries, too, which I must admit are selfish. How will I deal with her not being around to light up my life and mess up my kitchen? How will it feel to fly home from New York without vegetarian duck in two plastic bags? Will the joy of her freedom heal the pain of my loss?

It makes sense to prepare for her departure, emotionally at least. Perhaps, like she has, I can sprout wings and see where they take me. Flying at fifty is allowed, I think. It's the life equivalent of the Masters tournaments in sports: the action is less flashy than the younger players', but it is skillful and studied. And this way we two flyers, carrying our entwined histories and playing in our different leagues, can meet sometimes in Chinatown. We'll have roast duck and steamed dumplings and recount our separate adventures.

*Victoria Moran*

# Here and Now

*Love is a roller coaster. Motherhood is a whole amusement park.*

Cathy Guisewite

If there's one word that describes the life of a single parent, it's *hectic*. Even though my kids are older now, it doesn't take much for me to remember the feeling of having too much to do and far too little time to do it. I thought I'd never have a moment of rest again. But here I sit in a quiet house, wondering how time could have possibly passed by so quickly.

I remember one particular week when I thought I'd lose what little remained of my sanity.

"Mom, you went to Noel's stuff last week. You have to go to my pom-squad performance this Friday."

"No way, Serena!" argued Nik. "Mom is going to my gymnastics meet."

With my head spinning, I told all three kids to sit down. I walked to the living room, dreading what was sure to become one of our Schiller showdowns. *Why does it always have to be so overwhelming? Why does it always have to be so difficult?* I thought as I steadied myself for the onslaught. Each child tried to persuade me to attend his or her activity, leaving me feeling pulled in too many directions. Finally, I managed to coordinate our schedules so that I could attend all three events. Everyone seemed satisfied with the results, but I was emotionally exhausted. That was Sunday.

The rest of the week was nonstop activity. Monday, I managed to get myself to one meeting and the kids to another. Tuesday was Nik's gymnastics meet. I arrived in time to see him compete in the vault event, his favorite. Wednesday night meant school for me and a quick dinner for the kids. Thursday night was Noel's ballet practice, and Friday night brought Serena's halftime performance with the pom squad.

As I drove home from work on Friday, I hit heavy traffic. All I could hear was Serena's reminder to me that morning: "Mom, you can't be late! I need your help with my hair!" Pulling into the garage, I raced upstairs to see the panic on her face. We made it on time—barely.

By Sunday night, I needed another weekend to recover. *Lord,* I prayed, *I'm not ready to start again. When will I ever have time to myself? I am tired of this routine. I'm tired of hurrying. I'm tired of scheduling. Please help me get through the week ahead.*

Now the days of rushing are behind me. And the truth is, I miss them terribly. Three months ago, I watched Serena walk across the stage to receive her college diploma. Waves of precious memories (and, yes, the not-so-precious memories, too) flooded my soul—gymnastics meets, ballet recitals, pom-pom performances. I reflected back to the daily grind of what felt like the tedious and overwhelming pace of our lives. But those days really were precious. They were filled with tender moments and simple pleasures, like sharing my son's pride in his accomplishment, watching my daughter shine on a stage and helping my teenager get her hair just right. Those are the parts of being a parent that make all the chaos worthwhile.

Yes, life with children can be difficult, especially when you're on your own. Yet very soon, sooner than you think, you'll be asking, *Where has the time gone?* And the house will be quiet. Too quiet.

*Barbara Schiller*

# Marissa

*The more faithfully you listen to the voices within you, the better you will hear what is sounding outside.*

Dag Hammarskjöld

Marissa sat on the carousel horse, and I stood alongside her, my arms bracing her little long-legged body against the painted saddle. I glanced over to the crowd and saw my husband Tim watching us. And for a reason I didn't understand, I felt a terrible yearning, a need to freeze-frame the moment and etch every detail of him into my brain, from his pale and lightly freckled face and intent blue-green eyes to his blue denim jacket.

Two weeks later, he was dead. And there I was, a thirty-four-year-old widow with a three-and-a-half-year-old daughter and a slew of people throwing advice at me. Some of it was good—a lot of it wasn't—and all of it said more about the folks hurling it at me than it did about me and my particular situation. One woman, however, sounded a note that proved to be just as prophetic as the yearning I'd felt on the carousel that cool June evening.

"That little girl," she told me emphatically, "is going to be your salvation."

I rejected the notion. *It's not fair to expect her to be all that,* I remember thinking. *I have to get through this on my own.* And I set about trying to hammer out a new world from the debris of our old predictable one. I put Marissa in preschool three days a week, found a counselor I felt comfortable working with and forced myself to start writing again.

All of which were good, necessary things to do. But I was so intent on showing people—and myself—that I could handle, by myself, what life had thrown at me, that I had become more of an automaton than a person and a parent. I didn't neglect Marissa: I looked after her, gave her more toys than she needed and more animals than we both needed (our cat population shot up past the "sufficient" mark, and we acquired bunnies and even, for twenty-four hours, a pygmy hedgehog who loathed us). But my heart-spring was broken, and I couldn't respond to Marissa fully—then I would have to feel, and I wasn't ready to do that yet.

I resented having to be a two-in-one parent carrying the burden of all the responsibilities, while well-meaning friends and relatives got to take Marissa places and do all the fun stuff with her. I got tired, too, of feeling like I couldn't even have the luxury of being sick. I mean, if I did give into a sinus infection or a twenty-four-hour virus, wouldn't this Popsicle-stick-and-masking-tape world of ours simply fall apart?

"Oh, I know just how you feel," some of my friends in rocky marriages would say. "I'm like a single parent myself."

*You're not!* I always wanted to scream back. *Your children's fathers are living and breathing. They might not help much, but they're* there. *It's* not *the same.*

I was having an aggravated case of feeling sorry for myself. It was only natural, I suppose, but it wasn't getting us anywhere. So, as the numbness slowly receded, I made a conscious effort at being me again. Or, rather, a me who'd gone through a war and had the scars to prove it, but who was also tougher and more willing to try new things, both for Marissa and myself.

I'd been telling her ever since she was old enough to understand that "it's just the two of us now—we have to be a team." Well, now we truly started being one. I'd never been that wild about traveling—and I was more than a little daunted by the prospect of going it alone with my daughter—but now, I made a point of it. I'd never ridden a bike or been good at sports, but I bought Marissa a bike and pushed her along till she was ready to solo. We went horseback riding together for a year or so, then went on to doing Tae Kwon Do together. We dressed up for Halloween together, and she was on my business cards as my official partner when I was breeding Abyssinian cats. The secret, as I learned, was in focusing not on what we had lost but on what we still had: each other.

We no longer breed Abyssinians, and Marissa now prefers me to be a noncostumed, sensible mom on Halloween. But we play Scrabble, go for hikes and watch *Gilmore Girls* together. I help her with her homework and her butterfly garden; she has introduced me to Harry Potter and Nintendo, and occasionally lets me hang out with her and play horses. We discuss my dates and her friends, and she sometimes contributes titles or suggestions for my stories and essays.

There are fights and tantrums—on both our parts—but there's a lot of clowning around and laughter, too. And when she won a tiny red and white cloth bear (known as Scarlett) at the carnival recently, she insisted on putting it in my room, saying it would be "our bear."

Sometimes when I look at her, I catch glimpses of the person she is becoming: a funny, intuitive, astute young woman with all her dad's directness. There's a reason that *Gilmore Girls* is one of our favorite shows: the playful verbal sparring and camaraderie between single mom Lorelei Gilmore and daughter Rory mirrors our own, uncannily. Marissa is my companion, my joy, my partner-in-crime and my comforter when I am down or sick. There's still a terrible yearning when I think back on that night on the carousel and what followed, but there is also Marissa. In short, that little girl has indeed been my salvation.

*T. J. Banks*

# Well Enough

*You have to accept whatever comes and the only important thing is that you meet it with the best you have to give.*

Eleanor Roosevelt

I had fallen asleep on the sofa, TV humming away in the background, when I was awakened by a kiss on the cheek—a kiss from my broad-shouldered, stubbly faced eighteen-year-old son, Dan. I groggily opened my eyes and smiled at him, glad to see he was home safely on this summer night before he was to go off to college three thousand miles from home.

"I love you, big guy," Dan said. "Very much."

"I love you, too, Dan. Very much."

We smiled at each other. He patted me on the shoulder and went to his room. I lumbered to my feet, downed a glass of water and returned to the sofa, where I sat, pondering this state of life known as single parenthood.

I'd raised Dan and his sister, Laura, now fifteen, on my own since they were ten and seven. When I use the phrase "on my own," it highlights the many faces of single parenthood. A single parent, whose ex-spouse lives a mile away and takes the kids on a regular basis, is a very different sort of single parent than the one who lives in an unfamiliar city with no close friends or relatives nearby and no child support to help. I was somewhere in between, closer to the latter. I received no child support and had a couple of people nearby who helped on rare occasion. My children's mother had had almost nothing to do with them for years, and had died a year earlier. So when I say "on my own" it really feels like I've done it alone for the most part.

Dan and I had locked horns over the years but were always close, always loved and respected each other. He was a sweet kid, but not always the most demonstrative, so a kiss and an "I love you, Dad," was always a treat for me.

I sat there and thought about raising Dan and Laura, about how this had been the best experience of my life, and how I hoped dearly it had been a good thing for them. From all outward appearances, they were happy, normal, well-adjusted kids. Having roamed the halls of their schools more than a few times, I could say with confidence they were doing much better than many of the children of "traditional" two-parent households. Much better.

I remembered the five-year, three-state custody battle that wiped us out financially and tested us emotionally and spiritually beyond what I ever dreamed possible. I remembered the happy ten-year-old boy who couldn't understand why his mother wanted his sister but didn't want him, and the tears he'd shed trying to fathom that. I remembered the little girl who was nearly catatonic for two weeks when a judge she never met ordered her to leave her mother and come live with Dan and me.

I reviewed some of the hundreds of moments we had spent together, the three of us, and whether they were fights or trips to the store or working on homework or simply sitting and talking, they were all wrapped up in my mind like tiny precious gifts.

We had come through all of it, not just intact, but stronger, closer—happier.

And now, this little boy with the bushy blond hair and the squeaky voice had become a man with a perpetual three-day growth of beard, muscles bigger than mine and a talent for jazz drumming that came from some gene pool I knew nothing of. And he was about to go off to college in California.

I got up and walked into his room, where he was getting ready to go to sleep.

"I love you, Dan. I'm really going to miss you."

He looked at me with that eighteen-year-old's "okay, we already did this tonight," kind of stare. But then, he came over, hugged me and said, "I'm going to miss you, too."

I said good night and closed his door.

I'll never know if I did this single-parenting thing right, but at that moment, I knew I had done it well enough. And I knew it was the best thing I had ever done.

*Joe Seldner*

# READER/CUSTOMER CARE SURVEY

CE1

We care about your opinions. Please take a moment to fill out this Reader Survey card and mail it back to us. As a "THANK YOU" you will receive a valuable coupon in the mail towards future book purchases.

Or, go to **http://survey.hcibooks.com** and fill out our online survey, to receive an INSTANT COUPON as well as a SPECIAL GIFT available only online!

## Please PRINT using ALL CAPS

First Name |_|_|_|_|_|_|_|_|_|_|_|_|  MI. |_|  Last Name |_|_|_|_|_|_|_|_|_|_|_|

Address |_|_|_|_|_|_|_|_|_|_|_|_|_|_|_|_|_|_|_|_|_|

City |_|_|_|_|_|_|_|_|_|_|_|_|  ST |_|_|  Zip |_|_|_|_|_|—|_|_|_|_|

Phone # ( |_|_|_| ) |_|_|_| — |_|_|_|_|  Fax # ( |_|_|_| ) |_|_|_| — |_|_|_|_|

Email |_|_|_|_|_|_|_|_|_|_|_|_|_|_|_|_|_|_|_|_|_|

**(1) Gender:**
____ Female    ____ Male

**(2) Age:**
____ 12 or under
____ 13-19
____ 20-39
____ 40-59
____ 60+

**(3) Marital Status**
____ Married
____ Single
____ Divorced/Widowed

**(4) Did you receive this book as a gift?**
____ Yes    ____ No

**(5) How many Chicken Soup books have you bought or read?**
____ 1    ____ 2-4    ____ 5+

**(6) How did you find out about this book?**
*Please fill in ONE.*
1) ____ Recommendation
2) ____ Store Display
3) ____ Bestseller List
4) ____ Online
5) ____ Advertisement
6) ____ Catalog/Mailing
7) ____ Interview/Review (TV, Radio, Print)

**(7) Where do you usually buy books?**
*Please fill in your top TWO choices.*
1) ____ Bookstore
2) ____ Religious Bookstore
3) ____ Online
4) ____ Book Club/Mail Order
5) ____ Price Club (Costco, Sam's Club, etc.)
6) ____ Retail Store (Target, Wal-Mart, etc.)

**(9) What subjects do you enjoy reading about most?** Rank only *FIVE*. Use 1 for your favorite, 2 for second favorite, etc.

| | 1 | 2 | 3 | 4 | 5 |
|---|---|---|---|---|---|
| 1) Parenting/Family | ○ | ○ | ○ | ○ | ○ |
| 2) Relationships | ○ | ○ | ○ | ○ | ○ |
| 3) Recovery/Addictions | ○ | ○ | ○ | ○ | ○ |
| 4) Health/Nutrition | ○ | ○ | ○ | ○ | ○ |
| 5) Christianity | ○ | ○ | ○ | ○ | ○ |
| 6) Spirituality/Inspiration | ○ | ○ | ○ | ○ | ○ |
| 7) Business Self-Help | ○ | ○ | ○ | ○ | ○ |
| 8) Teen Issues | ○ | ○ | ○ | ○ | ○ |
| 9) Sports | ○ | ○ | ○ | ○ | ○ |

**(14) What attracts you most to a book?**
*(Please rank 1-4 in order of preference.)*

| | 1 | 2 | 3 | 4 |
|---|---|---|---|---|
| 14) Title | ○ | ○ | ○ | ○ |
| 15) Cover Design | ○ | ○ | ○ | ○ |
| 16) Author | ○ | ○ | ○ | ○ |
| 17) Content | ○ | ○ | ○ | ○ |

FOLD HERE

Comments:

*Do you have your own Chicken Soup story that you would like to send us?* Please submit separately to: Chicken Soup for the Soul, P.O. Box 30880, Santa Barbara, CA 93130

"You've been both a father and mother to me, Dad, so I got you a Mother's Day card."

# Sometimes,
# God Sends a Cockroach

*God speaks to all individuals through what
happens to them moment by moment.*
                                                J. P. DeCaussade

Sometimes, it seems God sends catastrophic things into
the world to get the attention of the human race. Floods,
plagues, the parting of seas have all served as reminders of
a presence greater than our own. Often, these tragedies
serve as catalysts for people to pull together and unite.

I have noticed that God sends reminders to us individu-
ally as well. On a much smaller scale, we have all received
gentle indications that we are not alone, and that together
we are stronger. It's like someone interrupting your daydream. They call your name or tap you on the shoulder,
and you're shaken out of one reality into another. But God
has to find other ways to get our attention. In my life, God
sent a cockroach.

The night of my forty-second birthday, I had just returned
home with my son from playing miniature golf. He was

seven years old, and we were both struggling with the divorce that had shaken our small family. We argued, though the actual cause of the argument is long gone from my memory. All I remember is both of us feeling sad and angry and tearful all at once. In the midst of what was a very irrational, emotional scene, my son looked over at the patio door and said in awe, "Mommy, *that* is the hugest bug I've ever seen!"

I looked behind me to see, indeed, one of the largest cockroaches I've ever seen. Some people politely call them water bugs, but you know what they really are. And in our town, when they spray the sewers, they come up through the drains and say, "Howdy!"

I loathe them.

But in a split second, that bug became our deliverer. My son and I became instantly united against the bug. It was no longer me against him or him against me. It was *us* against Godzilla. We rid our home of the bug, closed all the drains and snuggled into bed, laughing at our pest-control heroics. We reminded each other that we love each other no matter what. And as I dozed off, I actually thanked God for the cockroach.

Since that time several years ago, God has often intervened in moments such as those. Just last week, my now preadolescent son told me that I "just don't get it sometimes," as we left to get ice cream, hoping to lift our foul mood. Driving down the darkening street, something caught our eye, and before we knew it, we were both out of the car, fascinated with a young king snake crossing the road in the twilight. Another moment of unification took place. The mood lifted. It was like God saying, "Hey, look at this. Look at this cool snake." I no longer think it odd or coincidental when these things happen. I relax and believe in a God who sends me exactly what I need at the moment that I need it. These moments have become part of our history, our family storytelling.

Sometimes, God sends a cockroach; sometimes, a snake. I always know the message behind it: Unite. Work together. Love one another. And do it right now.

*Victoria McGee*

# Mom Has a Wicked Curveball

*It takes a village to raise a child.*

African Proverb

The boys of summer are full swing into their season. After watching a major-league baseball game on TV, my son, Daniel, digs into the closet for his plastic bat, ball and miniature baseball glove.

"Come on, Mom," he says, "let's go play ball."

I know I won't get any peace until I go to the nearby ball field with him to play his unstructured, invigorating version of baseball, so I throw on my well-worn New York Mets cap, grab my own battered glove and we're off.

On the way to the park, it strikes me as singularly sad that this little boy has to play baseball with his mother. Not that I'm a slouch; after all, I was a softball star in high school and college, and I'm still a mainstay on my church and work softball teams. And it's not that I don't love baseball, because I do. It's just that sometimes I wish my son had someone else to play ball with him. Someone male.

Being the single mother of a growing boy is one of the most difficult things I have ever done in my life. There is only so much that I, as a woman, can teach my son. I can sit beside him in the bleachers at the ballpark and describe the action on the diamond with good authority. I can teach him how to pitch, how to get the flowing rhythm of the wind-up, stretch and delivery beautifully and grace-fully in sync. I can show him how to bat: "Keep your stick off your shoulder! Raise that back elbow! Choke up! Step into the pitch and follow through!" I can show him how to hit first base with his outside foot, so he can have a straight path to second without going too far out of the baseline. I can show him how to scrabble sideways, glove low, limbs loose, in pursuit of a hard grounder hit to him at second base. I can teach him the duties of a good catcher, including how to block the plate with his body so a run won't score, taking the jarring impact without a murmur. This is the way I play ball myself. I can coach him well, and he will be a good player.

But there are so many things I can't teach him. While I can tell him how he should act as a young man, injecting a womanly wish of how men should behave, I can't tell him how to be a man. I don't know anything about the subtleties and secrets of manhood. I can play at men's games all I want, and play them convincingly, and my son will learn something. But it won't be the same as hav-ing a man in his life, someone he can admire, relate to and learn from.

I search out role models for him, but it's easier said than done. I'm choosy—I have to be. I want Daniel to become a good, brave man who respects women, loves equality and diversity, and is strong and sure of himself. Although all these qualities may not be embodied in only one of the men who take it upon themselves to be part of my son's life in the absence of a full-time father, there are enough men around who, together, give my son an excellent overview of the man he has the potential to become.

I want my son to have Frank's social conscience, Alan's sense of humor, Darren's work ethic and Steve's gentleness. I want him to have Phil's love for his mother, David's devotion to church and family, Tony's eagerness for education and Ted's spirit of fun. I want him to have Larry's quiet calmness, Levon's friendliness, Bill's helpfulness and Ben's sense of adventure. I want all these attributes for Daniel and something more. I want him to take everything he learns from these men and, one day, pass it on to another boy—making a connection that continues unbroken.

I hope my son gets to play baseball someday soon with someone who, during the game, will also teach him about some of life's nuances. Someone who will talk to him in a way that I can't—as a man to a boy, with a man's point of view and a masculine sort of love. My son will be very lucky to meet a person like that.

Meanwhile, I have this quiet little fantasy:

The World Series has just ended. My son, the Series' Most Valuable Player, has led his team to victory by pitching a perfect game: no runs, no hits, no errors, no walks. It awes everyone that someone so young can pitch so flawlessly.

"Who taught you to pitch like that?" a reporter asks.

My son smiles. "My mother," he says. "Mom has a wicked curveball."

*Tanya J. Tyler*

# Remainders

*Cherish your human connections: your relationships with friends and family.*

Barbara Bush

When I call my daughter, who is at her mother's on this dark winter evening for her visitation week, I can hear something wrong in her voice. An emotional quality that a phone cannot disguise. A troubled feeling that needs to escape and come home. Rose is also irritable and short with me; I know she's wishing this conversation would end.

"What's wrong, sweetie?" I ask, in my most welcoming tone, desperately not wanting her to hang up.

And then without warning, it is freed. "Keith Jensen committed suicide today. He tied a rope to his bedroom door and jumped off his bed."

A long pause. Now we are connected. "School was weird. There are so many rumors. We sat in small groups in Mrs. Spence's English class and tried to talk about it. Some of the kids were crying because the last words they said to him were, 'Shut up, Keith!' No one could do any work. I flunked my math test."

I look out the kitchen window at the drifts of heavy snow. I am suddenly shivering, but not from the weather.

I ask Rose if she knew Keith well.

"Everybody knew him. He seemed happy. I never would have thought he would do something like this. I don't understand."

She talks on with emotion and without hesitation, as if she is the river and I am the ocean she yearns to flow toward. I listen without interruption. Then, out of nowhere, my daughter says, "Don't worry, Papa, I would never do anything like that."

It's our long-standing tradition that, when we are separated and end our telephone conversations, we each say, "I love you." Tonight, there is nothing automatic in our good-byes.

I put down the receiver and get out the family album that holds her class pictures for each of the last seven years. I find Keith and Rose in Ms. Anderson's third-grade class and in Mrs. Strong's fourth-grade class. There is nothing in Keith's face that forewarns what happened today, nothing to prepare any of us for the idea of a twelve-year-old going through the elaborate measures of hanging himself. He is smiling out at me, along with the other children I have watched over the years: in the noisy playground at Russell Elementary School, onstage at the annual holiday concerts and at my annual visits on Career Days to talk about writing.

That's when I remember Keith, just for an instant, like a light drop of rain. He's at the edges of the classroom on one of the days I visited. I see him looking at me. I recall his eyes and his smile. Maybe the dark-brown color of his hair. And that is all I remember.

When I look at Keith's picture, I think of all the children I've known in my life. I remember how I've watched them grow. I remember the times I've teased them, held them, despaired as their parents split up to form new families. And I've been inspired by their bravery in the face of it all. I think of the connection they share with all the world's children, and of how their lives ripple through our community, affecting each and every one of us.

I continue turning the pages of the album, watching our lives—my daughter's and mine—take form. I am driving a tractor raking fall oat straw in northern Michigan; I am balancing baby Rose on the hood of our ancient green truck at a Reno rest stop; there's Rose playing cello; and her mother holding her wrapped in a towel fresh from a bath, both of them radiant.

More pages: Rose with tricycles and summer Popsicles; twirling a dance, eyes closed, in the western wind in a blue corduroy jumper and white tights; she is climbing trees and sniffing North Coast rhododendrons. She walks under the half-light of a redwood forest holding my hand and dancing with me, her feet on my own for balance. In every photograph, her fingers are busy, her eyes twinkling and her face reflects the light of each day.

A child's life, with my own intertwined, is held within the covers of this photo album. I can hold each picture and slip into a time frame of emotions. This is what I'm looking for tonight: a reckoning, a validation that the years just didn't pass without notice. I want to remember everything about my daughter. Photos are not easy to look at. Memories are never simple. I can't easily untangle the joy from the pain, and if I am to survive separation and divorce, I am forced to choose the better moments of our lives. What fine actors we ultimately must become.

All the rooms and houses stare back at me. Meals, friends, seasons and landscapes of desert and rain. Precious fragments of field and wood. Mountain ranges I still climb at night in my bed. All the western towns where I tried to hold us together, but failed. I guess these years are finally catching up with me.

I close the album. I am haunted tonight. I hear Rose's voice again: *Don't worry, Papa, I would never do anything like that.* I am holding still in this room, searching for faith with my own small remainder, affirming one child, remembering another.

*Stephen J. Lyons*

# 6

# GETTING ALONG AND FORGIVENESS

*I*magine all the people living life in peace.

*John Lennon*

# Second Chance

*Forgiveness is the final form of love.*

Reinhold Niebuhr

Stomach cancer claimed my mother's life three days before my second birthday. My father was devastated and never fully recovered from the heartbreak Mom's death caused him. He raised me alone, and although it was just the two of us in the house, I never really knew him. My mom's battle with cancer had been long and expensive. Insurance only covered so much, and Dad was forced to work crazy hours to keep my stomach full and the bill collectors satisfied. He wasn't home very much and was rarely in a good mood when he was home. His absence forced me to become very independent, and by the time I was twelve, I was pretty much on my own.

Left alone to do as I pleased, I was wild and developed a serious drug problem by the time I was fifteen. I did whatever it took to get high, and most times, that meant stealing from my dad. I'd slip a ten or twenty out of his wallet, pawn off something small from around the house, or invent some unforeseen school-related expense. It didn't take him long to realize what was going on and confront me about it. He screamed the usual fatherly threats, and I countered with the usual obscenities of a defiant, undisciplined teenager. It climaxed when I threw and landed a punch and stormed out of the house, never to return.

I spent the next seven years bouncing around from one city to the next. Each move was supposed to be a fresh beginning, but ended the same way. I'd get into some kind of trouble with the law, or run up a tab with some drug dealer and be forced to run. I'd scrape up a few bucks, hop on a bus and move on, in search of greener pastures. Normal living was nothing but a pipe dream. I felt incapable and unworthy of living a normal life. I hated myself for what I had done to my dad.

Most recovering drug addicts will tell you that they were only able to get clean after hitting rock bottom. I met someone who helped me get clean before that happened. I was lucky. Her name was Gina. She was a bartender at Bob's Bar and Grill, a place I frequented. We struck up a casual bartender-patron friendship that slowly turned into something deeper. She knew about my addiction, but looked past it to see the real me. I fell crazy in love with her, and to my amazement, Gina fell in love with me.

Together, we confronted my addiction head on. With her love as my inspiration, I entered a rehab clinic, and on my first try, kicked my habit cold. She visited as often as they'd let her, and kept me strong with her smiles and kisses. Two weeks after I got out, we were married.

With a renewed attitude toward life, and the confidence gained from my recent accomplishment, I enrolled at the local community college. Gina kept her job and got her boss to hire me part-time. We struggled financially but somehow managed to make ends meet until I graduated with a bachelor's degree in hotel management. I found work at a five-star resort as a front-desk manager and earned enough to allow Gina to quit her job, and for both of us to concentrate on starting a family. On June 19, 1995, Dr. Barnes gave us the good news: we were pregnant.

Our daughter, Jennifer, was born on March 14, 1996. She was indescribably beautiful. God had blessed me with a new life, and with Jennifer's arrival, it was now complete. For the first time in my life, I was truly happy. I thought often about tracking down my dad, but never did. I felt too guilty, too scared to face him.

Just three months after my daughter's birth, God, in his mysterious way, tested the strength of my resolve and challenged my sobriety. On her way to the grocery store, a car ran a red light and struck Gina's car on the driver's side. She was killed on impact. I was home with Jennifer when the police officer called to inform me of the accident. I took solace in the fact that Gina hadn't suffered and probably didn't even see it coming. I hung up the phone and stared at Jennifer, who slept soundly. Tremendous grief enveloped me; I feared I couldn't handle taking care of Jennifer by myself.

The next few months were filled with anxiety, fear and depression. I found day care for Jennifer, went back to work and struggled mightily to stay sober. The emotional pain was relentless, and I was tempted every day to turn to my "old friend" for relief. Jennifer was the only reason I didn't. I would sit for hours, just staring at her, begging God for the strength to stay straight for her. I begged God to ease my pain and misery because I missed my wife so much.

One evening, after putting Jennifer down in her crib, there was a knock at the front door. I hurried to open it, and when I did, I saw my father standing there. He looked older and had less hair, but it was definitely him. He was obviously nervous and just stood there staring at me. I stared back. Several seconds had passed, when I broke the silence and began sobbing uncontrollably. My dad grabbed me, and we hugged each other tight. We stood there at the door and wept together.

"I'm sorry," I cried.

"No, son. I'm sorry."

The tears continued to flow as we held our hug. I released him and wiped my eyes. I invited him into my home; he came in and sat on the couch. I sat in my easy chair and looked at him, both of us trying to control our emotions and our tears.

"How did you find me?"

"It wasn't that hard, son. I have a friend who's made a business out of doing this sort of thing. I gave him a few bucks to track you down. I would've called but . . ."

"But what, Dad?"

"I didn't want . . . I didn't want you to say no."

I buried my face in my hands and wept again. He rose and came to me. My dad stood next to me and held me as I let out all the guilt and remorse I had carried around for years. Through my sobs, I begged his forgiveness.

"If I could take it back I would, Dad! I've hated myself for a long time because of what I did and what I put you through. You didn't deserve . . ."

"Stop it, son. Stop it! It was me; it was all my fault. All of it."

We talked for a while more, each of us trying to out-apologize the other. I still hadn't introduced my dad to his granddaughter, and I figured it was time.

"Dad, I have a daughter."

He looked surprised at first, then elated. It was the first genuine smile I can ever remember seeing on my father's face.

"Her name is Jennifer."

"Can I see her?"

I walked him into Jennifer's bedroom, and we both stood over her crib, watching her sleep. My dad stared at her as tears welled up in his eyes.

"She's got your mother's eyes."

"Yeah, I noticed that. Her mother passed away three months ago."

He looked at me with pity and concern, then grabbed me by the arm and led me out of the room.

"Son, I've made so many mistakes in my life. The biggest by far was letting you walk out of that house. I never got over your mother's death. I let my grief come between us. I love you; I always have. Don't make the same mistakes I made. Let nothing interfere with your relationship with your daughter. It is the only thing that matters. Her love for you will make life worth living. You are here to take care of and love that little girl. It'll be very difficult at times, but keep what happened to us fresh in your mind, and don't let it happen with her."

My dad stayed with us for two nights and then flew back home. I took his words to heart. They are always with me for inspiration and encouragement whenever things get tough.

Two months after his visit, I asked my dad if he would consider moving in with us to help take care of Jennifer—and me. He quickly accepted the invitation and moved in four days later. I miss Gina, and some days are harder than others. But I know she looks down at us and smiles because we are doing well, and Jennifer is happy.

Sometimes, a second chance is all it takes.

*Michael Shawn*

# In Times of War, a Little Peace

*For every minute you remain angry, you give up sixty seconds of peace of mind.*

Ralph Waldo Emerson

Like many New Yorkers', my phone rang off the hook on September 11, 2001. Friends and family across the country wanted and needed to touch base, to make sure that my son and I were safe. What surprised me was that most of the messages were from my ex-husband, who lived in Tennessee.

He left messages at my office. He left messages at my home. He left messages on my cell phone. This from the man who had never picked up the phone to check on my health or well-being since our divorce. With each message he left, his tone was more and more frantic. His final message was simple: "Please call. I want to make sure you and TJ are safe."

What my ex-husband didn't realize was that my entire building had gone into lockdown directly after the attacks on the World Trade Center. As a communications coordinator for my company, I was immediately pressed into action to alert our offices nationwide of the state of events, as well as coordinate comfort areas for the many employees who had family members working in the towers.

I was called into my CEO's office after the first tower was hit, and I didn't return to my desk until sometime after 1:00 that afternoon. When I was finally able to reach my ex-husband, I was shocked at the obvious tears in his voice. "Thank God, thank God," was all he could say for the first several minutes. Since he was a native New Yorker, I knew my ex would have been deeply affected by the events of September 11, but I had no idea that simply knowing we were barely thirty miles from Ground Zero would shake him to the core.

For the first time since our divorce, my ex listened to me intently as I quietly explained how my team had watched, first in confusion and later in horror, the New York skyline that we can see at a distance from our office windows. Once I had entered the CEO's office, it became a horrific ping-pong game of watching the events out the window and the coverage on CNN.

My ex never interrupted, not once while I shared how many of my co-workers had broken down sobbing, knowing that family and friends were trapped in the wreckage. He offered no complaint, no words of recrimination, as I explained why, for the past five hours, I hadn't checked my messages because I was seeing to the needs of people at my company. He offered no criticism when I told him I had just checked in with our son's school a few minutes earlier, and all was well with our son. He offered no suggestions, no orders, no advice when I told him I would talk to our son later about the events. When I had finished, he simply said, "Thank you for calling me. I was so worried. Thank God you are both okay, and your family is safe."

To understand the enormity of that statement, you need to realize that just a few months prior, my ex and I could

barely speak to one another without a conversation evolv-
ing into a screaming match. We both had such extreme
views of our past and how the events of those times had
fractured our family. For the past five years, we had both
held on to such hurt and anger it was little wonder that
we couldn't ever find a common ground.

The catalyst for our tentative peacetime agreement was
actually the request of our ten-year-old son. While consid-
ering vacation ideas in July, he asked me to take him to
Tennessee to see his dad. When I began to offer my long-
standing reasons as to why this was not a good idea, he
quietly said, "You may not be ready to go, Mom, but I am."
Those words stuck with me for days, and finally, I realized
he was right. I might never have been ready to make that
first step toward peace, nor might his father, but our son
was ready. He became an ambassador of peace between
two very hostile countries.

After a great deal of consideration, I realized it was time,
at least for me, to put the past to rest. I was tired of fighting. I was tired of always being angry, regardless of how
right I knew I was. I made the reservations, and in August,
we visited my ex-husband and his wife for a short stay. I
am not saying it was easy, or problem free. There were
many tense moments, but overall, it was a tenuous beginning at peace.

The phone calls on September 11 were further proof
that some things are just more important than holding on
to anger and pain. When tragedy strikes, some things—like
family and children—matter more than who is right and
who is wrong.

I sense a difference now in my relationship with my ex.
We actually have conversations when he calls. He asks me
about my job and listens patiently as I express how difficult it has been to talk to the many families and firefight-
ers, to be involved in the arrangements for the funerals

and memorials for those who died so tragically. He offers compassion when I express how tired I am from the many hours I have been working, and he quietly discusses what his company has done to assist in the relief effort.

We talk about the friends we shared long ago, and how many of them were affected by the tragedy. And mainly these days, we calmly talk about how all of this has affected not only our child, but also his stepchildren, and what we can do together to help them. Just last night, we discussed ways to help our child through a difficult problem he is struggling with, and there were no words of blame or recrimination. Although we are not yet at the point of being "one big, happy family," our lives, which we thought had been destroyed by pain and bitterness, are beginning to heal.

We are learning how, in a time of war, to come together and offer our child a more peaceful existence. And our child, who in a way has been a refugee from a war-torn country, seems happier. Despite the fear he has about the world around him, his own little world has found peace at last.

*Patricia S. Brucato*

"Oh, hi, Helen, I'm just multi-tasking. How about you?"

# The Magic Spring

*Only love is real; everything else illusion.*

Carole King

When my husband and I divorced after six years and two children (if you didn't count ourselves, in which case, there were four), I faced a dilemma shared by every single mother: how was I to convey to our confused offspring that it was okay—even eminently desirable—to go on loving both their parents, even though it was obvious to them that one or both of these same parents had screwed up somewhere, and badly?

I tried often to explain this concept of loving both of us equally, and I failed every time.

"Daddy still loves you both very much," I would say, hopefully.

"If he loves us, then why did Daddy leave us?" they would ask, sad and mystified.

Unfortunately, I couldn't in good conscience share the answer that sprang most readily to mind in those first raw days of single parenthood, which was, "Because he's a jerk!"

This might not have been entirely accurate, but it worked for me.

Holding that thought at bay with some effort, I would mouth that oft-repeated platitude: "Mommy and Daddy just need some space, honey."

Whatever that statement meant (and even I wasn't sure), it was generally greeted with blank looks from both of my young children.

Meanwhile, through each paternal visit, my children struggled with their feelings of disloyalty. They knew they loved and missed their dad, but felt terribly guilty mentioning that fact to me, if only for practical reasons. After all, I was now the sole arbiter of their arguments and judge of their punishments. They no longer had an alternative for appeal, and this situation created tremendous ambivalence in my children.

Early in their lives, they had learned to take their grievances against me to their father for support, and vice versa. Now if they were mad at me, the only source of comfort lay squarely in the enemy camp. It didn't seem right to any of us when they had to grudgingly apologize or deny their anger so they could climb into the only lap available—mine.

Finally, one day as she sat on my lonely lap in our small Berkeley, California, living room, my five-year-old daughter articulated her guilt.

"I'm feeling bad, Mommy," she sobbed as I held her. "I still love Daddy, and I miss him—even though he left us . . . even though I know you're really, really mad at him."

How had she picked up this intelligence? I was sure I hadn't done any shouting or overt sniveling when I spilled my pain into the telephone talking to my best girlfriend and confidante. I had been so careful to maintain a neutral stance around the children.

"And is it okay to kind of like his new girlfriend, too?" asked my son, innocently.

I didn't have a snappy answer for that one, so I mumbled something that was meant to be reassuring, slinking off to the kitchen to lick my reopened wounds.

At a loss to help them, I took my problem to an older, wiser single mom, and she gave me the solution I craved, in words I knew the children would instantly understand.

"Tell them this," she said. "Love is not a pie that must be divided into portions, my dear. It isn't something you get more of if you've been 'good,' or less of if you've been 'bad,' and then it's all eaten up and gone. Love is an ever-flowing spring from whose infinite bounty anyone can drink, anytime one chooses, and one may share a cup with others anytime one chooses, and never feel that by so doing one is depriving someone else, because it is a magic spring that refills itself instantly, and there is always enough to go around."

I couldn't wait to tell the kids, and once I did, they couldn't wait to offer a generous drink to their father on their very next visit.

And when they came home again, they offered their brimming cups to me, because in their sweetly giving hearts, they knew my thirst.

*Mary Lynn Archibald*

"Oh, sure! Now that I have a paper route
they both want custody."

# It Can Work

*People who fight fire with fire usually end up with ashes.*

Abigail Van Buren

I recognized Melissa the moment she entered the conference room for the job interview. I hadn't seen her since we had met, approximately ten years earlier, but she was someone I could never forget. I had often wondered how she was doing and what had become of her life.

I remembered that hot summer day many years before, when I received a call on the office intercom from Judge James Jones summoning me to the east courtroom. As I opened the ornate double doors of the courtroom, I noticed the clenched teeth and exasperated look of the judge as he peered down from the bench at the meticulously groomed attorneys and their disheveled clients. In the audience section of the courtroom sat three young girls, on the edge of their seats, gripping each other's hands. Before everyone in the courtroom could turn around to see who had entered, Judge Jones authoritatively broke the silence, "Mr. Mediator, please approach the bench."

As I walked down the aisle, I could not help but notice the looks of the three girls. Their eyes were red and moist from crying, but the eyes of the girl in the middle were different; they appeared locked on me in desperation. They reminded me of a drowning person, looking up from the water at a lifeguard as she takes her last breath.

Before I had even reached the bench, Judge Jones continued, "I have been engaged in four days of testimony, both sides alleging the other is unfit to be a parent. I have also observed the suffering these three young ladies have experienced throughout these past few days. I can only imagine what they have endured during these last months. I now have before me the question of residential custody. I am inclined to refuse residential custody to either parent, but since we now have a divorce-mediation program, I am requesting assistance."

Turning toward me, the judge continued. "Please meet with the parents and their children. If an agreement can be reached, I will approve it."

Judge Jones then leaned forward and spoke directly to the parents. "You both profess to love those three girls. If you really do, you will abandon your petty, selfish behavior and be the parents these young people deserve. If you do not, and you come back before me, neither of you will be happy with my ruling."

With the judge's directive, I led the family to my office. Actually, it was Melissa, the young girl whose desperate look had caught my attention, who led the group. She almost sprinted down the hallway, dragging her sisters and parents behind her.

Melissa kept saying to everyone, over and over, "This will work. This will work. This is our last chance."

Over the next few weeks, with Melissa constantly supporting and prodding her parents to work something out, the parents dug through their anger and reached an agreement on custody and a parenting plan for their three children.

The reason I remember this case so well is that it was so surprising when the agreement was reached. Because of the depth of the parents' anger and their long pattern of conflict, even their own attorneys had predicted additional costly and lengthy hearings, years of returning to court and three emotionally scarred children.

But no one had imagined the determination of a fifteen-year-old girl, who saw her world crumbling around her and decided to do everything she could to try to make things better.

All the mediation skills, counseling and divorced-parenting education could not lift the parents out of their own inner pain, but the courage of this child somehow got the parents to focus on their kids, rather than on themselves.

This was one of the first success stories of our new divorce-mediation program. This family never had to come back to court. I never got the chance to find out how Melissa turned out until she walked into that job interview ten years later. With confidence, grace and a maturity that exceeded her age, Melissa sat down at the conference table.

"I have been preparing for this moment for many years," she began. "My college friends always talk about the point in their childhood when they decided they wanted to be teachers or doctors. I can easily remember the moment I knew what I was going to do with my life. Actually, it was in this very courthouse.

"I can remember that day, when I felt the lowest I have ever felt. I was scared I would be separated from my parents and my sisters. I was scared that the rest of my life was ruined. I was scared, as most kids are, that I was somehow responsible for my parents' anger, their fighting and their divorce.

"I prayed and prayed for a solution, but thought all was lost until the judge ordered mediation. Although I did not have a clue what mediation was, I knew it had to be the answer to my prayers.

"I had spent three long days in a big, cold, scary court-room watching a process that seemed to bring out the ugliest side of my parents. As the judge ordered our family out of the courtroom, I thought I could actually see light at the end of the tunnel as we walked down the hall and into that bright, cheery conference room with a big, inviting round table. The room overflowed with hope, and I kind of knew right then what I wanted to do with my life."

Melissa calmly continued, "The whole mediation process seemed magical at that time. I saw my parents slowly begin to focus on us kids, and for the first time in years, put aside their own problems. I observed my parents learning all over again how to communicate with each other and how to talk to each other without being angry, at least when it had to do with us.

"My sisters and I survived, and have all turned out great. I decided I wanted to do anything I could to help kids who are in similar situations, so here I am. I received my medi-ation certification this past May, and would be honored to work as a mediator in this judicial district." Melissa then took a deep breath and leaned back in her chair.

I hired Melissa that same day, and she is now one of the most respected and successful child-custody mediators in the state.

*John K. Steelman*

# The Little Train That Couldn't

*To understand is to forgive, even oneself.*

Alexander Chase

When my son was three years old, he was given the old fashioned, long-playing record of *The Little Engine That Could*. He listened to it often, and it always made him smile. His world was a hard one, and he and his sister and I struggled to get by, to survive in a world without benefit of alimony, child support or state welfare help. He had few possessions, but since he was still a child, he had fun in spite of this. My life, even though it was hard, was easier because my children were in it.

So often during those days, I wondered how my meager earnings would pay the bills, buy the food, take care of all those extra expenses that pop up when you're raising children. I worked nights so I could spend as much time as possible with the children when they were awake. Like so many single parents, I had no idea that I would be the sole supporter. But the difficulties were always made easier because my children were happy and loving, compassionate and smiling, oblivious to their mom's hard work.

Boys will be boys, and one particular day my son was especially spirited. By evening, with all my patience depleted,
I simply lost my temper and lashed out in response to his
antics, grabbing his favorite record off the turntable and
breaking it. *Oh, dear! What have I done?* I scolded myself. I
sent them to bed with such a heavy heart, I couldn't even
look either of them in the eye—those big, innocent, questioning eyes, which as much as said to me: *What happened
to Mommy? What made her voice so loud and her face so mean?
Does she still love us, or will she leave like Daddy did?*

Needless to say, I got no sleep that night, confused by
how his behavior, which was so benign—after all, he was
just a three-year-old boy acting a bit rowdy, nothing
more—could make me lose my temper and actually
destroy something that didn't even belong to me. I wept
tears of guilt all night. *What if it happened again?* I wondered.
*How could I have been so mean?* He certainly didn't deserve
my harsh words, and the pain of my actions almost ripped
my tired heart in two. I was in actual, palpable pain; my
heartache consumed me, body, mind and soul.

By the time morning came, I was so ready to apologize,
I couldn't wait for him to awaken. I did apologize; I did tell
him I was so very wrong to do what I had done, for he did
not deserve that at all. And just like a child, he was soon
out playing, acting as though the incident never
happened. Ah! The unconditional love of a child! This is
their gift to us, and for some of us, through our children
we truly experience freedom in loving and interacting for
the first time.

It was a long time before this lesson of my temper
finally made itself clear to me: it was okay to mess up, as
long as I said I was sorry. What was most important was
to sincerely and contritely apologize for my mistake, for
my misbehavior. As I contemplated my actions in those
moments, I realized I wasn't perfect; I wouldn't always be

able to be judicious. After all, I was simply a young, newly divorced woman trying to figure it all out as I went. Raising children on my own was going to teach me as many important lessons as I would teach them. And this most important lesson, of messing up and then saying I was sorry, taught my children that when they messed up, they could also say they were sorry, and life would be good again.

We all make mistakes; we all misstep along the way. But as we learn and grow, we teach our children, so they, in turn, can learn and grow. From time to time, after that terrible day, I would feel the pressure of life on my tired shoulders, the weight of survival and the slings and arrows of oppressive landlords, nasty neighbors and assorted difficulties, and I would begin to lose my temper and raise my voice. In that moment, I would step outside of time and remember that day when I broke my son's favorite record. Remembering, standing outside myself, would give me enough time to reconsider, to lower my voice, to simply say: "Mommy's having a rough day, so let's give me a break and calm down."

I know I didn't always do my best, didn't always take the better path, but I had learned to apologize when I needed to and to make sure the laughter well outweighed the sorrow of the day. And doing it that way, each and every day became a single pearl, one after another; and now I have a string of pearls, each one a perfect representation of what it means to be human, to grow, to evolve and to love. I learned it all in feeling the love our children give us without question, without judgment.

Recently, I was talking to my daughter and told her I worried I had been too hard on her and her brother when they were young, always scolding and complaining, and that was my only regret. She looked at me and said, "I don't remember that. I just remember laughing." Her brother said the same thing. After all the years of self-doubt, all the nights of wondering how I could let my frustrations spill over and of how I could have done better, now that they are grown and on their own, they look back on their childhood as having been filled with love and laughter. They don't care about the things they didn't have. They only remember what they *did* have: unconditional love, the perfect gift that keeps on giving.

*Barbara Stanley*

# Forgiving My Dad

*Forgiveness does not change the past, but it does
enlarge the future.*

Paul Boese

My story begins . . .
I am being raised in a single-parent home
With my mom, my grandmother and aunt.
Raised with a lot of love from my three moms.
My dad is another story.
So this is dedicated to him
And to all dads who aren't there for their kids . . .
Many because they can't, many because they choose not to.
The last time I saw my dad, I was going to turn six.
I still remember when he gave me a big hug;
That's something I'll never forget.
I will soon be twelve.
I sometimes wonder if he ever thinks about me
The way I think about him.
He never remembers my birthday
Even though I always remember his.
I used to send him a card for the holidays;

He never remembered me.
In school, all my plays, awards, my mom is always there
Even though she has to miss work;
But she makes it to all my school activities.
I wish he could know that I'm not a bad kid.
I make good grades, I have a lot of friends.
When I see my friends with their dads
I wonder "what if," Dad . . .
Even though you choose to not be a part of my life,
I want you to know I will always be here for you
Whenever you choose to be a part of my life again.
Because I will always love you no matter what happens.
So Dad, if you are out there and you are reading this,
Please know that I do love you and forgive you.

*Sincerely,*
*Your son, Joseph*

*Joseph Salazar*

[EDITORS' NOTE: *Joseph is autistic and spends hours and hours at his computer, intently focused on writing.*]

# A Turning Point

*A chip on the shoulder is too heavy a piece of baggage to carry through life.*

John Hancock

As everything unraveled in our twenty-five-year marriage, and my husband moved out of the only home our daughter had ever known, I felt a huge sense of relief that my daughter was twenty. It made everything simpler. Or so I thought. Because she wasn't a minor, I didn't have to negotiate custody arrangements and child support, didn't have to put up with his coming around to see her, didn't have to try to explain the inexplicable to a young child. Mostly, though, I was relieved because I thought it would be less complicated emotionally for her at that age. She was a young adult, away at college, not subject to the day-to-day difficulties or emotional turmoil of her parents being in two households.

In an attempt to ensure that my crushing hurt did not affect their relationship, I had said to my daughter and her dad that the nature and quality of their relationship from that point on would be up to them. I would not interfere, but neither would I facilitate. I tried to be glad when I saw his phone number on the phone bill from her college dorm; but I'll confess that on more than one occasion in those early days I slipped into revenge fantasies, wishing with more than a little shame that I could be one of "those" divorced parents who use their children to "get at" an ex-spouse. Over time, my anger waned in intensity, but on occasion glowed white hot, briefly and unexpectedly, for reasons that still elude me. At those times, I exercised that remarkable ability most women have to feign pleasantness and serenity while simultaneously holding down an ugly knot of hurt and anger that clamors for attention.

I observed my daughter's next few years from afar as she concentrated on her studies; became active in a sorority; made new friends; played on her university's tennis team; enjoyed snow-skiing, camping, boating and beach trips with friends; and fell in and out of love. I naturally wondered what impact the end of her parents' twenty-five-year marriage might have on her. From all I could see, though, my daughter's strong spirit, sense of independence, self-confidence, good humor and zest for life were serving her well. After a while, I even allowed myself more than a few moments of self-congratulation on having handled things in a way that had left her relatively unscathed.

Reality hit hard one evening during her Christmas vacation, six months before she was to graduate from college. That's when my daughter taught me an important lesson: children whose parents divorce are forever changed, regardless of their age or life situation. Sitting at the dinner table that night in my new house, which still didn't feel like home to either of us, she hesitantly told me she was dreading her college graduation.

"All my friends' families will be coming, and there are dinners and receptions all weekend," she said, putting her elbows on the table her father had sanded and stained when she was a little girl. "And every time you see or talk about Dad, you cry all the time and feel sad. I can't tell one of you not to come. You're my parents. But . . . well, I don't even want to go through graduation."

I felt as though I'd been hit with something big and hard.

I couldn't breathe. And then tears—the tears I usually fought back so well—began to course down my cheeks and drip onto my chest. I felt hot, and the light over the table seemed to spin and flash as I struggled for composure. I was stunned and stung. Stunned to discover that my involuntary tears had cut so deeply into her life and soul. Stung that my hanging on to sadness and a sense of loss were responsible for her wanting to skip such an important milestone in her life. I didn't believe for a second that she would really miss the festivities, but knowing that she saw my continued grieving as an inevitable dark cloud over her graduation weekend was devastating.

I've always believed that actions follow thoughts. Now would come a test of that belief. "I know it wasn't easy to say that," I managed to say. After a pause and a big sigh, I continued, with a note of determination in my voice that I didn't feel. "It's six months until graduation. You know both your dad and I love you and want your graduation and all your special moments in life to be unmarred by what's gone on between us. I promise you that on your graduation weekend, you don't have to worry about my crying. We'll be fine."

And we were. Tears did fall that day, but they were shared by my ex-husband as we stood arm in arm, watching the daughter we'd raised walk across the stage to accept her diploma. He even carried an extra handkerchief for me, as he had all those years we were married. That's when I knew that my choice to spend time with him during the months after her sad dinner-table confrontation had been worthwhile. By "practicing" being cordial and friendly, by sharing conversations and meals, by saying why I was doing this, I moved beyond the automatic response of tears. I think we actually ended up enjoying ourselves after a while; and it wasn't long before I realized that forgiveness had crept into my heart, softening that hard knot of anger and hurt.

It was a turning point, not only for the three of us, but for our extended family and friends, as well. Now my sister and mother and friends can once again be friendly toward my ex without feeling disloyal to me. The cordiality and friendliness we felt that spring weekend has continued in the years since, making subsequent visits more enjoyable for everyone. And now we're all immersed in planning for another milestone: our daughter's wedding. In the fall, my ex-husband and I will sit side by side once again—this time in the front pew at the church—perhaps sharing a handkerchief once more.

A beloved teacher once said to me, "Forgiving may help the forgiver more than the forgiven." She was right.

*Susan Carver Williams*

# A Special Bond

*It is through cooperation, rather than conflict,
that your greatest successes will be derived.*

Ralph Charell

Seventeen hours of confinement inside the Boeing 747 provided endless opportunities for reflection, as well as anticipation of the most significant event of our lives. Susan, my wife of five years, sat beside me lost in the six-inch image of an in-flight movie. Outwardly she appeared unfazed by the fact that we were headed to central China, where in two short days we would be united with our first and only child: a little girl born in Anhui Province two years and four months earlier. The photos and bio forwarded to us by the Chinese government's adoption agency provided information such as height, weight, age and health status. But something more than simple images on paper had been given to us. In my heart the beginning of an incredible love was stirring, the likes of which I had never known before.

My reflections took me back to rural Long Island, where I grew up in a typical middle-class family. Who would have thought that at fifty-two years of age I'd become a global dad? I always was a late bloomer. With navy, college, career and a string of unfulfilling relationships, the thought of children had always been a "someday" thing. Now, "someday" was rushing toward me at six hundred miles an hour, and I was scared to death.

Han Dong Cheng was scared, too. Her gut-wrenching screams echoed through the orphanage as she was handed over to this strange-looking couple. In time, she wore herself out and began surveying her new situation. She was a beautiful little girl with jet-black hair, bright brown eyes and, when it finally appeared, an incredible smile that lit up the room. Through the camera lens, I watched her and Susan share some playful moments. I was quite happy to just watch this exquisite little creature begin to open up and relax. But, while Jordyn Nicole (her American adoptive name) and her new mommy were beginning the bonding process, Daddy was persona non grata. She was extremely fearful of me and wouldn't allow me within arms' reach, turning away in tears whenever I approached. This heartbreaking sequence occurred several times over our remaining ten days in China. It tested the limits of my emotional strength and maturity to understand and accept it. I was only able to cope by telling myself things would be different once we got home—or so I thought.

Susan and I had been having marital difficulties for some time, and despite our best efforts, the marriage wasn't working. Truth be told, we should have been going to divorce court, not China. I now thank God every day that we chose China instead. For the time being, it was easy to put our personal issues aside as the presence of our new daughter provided a renewed sense of excitement in our otherwise unhappy marriage. This was tempered, however, by Jordyn's continuing negative reaction to me. It was many days before I could come close enough to touch her and attempt to hold her.

Days turned into weeks, and slowly but surely, I began building the relationship with my daughter that I had wanted for so long. Eventually, I could actually hold her, and I could tell she was beginning to accept my presence in her life. To my delight, Daddy became a jungle gym, a clown, a horsey—anything to strengthen our developing relationship. Her laughter began to fill our house and fill my heart. Even though I knew I was lagging behind Mommy, I felt a definite bond forming between us. She was turning into an extremely happy little girl, adapting to her new life in a way that indicated all would be fine if we just gave her lots of love and let it happen in God's own way.

Just as my relationship with Jordyn blossomed, my relationship with Susan withered. There were two camps: Mommy and Jordyn and Daddy and Jordyn. As difficult as it was, we both placed Jordyn's well-being first and strove to never jeopardize her happiness or undermine her relationship with the other parent. We focused on our respective relationships with her, overcompensating with huge amounts of love and attention. Divorce was inevitable, but we stayed together long enough to cement my growing bond with our daughter.

Twenty months after the trip to China, our divorce was final. After much negotiating, we agreed on joint custody and to live close enough to each other for frequent visitation. We were able to agree on nearly all issues, and I realized what a welcome relief a divorce could be for an unhappy marriage.

Over the following months, my relationship with Jordyn continued to grow. This little girl, who only two years before was a complete stranger, had become my daughter in the full sense of the word. The stirrings of love I felt those many months before had fully blossomed, and

I knew I couldn't possibly love her more had she been my biological daughter.

Today, my six-year-old daughter and I share a special love and bond that has been strengthened by all the difficulties we went through. She taught me that patience, love and understanding can transcend all obstacles. We are one human race created by God, transcending borders and nationalities, colors and races, philosophies and religions. We can love one another, whether we live next door or halfway around the world.

Nearly every day, I hear the words that once seemed so elusive, and that still cause a catch in my throat each time I hear them: "I love you, Daddy."

*Ed Mickus*

"I'm making cheesecake, Daddy.
Do you like Roquefort or pepperjack Muenster?"

# 7

# GOING
# FORWARD

*For lo, the winter is past,*
*the rain is over and gone.*
*The flowers appear on the earth,*
*the time of singing has come,*
*and the voice of the turtle*
*is heard in our land.*

*Song of Solomon 2:11–12*

# The Walk Away

*The best thing about the future is that it comes only one day at a time.*

Abraham Lincoln

She will walk away.

I will watch her skip up the blacktop walk, pass the wooden carving of the Road Runner and melt into a sea of five-year-olds. Kindergarten.

She now enters the system, a world that for the first time does not include me. Yesterday, there was preschool, Sunday school and day care. But those were tiny steps. Today, she leaps; this is The Show.

Is it wrong for me to wish it away? To go back five years and start again? Back to the days when she weighed less than the handlebars on the pink and purple two-wheeler she now pedals down the walk?

It has come too fast, this walk to school. Daddy still holds a good deal of attention in her world, the first to hear the vital details at the end of the day. She still needs at least three kisses before she falls asleep. And she still asks me to sing "Joy to the World" (the 1970s hit by Three

Dog Night, not the Christmas carol).

But not for long. There should be "baby years": one baby year equals three calendar years. We could slow the ruthless rush of time that leads up to the "walk away." Five years alone with her has not been enough. Baby years would give me ten more. Ten more years for her to say, "I love you, Dad," just because she wants to, not because she wants money for the movies or the keys to the car.

So many times I've heard, "Enjoy her now, she'll be gone before you know it," without understanding. Yes, I knew this baby thing wouldn't last forever. But what's so great about dirty diapers, juice stains on the carpet and crayon marks on the wall?

Now, I understand. Now, she walks away.

Soon, I will not be her entire sphere of influence. In fact, it has begun to happen already. She will have her own friends, her own relationships, her own world. I remember the first time she said, "Daddy." She was on the living-room floor, sitting among the juice stains that would later trigger the removal of the cream-colored carpet. Her words now take a different tone. There is a new attitude as kindergarten nears. Now, when I ask her to fetch a Diet Coke, she sometimes answers, "I think not." I still don't know where that came from.

Kindergarten is the first marker on the walk toward independence, the walk that soon will turn into a trot. And then a run.

My eyes tear up as I hold my little girl, and she holds me. I wonder what I did to deserve such delight, never thinking that, one day, I am supposed to let her go.

She wakes from a dead sleep smiling if she feels my kiss on her cheek. Reading her a story is not enough. She must be on my lap, playing with my fingers and leaning her head into my neck while listening to *The Cat in the Hat*

*Comes Back.* Tomorrow, she will read books I may not understand.

Five years used to mean the span between high-school graduation and the first class reunion. It was the amount of time between visits with an old army buddy. Now it is the time since my daughter was born, and kindergarten marks the anniversary.

Kindergarten is another reminder that the clock does not stop. It ticks off the passage of time in my life, as well as in my little girl's. I grow older. She grows up.

Today, she cannot grasp the concept that, someday, she will move away. Sometimes, she talks of her "husband," asking which bedroom in our house will be his. I explain that she will have her own house one day, but she doesn't want to hear it. Soon, she will scream to get out of my house, and because God made teenagers the way he did, I probably will wish it so. I can't imagine it now, but it's coming. Kindergarten reminds me.

This September is more than the fade-out of just another summer. It is the bittersweet twilight of a time I will always remember with a smile and a tear.

Kindergarten is here.

And she will walk away.

*Jeff Barr*

# It's Never Too Late to Pursue a Dream

*I don't know anything about luck. I've never banked on it, and I'm afraid of people who do. Luck to me is something else: hard work.*

Lucille Ball

I grew up in a single-parent family. My mother raised my two younger sisters and me, without the benefit of a dad around, since she had divorced my father when I was six.

I was a bright student growing up, but between the time I was sixteen and almost nineteen, I drifted away from learning, from the friends I used to hang around with and from everything I loved to do, including acting. I started hanging around a group of kids my mother didn't approve of and, I hate to admit it, she was right. A lot of them were trouble.

One unusually calm day in my otherwise chaotic household, I sat alone in the family room waiting to hear the sound of the mail being dropped into our mailbox. I was nineteen and had finally decided to turn my life around. I was desperately awaiting the response to my application to the American Academy of Dramatic Arts. Yet as I sat there, something felt off balance. Something was definitely about to change—I sensed it; I just wasn't sure what it was. Without a doubt, I knew I wanted to attend this school to study acting, but if someone had asked me then, I doubt that I could have defined my reasons clearly.

Laced with a divine message, the letter did come that day. I grasped it in both hands and sat down. As I silently pep-talked myself into opening it, I saw the dreams that had been brewing inside me since childhood flash before my eyes. I carefully opened the envelope and stared coldly at the "Thank you, please try again" that screamed at me from the page. A single tear trickled down my left cheek. And as that tear reached my chin, I placed my hand gently over my stomach and finally admitted to myself what was changing . . . what was now brewing inside me.

I got up and drove myself to a clinic for a pregnancy test. It was positive. I was going to have a baby. Right after graduating high school, at age nineteen, I gave birth to a beautiful baby boy and became a single mother. My life was dramatically altered—forever.

Seven years later—seven very tough years later—I sat outside one evening after putting my son to bed. As I admired the sparkling stars that filled the sky, various thoughts ran through my mind, thoughts of all the joys and challenges I had experienced since having my son. But most of all, I thought of all the dreams I had yet to fulfill that sat idle in the back of my mind. The further and further I pushed my dreams aside, the more I began to believe that what I once wanted so badly was no longer possible. Then, as I lifted my head back up to that darkened but glittery sky, I saw something I had never seen before: a shooting star. It amazed me. And for some reason, that shooting star caused me to ponder my inherent love of acting and my failed attempt at attending the American Academy of Dramatic Arts.

I spent the next few days in a glowing state of realization, believing I still had a chance no matter what my circumstances had become. There could be a second chance for me. My life had shifted focus for a while, but I never completely lost sight of my dreams or my purpose.

As a single mother who knows the reality of a utility bill staring her in the face, it would be very easy for me to choose to settle into a decent job with good pay and benefits, even if it meant I would have to answer phones or do paperwork for the rest of my life. Instead, I'm giving my dream another shot. Yesterday, I applied to the Academy once again, at the age of twenty-six.

When I was nineteen, I couldn't see the bigger picture. The bigger picture turned out to include an active little boy who stopped me in my tracks—for good reason. I just wasn't ready to pursue my dream then. Now, I am.

It has been said you can only be as good an actor as you are a person. The seven years I've spent as a single mother have taught me to be resilient, to face life realistically and to forge ahead, no matter what.

So, once again, I await the sound of the mail being dropped in the mailbox, and know that my dreams are within my reach.

*Heidi Cole*

# Weekend Dad

*I love the man that can smile in trouble, that can gather strength from distress and grow brave by reflection.*

Thomas Paine

When you were born, the angels sang;
it echoed in my tears.
To see your face; you stole my heart
and quelled my darkest fears.
We brought you home, the sweetest gift
and placed you in your bed.
I promised, "I'll be with you,"
then kissed you on the head.
Those nights we rocked together,
the world all sound asleep.
I shared my every secret,
you never made a peep.

But time went by, the cruelest times
when Mom and I would fight.
We built a bridge between us

to cross one dreadful night.
In different ways, we both had grown
and changed an awful lot.
It wasn't for the better;
it tore our lives apart.
United, both unhappy;
alone, we stood a chance.
Deciding on the latter,
I grabbed my shirt and pants.
And there you stood in sorrow,
your arms extended wide.
You screamed, "I'm sorry, Daddy!"
It haunts me still, inside.
I held you tight within my arms
and rocked your fears to sleep.
Reminded of our secrets,
my soul began to weep.
For you, I wanted so much more,
not parents who just yelled.
I cried, "It's me that's sorry!"
then took the path to hell.

Your mom and I said bye in court,
that pain I can't describe.
A stranger made decisions
affecting all our lives.
The judge said you belonged with Mom,
it hurt, but I agreed.
For no one can replace Mom's love,
not even dads like me.
I've stood and fought for so much less,
but your life's valued more.
So never would I pull and tug,
the son who I adore.

They ordered I pay child support,
I laughed, "To clothe and feed?
As long as I am drawing breath,
my boy will never need!"
They couldn't know our secrets—
that you were all I had;
That I'm not just your father,
but me, who you call Dad.
And then I got my sentence:
I'd see you twice a week
and every other holiday,
my eyes began to leak.

And now I write this verse for you
from my heart—which you own.
Reminding you that where I live
will always be your home.
That your life was conceived in love
and no fault should you hold
for folks who couldn't make up,
or life, which can be cold.
So when you blow your candles out
or pray at each day's end,
just know that, "I am with you.
I'm Dad, your very best friend."

                              *Steven H. Manchester*

# Small Moments

*What is life?*
*It is the flash of a firefly in the night.*
*It is the breath of a buffalo in the wintertime.*
*It is the little shadow which runs across the grass*
*and loses itself in the sunset.*

Crowfoot, Blackfoot warrior and orator

It's easy to forget how precious our moments with our children really are. It's easy to get so busy being grown-up, with grown-up jobs and grown-up pick-up-the-dry-cleaning, take-out-the-trash, do-the-laundry times, that we forget the simple enthusiasm for life our children find in puppies and snowmen, butterflies and boxes of new crayons.

Of all people, I should know better. I should know to cherish each day with my daughter, Sophia Rose, to savor each precious second. She's ten and growing fast. Soon, her interest in puppies and snowmen will give way to makeup and girlfriends, and then parties and boys. I have awhile still to revel in her childishness and in the beauty of her discoveries. Last week, she discovered baby mosquitoes wriggling in the dog's outside water bowl, and she called it to my attention, fascinated by the scientific phenomenon that they would someday fly instead of wriggle, and eat people instead of drink water.

I've been told more times than anyone can count that she is "such a blessing, all things considered," and that I must find it "easy to cherish each moment." That after my life journey so far, I must be an ideal mother, always ready to be attentive.

I am not. I know I should be, but I am not. Sometimes I get cranky or hungry or just plain exhausted. Single motherhood is a wonderful experience, but parenthood in general can weary even the most buoyant soul. Sometimes I forget how precious she is. Sometimes I forget to love the small moments.

I have a special reason to cherish each moment. I really do know better than to waste a moment of her time with me. You see, Sophia is my third child. Long before she was ever thought of, her father and I were on vacation in England with her older brother and sister. At the time, my son, Jeremy Winston, was just over four years old, and his baby sister, Amelia Louise, had just celebrated eighteen months. We were enjoying a day of sightseeing when a car hit us at nearly seventy miles per hour.

Both children died in the crash.

I was gruesomely injured and nearly died, too. I lay on my back in a hospital bed for months, waiting to learn to walk again. All the while, I grieved for my children. Tears rolled down my cheeks, trickling into my ears. Only parents who have lived through what I have know how much I miss my sweet babies.

In those darkest of hours, I swore to myself that if I ever walked again, I would not take my legs for granted. I swore I would never take anything for granted again. I assured myself that, if I ever had another child, I would never raise my voice. I would be the perfect mother. I would, I would, I would. . . .

Sophia was born about two years later. I was on crutches for much of the pregnancy, and in extreme pain. When she was born, she brought such joy into our decimated lives. I was thrilled with this perfect little girl. We named her Sophia, which means wisdom in Greek, because we wanted to have gained wisdom from our ordeal. We gave her the middle name Rose because there is a Scripture that promises that the "desert shall blossom like a rose," and our hearts had been a desert for so long.

Yet, life took another turn when I divorced Sophia's dad two years later. Mired in my own problems—emotional, financial, mental, spiritual, physical and others—little Sophia got lost in the shuffle. Sometimes I would forget that each moment is precious. Sometimes I would forget that she's one breath away from being dead, just as I am. Just as we all are. Sometimes I would forget the gaping wound I felt when I buried her brother and sister nearly twelve years before.

You would think I'd never forget something like that, wouldn't you? You would think that I, of all the mothers you might know, would spend every moment being joyful for what I have now, grateful and happy. You'd think that each page of perfect fractions she brings home from school, each lumpy ceramic project she hauls home in her backpack, would send me into bliss. Sometimes, it does; sometimes, it doesn't.

I know in my heart that my relationship with her will last the rest of our lives. I know that this is the one person who will count on me, and someday, I will likely count on her. We have the special bond that forms between single parents and their children. I know that I am creating in our lives an example of a mother who is doing the best she can to be present in the moment, to exult in butterflies and mosquito hatchlings for now, and perhaps enjoy choosing just the right shade of blush in a few years. I know that while she is small, it's my big chance to savor the small moments.

*Wendy Keller*

# What I Know Now

*Life is the first gift, love the second and under-
standing the third.*

Marge Piercy

While at the park, basking in the glory of a perfect
spring day and pushing my young son on the swings, I
was pleasantly aware of the sweet chattering from another
child nearby who was even younger than mine. His
"momma" was struggling to pluck him up off his hands
and knees from the sandpit, where he was gleefully covering himself in Texas dust. His words stung me as they
floated up and hung in the air, echoing in my ears, "No, no,
no, I want to go to Daddy's house!"

My heart sank as the memories of my own fatherless
childhood flooded my mind, and I glanced over at my
husband, whose own daddy had also been absent from his
life. We both sighed knowingly as we desperately wished
the memories away and refocused on our own child—
determined to escape the haunting thoughts that it could
possibly happen to us. Bewildered, the young mother
finally succeeded in lifting her child up off the ground. At

the time, I wondered whether it was sadness or wisdom I saw in her eyes.

Many years have passed since that memorable day in the park, and despite our best efforts, determination and desperate wishes, my husband and I were unable to hold our marriage together. I have since come to know that young mother's very same bewilderment whenever my son hollers for all to hear that he wants to go to Daddy's house.

The memory of that young single mother struggling over her child returns to me on such occasions. It is always the first thought in a long succession of memories that march through my mind—beginning when I was a young girl sobbing uncontrollably as I watched my father drive away to move to Florida, and continuing through each and every one of my life's highlights, which always seemed to lack an important element: my father. The chain of memories ends with the vision of my own son's face crinkled up at me in rigid defiance, insisting he wants his daddy.

I am instantly forced into a critical self-evaluation on how I'm doing as a single mother. The man responsible for creating me was never around to carry me in his arms when I fell and hurt myself. He wasn't there when I was inducted into the National Honor Society or when I made the All Stars' team for softball. He missed out on all the joys and heartache of my childhood. He even missed out on being a grandfather. My mother strove to fill the void. Despite the daunting task of raising five children alone on her meager earnings as a waitress, with no financial or emotional support from my father, she was strong, she worked hard, and she did the best she could with what little we had. Somehow, she even managed to surprise us at Christmas and to sew pretty dresses for me to wear to special events.

I have come to realize that not having had my father around has made me a better parent. Because he didn't teach me how to throw a baseball or ride my bike, I know how important it is to play with my own child. Because I never knew the feeling of making him proud, I cheer the loudest and praise every important landmark in my son's life. Because of my own childhood longings, I volunteer at school and steal kisses and hugs from my son during his day. I talk to him and listen to him. I stand over his bed while he sleeps, and thank God for him each and every night. We giggle together, sing silly made-up songs and daydream about his future and what great things he will do in his life.

As I stand here faced with my son's demands to go to Daddy's house, I slowly kneel down, wrap my arms around him and whisper softly to him that I know just how he feels. He relaxes into my hug and whispers back to me that he's sorry, that he loves me, that I'm the best mommy in the world. Together, we cling to this precious moment in time, reluctant to let go of one another as we smile through our tears.

The little girl I used to be, who was full of so many doubts and fears of raising her own child, cheerfully skips away, humming joyfully.

*Ellen Barron*

# Two Pairs of Eyes

*In the darkest hour the soul is replenished and given strength to continue and endure.*

Heart Warrior Chosa

When I returned home that day, the babysitter was waiting for me with an alarming message: "Call Linda right away. Something terrible has happened."

When I called, I couldn't quite understand Linda's tear-garbled words: "They found Don's truck on Bundy Road. There was a fire. There was a body in the truck."

"I'll come over right away," I said.

I drove off, realizing I hadn't learned whose body was in the truck. I knew it was Don's weekend to have their eleven-year-old son, Jason. *Whose body was in the truck?* I worried ever more urgently as I approached their house. Jason was the first person I saw as I knocked on their kitchen door, a momentary relief, short-lived as the enormity of the truth dawned: Don had died. Jason was fatherless.

I sat next to Jason, patting his back as he sobbed uncontrollably. What the loss would mean dawned on him bit by bit: "My dad won't ever see me get straight As again. He won't see me graduate from high school." While his shoulders shook with grief, my heart broke for him.

Sitting with him at their kitchen table, I relived sitting next to my own son four years earlier when the meaning of a parallel loss dawned on us: "We've been to the hospital this morning. The cancer grew too fast. Daddy didn't make it. He died." Jason's sobs were my son's. Jason's terrible new reality had been ours for four years: Daddy had died. Life would never be the same.

"I wish Daddy hadn't died," my son said later on the day of his dad's death.

"Oh honey," I replied. "That will always be our wish. That wish will never go away."

My son, then seven, was too young to infer the meanings that eleven-year-old Jason now saw immediately: *It means my dad won't be here for this . . . and for this. . . .* All the future lost moments telescoped into the present moment of grief.

Two days after my husband died, I had one of those moments that proves that, even in the midst of tragedy, life goes on. My son, struggling to let go of his training wheels, finally took off and rode his bike up the street for the first time on two wheels. He pedaled fast, thrilled with his newfound skill, full of the exhilaration the new freedom of movement gave him. I stood in our yard and watched, excited for his achievement and for the symbol of his growing independence and freedom.

But overshadowing that excitement was my longing ache for the pair of eyes that was absent—his father's. In that moment, I realized all the achievements my husband would miss, all the firsts, all the proud moments we would not share as parents. The enormity of being alone, a single mother, crashed down on me with overwhelming weight. But in that moment I also resolved to be enough.

I resolved to be sufficient. If I am the only pair of eyes my son has, so be it. I would just have to look at him doubly hard. I would have to see all his life enough for both my husband and me. I would have to see this and all the future moments through two pairs of eyes.

Later in the evening at Jason's house, we went back to the things his dad would miss seeing. "But remember, Jason," I said. "Your mom is like a mother tiger who will never let anything happen to her cub." Jason smiled and nodded his blond head. "The remarkable thing about your mom is that she will now be able to see your life enough for both your dad and for her. Moms can do that," I continued. "They can see for the one who isn't there. They can see through two pairs of eyes." I knew because I'd been doing it for four years.

If in marriage two can become one, so after death, by God's grace, one can become two. We find we can see through two pairs of eyes.

*Barbara E. Stephens-Rich*

# A Mother's Test

*Patience and perseverance have a magical effect before which difficulties disappear and obstacles vanish.*

John Quincy Adams

My mother and father were married for ten years before she discovered that he was having an affair. He begged her forgiveness and then promised he would never be unfaithful again. Although she was devastated by my father's unfaithful acts, she apprehensively gave him a second chance. She did so because she felt it was in the best interest of her three sons; she felt that we needed our father. When she discovered that he continued the affair, what little chance he had at regaining her trust and restoring the marriage was completely destroyed. Realizing that she could take no more, she kicked him out of the house and filed for divorce.

Though my father agreed to the divorce, and the proceedings went pretty smoothly, it was still the most difficult time of my mother's life. The decision of custody was left to us, and we all chose to live with our mom. She didn't have a job. When my parents married, they agreed that she would be a housewife and full-time mother. Although she finished medical school in the Philippines, where my parents had met, she wasn't qualified to practice medicine in the United States since she hadn't taken the ECFMG, the difficult cumulative medical exam that graduates of foreign medical schools have to pass in order to practice medicine in America. She did not have a driver's license, because my father didn't believe that she needed one. Because public transportation in the suburbs was almost nonexistent at the time, doing everyday tasks was very difficult for her. There were times when all four of us would hitchhike to Kmart.

Her entire family was thousands of miles away in the Philippines. I was five, my brothers were seven and ten, and we were not equipped to provide her with the kind of support that she needed. My mom cried an awful lot during those times! I remember listening through the walls of my bedroom at night, hearing her cry and repeatedly asking the Lord to help her get through this. After phone conversations with my father, she would cry uncontrollably. Each time I heard her, I would do what she taught me to do when I really needed something: I prayed to God. I prayed to God to make my mom stop crying.

Mom could've picked us up and moved us to the Philippines, where her parents were financially well-off. However, she wanted to be an American, and she wanted her kids to grow up as Americans. In 1979, I was in kindergarten, and my brothers were in second and fifth grade. They were in school all day, but I was out at noon. Soon after the divorce was complete, she registered for driving lessons. I went with her to every lesson right after I got home from kindergarten. After a few months, she finished the lessons, passed her driving test and got her driver's license.

She was getting alimony from my father to support the family, but it was only about one-tenth of what he was making as an anesthesiologist. She made use of the money, though. She bought a 1980 Toyota Corolla. She drove this little car to a facility that helped prepare her for that very important exam: the ECFMG. After ten years of not reading a medical book or gaining any medical experience, she decided to register for the examination.

While mothering three boys, she prepared to take one of the hardest exams in the world. For a whole year, she read for hours a day. She read book after book after book, and then followed that up by reading study guide after study guide. She went to Stanley Kaplan classes two or three days a week. She prayed, both at church and at home . . . oh, how she prayed. She was relentless. When it was time to take the test, we drove from Frankfort, Illinois, all the way to Des Moines, Iowa. A friend of hers, who had graduated from the same university in the Philippines as my mother, came with us. She was going to take the test, too.

We waited for months for the results to come in the mail. Her friend got her results first and she did not pass. When my mother's results came in the mail, my brothers and I crowded around her as she opened the letter. She began crying. Then, fighting through her tears, she gleefully screamed, "I passed, my darlings! I passed! Now we can have everything we want. I am so happy." I remember thinking after she said that, *I do have everything I want; Mom's happy again.* From that point on, she began laughing and smiling a lot more, and she stopped wasting tears on my father.

My mother never had to preach the most important lessons in life. She showed us by example: how to get up after falling down, how anything is possible as long as you are willing to work hard. She showed us not to give up on love. Although, at times, love may fail you, if you keep try-ing, you will eventually find the one who is meant for you. After she became the woman she wanted to become, she fell in love with and married a man who is truly deserving of her. They remain happily married to this day.

*Ervin DeCastro*

# Pictures of the Heart

*The past is our definition. We may strive, with good reason, to escape it, or to escape what is bad in it, but we will escape it only by adding something better to it.*

Wendell Berry

They were the worst two weeks of my life. My husband and I had just separated, in one of the most contentious and horrible ways possible. Everyone had been involved: neighbors, police, and hospital and social workers. I was a wreck; I could barely eat, think or even walk. Our two-year-old daughter was shuffled between us like a Ping-Pong ball, and I felt like there was nothing I could do. I had no idea what the future held, or whether there even *was* a future for any of us.

Somehow, I survived. I am sure now that it was only because of the help of family and close friends who chose to be near me and chose to give me hope. At the end of those two weeks, the phone rang.

"They're ready," a lady said when I picked up the phone. *What?* The words jumbled in my brain. The photos. The family photos my husband, daughter and I had sat for only days before our cataclysmic separation. I remember having picked out the pretty blue dress our little girl would wear and the smart houndstooth one I chose for myself. My husband had grudgingly agreed to have the photos taken. It wouldn't cost anything, I told him. The first small set was free, and payment was only required if we ordered more. I was determined to have a portrait of our "perfect" family in our tiny house—if only to remind us that we did have a family to hold on to.

Through the events of the past weeks, I had completely forgotten about the photo shoot. Tempted to tell the lady on the other line, "Throw them out; I'm not buying any," I hesitated. Those photos would be the only portraits my daughter would have of herself and her two parents, *together*. I thought of her future. Deep inside, I knew my marriage was over. But she still had two parents, and this was a picture from the past, a part of her life—then and always.

Picking up those pictures wasn't easy. The salesgirl, too, had recently become a single mother. When I told her my story and why I wasn't going to order any additional photos, she understood, so much so that she cried with me. I got home and hid the photos in the corner of my closet.

Years later, I took them out and showed my daughter. The excitement glowed on her face and I felt a tiny, bittersweet taste in my mouth, but nothing I couldn't swallow. Time had soothed the pain. I placed the photos in her hands. My daughter smiled and commented on how young I looked back then. Then I smiled.

*Joanna Emery*

# 8

# ON THE LIGHTER SIDE

*Good humor is a tonic for mind and body.
It is the best antidote for anxiety and
depression. . . .
It lightens human burdens. It is the direct
route to serenity and contentment.*

Grenville Kleiser

# Mystical, Magical Moments

*Nothing shows a man's character more than what he laughs at.*

Goethe

I'll be frank. This is an eloquent piece about poop.

I have three of what I call poop-manufacturing devices. The youngest is a small puppy, the oldest is a three-year-old boy, and the last is a one-and-a-half-year-old cute-as-a-button, entirely lovable, make-you-smile-at-the-simplest-things little human girl. I added the adjectives for the third device, not that the other two aren't also cute and lovable, but because I sometimes need to be reminded that the little girl is, in fact, human. My doubts stem from the fact that she generates entirely nonhuman smells that escape from the outside garbage can and find their way back into my couch cushions.

The following is the drama I call "my family life."

Upon returning home from work, the three output devices, having *not* output any material for the sake of saving such output for my enjoyment, decide that it's time to get to work. Of course, the day-care provider insists that the output devices never stop working, but I find this impossible to believe since, and I could be wrong, theoretically these devices simply cannot put out more than they take in. Should their input match their output volume-wise, then they would require a daily input roughly the size of a small Volkswagen.

Within fifteen minutes of returning home, it is soon apparent to me that the small, supposedly human girl has output something potent into her diaper (hereafter referred to as "the diaper"). Coincidentally, a diaper is the very same container that the small boy knows he should *not* output into, but does so anyway giving the following explanation: "No Daddy, no poop in the potty. Daddy poop in the potty. Robbie, diaper." So, not to be outdone by the supposedly human girl, the small boy also outputs. This sends the small puppy into an output frenzy, despite having just done the very same thing on the front lawn ten minutes earlier.

Now the stress begins (up to this point, it was only pain from the odor). Somehow, the small, supposedly human girl transforms herself into a professional wrestler about to be pinned. This transformation is triggered when she's laid down and I attempt to remove the aforementioned diaper. This is also when, for whatever reason, the little wrestler begins screaming bloody murder.

This causes the neighbors to call the police to report a case of child abuse.

The puppy shifts into red alert upon hearing the familiar Velcro sound of the diaper being taken off and waits for that brief moment when I slide the dirty diaper just out of reach of the wrestler's flailing feet while I feverishly clean the tush. Despite my knowing this will happen, despite my eyes continually scanning in all directions while also managing to be sensitive to what many call diaper rash (I call it "instant karma"), the puppy manages to bolt into the room, grab the diaper and drag it over the carpet just out of reach of my one free hand, the other *not* being free, since I have to hold the squirming body high enough off the carpet so as to avoid it becoming poop smeared. Throughout this ordeal, the other small human throws in expert commentary, "Oooooh, yuck!"

As the dog chews on the diaper, the wiped-as-clean-as-possible human transforms into a "greased pig," and the other, having somehow found the basketball hidden away on the top shelf of the linen closet, tosses the ball onto the greased pig's head.

It is at this point that the policeman knocks on the door.

The "greased pig" is screaming, having been bonked on the head with the basketball. The "ball player," having been reprimanded for causing potential brain damage, screams louder than the greased pig. The puppy, not to be outdone, barks uncontrollably. I smile at the police officer, who's never had children, and try to convince him that everything is perfectly fine. The dog also tries to appease the visitor by dragging the diaper to his feet as a peace offering.

We now have one small, screaming, naked child pulling on my pants pocket. An open diaper rests at the officer's legs. Yet more poop quite visibly smolders in the middle of the floor right near where we all stand. The puppy won't stop barking. And to top it off, the older boy who knows when, where and how to use the potty, has chosen *not* to do so and is now handing me his diaper full of poop. He, of course, is screaming because, in addition to the previous reprimand, runny poop is smeared all over his behind and running down his legs.

I can feel my head expanding as the smells accumulate, the sounds build up, and the tension increases. The policeman steps back, fearing exploding head particles, and begins to file a lengthy report.

But then something happens . . . *something mystical, something magical.*

When I pick up my little girl, she snuggles her tiny head into my neck and shoulder, then pats my back very lightly just as I do with her when she cries. The tension releases, the smells disappear, and my head returns to normal size. My boy stops crying as he realizes that if he hurries he can mow over the poop with his bubble-blowing lawnmower.

Ever receive a sincerely loving hug from a child? It's a mystical, magical thing. How can you compare poop to watching a toddler blow bubbles in the tub? Or when they shout with glee simply because you walk through the door in the evening? I look forward to each poop-filled day because every once in a while, quietly placed in between the boxes of cereal emptied onto the bed and the hands playing in the toilet, I receive yet another mystical, magical moment. These make everything that was once so overwhelming seem so very insignificant.

So, I may have several garbage cans full of freshly minted poop, and I may be on a first-name basis with both the police department and social services, but I also have happy, healthy children who are quick to jump into my arms each and every day. Of course, their diapers are full, but you know, it doesn't really matter. My children love me. And this single dad loves them.

*Rob Daugherty*

# Hannah's First Visit

*Joy is not in things, it is in us.*

Richard Wagner

There she sat, staring at me hopefully, blue eyes bright and sparkling; a tear could spill over at any second. This was Hannah's first visit to my apartment since I had started living on my own. I was ecstatic about our day together, but then the logistics overwhelmed me: a young, newly single dad with a two-year-old to entertain. I stared down at her, like looking in a mirror, and racked my brain for entertainment. I missed not seeing her every day and wanted to make this visit fun and special; I wanted to make this visit last. But my apartment didn't have all the toys she was used to, or the video library of movies she had at home. Her stuffed animals weren't here, and the crayons and lined paper I did have would become boring before long. *Had I forgotten to buy apple juice? Did I have enough wipes?* My heart raced. Above all, I just didn't want her to cry. Her toddler laugh could light up my heart, but her tears would always break it.

I figured that getting acquainted with the new place

might be the best idea. I took her little hand in mine and we began a tour of the three-room apartment, pausing at potential entertainment. Aha! The yo-yo on the shelf piqued her interest. Then I lost her to frustration, mere seconds later, when the toy unwound. The slide whistle from last Christmas went over well, but all too soon the noise grew annoying. The wall was lined with books, but none with any pictures. The neat-looking camera was too breakable to play with. The kitchen cupboards didn't have the right kind of food. But in the bathroom, at last, we found our salvation: a package of plastic barrettes.

It wasn't that Hannah had any interest in putting these fluorescent plastic rabbits and flowers in her own hair—she sobbed anytime anyone even so much as approached her with a ponytail band! She stared at me incredulously as I affixed the first pink tulip to a two-inch long strand of my own hair. Then another. Then another. Hannah had seen a lot of Disney movies, scores of Dr. Seuss books and gobs of string cheese, but never before had she seen a daddy (hers or anyone else's) walking around with colored barrettes in his hair. She broke out in peals of laughter, and I couldn't contain my own laughter in my relief at her happiness. I could hear her comfort in her relaxed giggles, and I smiled to see my daughter enjoying her daddy. She didn't need toys or movies—she just needed me.

The merry mood continued, and we laughed and played all afternoon until, too soon, it was time to drive her back home. I piled her into the car seat and headed across town. I caught glimpses of her through the rear-view mirror as often as I could on the drive and listened to her hum along with the radio. My heart sank as I gathered her up from the car seat and carried her up to her door. After some tears, I got her safely inside and returned to my empty car.

Heading back toward home, radio off this time, I decided to stop at the convenience store for a frozen pizza. Standing in line, kids kept walking by me and snickering. I figured they saw the heartache on my face. I was in no mood to be laughed at. When I got up to the counter, the clerk, too, didn't seem to take me seriously. By the time I got back to my apartment, I was livid. I missed Hannah and our wonderful visit, and my stop at the store had put me over the top. I stormed into the kitchen to deposit the pizza in the freezer and then wound my way to the bathroom. As I turned the corner, I caught sight of myself in the little mirror over the sink. I broke into laughter as I caught sight of my pink-tulip barrettes, and smiled as I remembered our wonderful day.

*C. J. Druschke*

"I'd love to, but I can't. I have my dad for the weekend."

# I Want It in Ink

*Children spell love: "T-I-M-E."*

Dr. Anthony P. Whitman

My son was nine years old and beginning to recognize he had a life to manage. Asking me to schedule a commitment to him for the following week, I picked up a pencil to write it in my calendar.

He said, "I want it in ink."

The lightbulb went on. He knew that when I wrote things in my calendar in pencil, they were subject to being rescheduled. He didn't want to be "rescheduled."

This was a reminder that children notice the littlest things, and if we are listening to them, we can learn a lot. Needless to say, from then on, I wrote all commitments to my children in ink.

*Dorothy M. Neddermeyer*

# Judgment Day

*A hero is a man who does what he can.*

Romain Rolland

When I am old and gray, judge me as a father by the number of times I said, "I love you," and how often I was able to say, "I'm sorry."

In a few days, the kids and I would mark the first anniversary of their mother's death. After dinner, we began talking about her, in a wonderfully casual manner—proof, at least in one way, that they were adjusting well.

"Have I been a good dad to you guys this past year?" I then asked daringly.

As expected, I was assaulted with, "Dad, be quiet!" and "Do you really want to know?"

I actually did. "I'll let you guys pick ten categories you want to rank me by. *Any* ten. You can give me any grade you want—and I promise I won't get mad," I said.

"Any grade?" Matthew asked, with a devious grin. "Are you sure we can give you *any* grade?"

"*Any* grade," I responded, with a growing reluctance. I went to get a pen and paper.

They started laughing—howling, actually—in much-too-eager anticipation.

"Should I be nervous about this?" I asked them. But it was too late.

"Laundry!" Mary shouted out, bringing all three of them to hysterics.

"Uh-oh," I grimaced. *They've gone for the jugular right off the bat. This could be tougher than I thought.* Comments about newly pink whites soon followed, as did complaints about missorted socks and a lack of timely folding. (I absolutely *hate* folding.) But after careful deliberation, they gave me a B. *Not bad*, I thought to myself, clearly relieved.

"Personal Grooming," Anne then called.

"What does *that* mean?" I asked. I hoped she was referring to frequency of showers, rather than helping to braid hair. She was, and an easy B resulted.

"Cooking," they said, almost in unison, obviously getting the hang of the adventure. They gave me a *very generous* B-, due largely, I'm sure, to the close proximity of a McDonald's to our house.

"Clothes Shopping: B." Still quite generous.

"Food Shopping: B+." (I'd taken immense pride in this area over the past year, and was secretly hoping for an A.)

"Cleaning: C+." I exercised my first protest, pointing out to them that *they* were the cause of virtually all the household debris. But the judges were unmoved.

"Studying: B-." I was "too strict" when it came to homework. (I'd accept that anytime.)

"Driving Around: B+." I clearly felt I deserved an A on this one, given the amount of time I had spent in the car ferrying them to practices, activities, friends' houses and so on. But I had *completely forgotten* about one of Mary's basketball games the previous week. So I agreed that the lower grade was warranted.

"Gift Wrapping: B-." *Do kids really care how birthday*

*presents are wrapped?* I thought that was an adult thing. Obviously not.

And finally, "Sports Fan." They gave me a well-deserved A. Far too many losing seasons had tempered my vocal competitive edge in the stands. I had reluctantly come to appreciate the value of simply *participating* in a sport, when a championship isn't even a remote possibility.

My overall grade as a dad?

"B," they declared. I'd done okay, according to the panel, but there was clearly room for improvement. We laughed and laughed, and they told stories about "surviving" me over the past year. It was a great moment, albeit at my expense.

After I tucked the kids in that night, I sat down and thought to myself that a B wasn't all that great. But then again, we had always been able to laugh. About their mom. About their *father*. In this past year, during which they could have been all too easily overwhelmed by sadness from their mother's passing, they had been able to find a wonderful measure of happiness.

Maybe as an extra-credit question I could have thrown in something like, "Don't Worry. Be Happy." It might have kicked my overall grade up to a B+. I'd settle for that this first year. *For that matter,* I thought, *a few additional chores for three discerning judges might do wonders to help bring up that C+ in cleaning. . . .*

*Richard Zmuda*

# The Dating Scene (Single-Mom Style)

*You had me at hello.*

Dorothy, from the movie *Jerry Maguire*

When you're suddenly single, after being married for a long time, dating is either one of the things you want the most or fear the most. For me, it was both. Compound that with being a mother of three *very* opinionated daughters, and you've got a recipe for a nerve-wracked single mom, wanting desperately to find love again, and yet very afraid to try.

I haven't been too good at the dating thing. After nearly two decades of being single, I'm just that: still single. Oh, I've had a couple of relationships, one so important he'll forever be a part of my life and my children's. But, for some reason or another, I've never been able to find the right guy.

I've dated several different men, usually just a dinner and a movie. The hard part was how to best handle these dates with three daughters who always had to have a say in everything I did, including my love life.

"Mom, I didn't like him at all. . . . His laugh is really

stupid," said one of the girls after an innocent dinner out.

"Geez, what was with that guy?" another daughter exclaimed, when I came home after another date.

"Wow, Mom, we all liked him!" they chimed in after yet another date. I think what they really liked was his cool car. I didn't like him at all—cool car or not.

I once went on a blind date, and it was a complete disaster. It cured me for a long time. Immediately after that horrible evening, I vowed to remain single for the rest of my life. I guess I'm keeping my promise.

Yet, I silently yearn for the "love of my life"—my "soul mate" (if there really is such a thing)—for "Mr. Right" to come along. I wait, and I wait . . . and I wait.

At heart, I'm a hopeless romantic, and I gauge the men I meet on two distinct experiences I had with two different men. I went out with each of these men once.

The first provided me with a memory worthy of a movie scene: I was going on a date with Mark, a tall, drop-dead-gorgeous, *GQ* kind of guy. He and I were to meet at a lake for a picnic lunch. He was late, and I was peeved.

I sat at the picnic table, drumming my fingers as if they were the hands of a clock ticking the seconds away. I was lost in thought looking out over the shimmery water when I saw a big, black dog swimming to shore. It was Mark's dog! He scrambled across the sand, shook himself off and bounced over to me. Wrapped around his neck was a bouquet of flowers tied in a plastic bag. I was stunned. Looking back at the lake, Mark was swimming to shore, too. He had parked across the lake, and had swum the entire width of the lake as a surprise. *Sigh.*

The other memorable evening occurred on my first trip to New York City early one December. I was staying with friends in the city, and a sweet, charming man I'd met briefly on one of my travels had promised to take me out on the town when I visited.

He arrived by taxi, and had planned a lovely evening for us. New York City is romantic all by itself, especially during the holidays with sparkling lights everywhere, but when it's coupled with a delightful, handsome man, it's all the more magical.

Bruce took me to a quaint, offbeat Italian restaurant. We actually had an intelligent, thoughtful conversation and a lovely meal. My birthday (which I had spent alone) had been two days before, so I felt like the celebration was being extended. Unbeknownst to me, he knew I had turned over another year, and after our meal, a surprise birthday cake was presented with the entire café, patrons and all, singing "Happy Birthday." Once again, I was stunned by a generous move on the part of a "suitor."

Bruce then took me to see the movie *Life Is Beautiful,* at the tony Paris Theatre, and afterward for a nightcap at the ever-so-elegant Plaza Hotel. The whole evening was topped off with a carriage ride through Central Park, with snowflakes falling gently from a partially moonlit sky. When he took me back to my friend's co-op, he literally waltzed me into the lobby, twirling me around as he hummed a little tune. *Double sigh. No, triple sigh.*

Is it unrealistic to wish, to hope, for this again, only on a more serious, permanent basis? By that, I mean, to experience romance and a meaningful connection, too, with someone you're attracted to, who can become a companion, a lover, a friend. Someone to fall in love with, and make it stick, once and for all. Someone who likes my daughters, and someone whom *they* actually like. That would be a miracle in itself.

I wonder sometimes if being a single mom all these years interfered with my chances to find love. Now that I'm a bit older, and the children are more grown-up, is it too late? I don't know, but this much I do know: at this stage of my life, after waiting for so long, I won't settle for just anybody. The next guy that captures my attention better know how to swim or hum a few bars. . . . That's all I've got to say!

*Nancy Vogl*

"She'll be right down. . . . She's shaving."

# Easter Baskets

*Faith is the substance of things hoped for, the evidence of things not seen.*

Hebrews 11:1

When I was around seven or eight years old, growing up in Pawtucket, Rhode Island, I got up very early one Easter morning and set out to catch the Easter Bunny. I didn't have far to go. In those days, we lived in a cramped one-bedroom apartment on the third floor of a tenement house—my mother, my sister and I—and every year, the Easter Bunny left our baskets of goodies on the back stairs.

That year, I had a plan. Armed with a carrot and a squirt gun filled with Welch's grape juice, I sat down in the hallway to wait. The carrot was a peace offering. The loaded gun not so much a weapon as the manner in which I preferred to drink my grape juice. I intended no harm toward the Easter Bunny; I merely wanted to corner him for a minute or two. The number-one question on my mind was, *Why did some of my classmates get live fluffy bunnies and fuzzy chicks, while my sister and I only got lifeless creatures molded from chocolate?*

I was nervous. I didn't know the exact penalty for a face-to-face encounter, but I suspected it no less a crime than, say, hiding behind the Christmas tree and catching Santa. *Would the Easter Bunny turn tail and speed off without leaving a single marshmallow Peep? Would my presence spook the creature into biting me? Could I catch rabies from a man-sized rabbit?*

Despite occasional bursts from my squirt gun, I fell asleep. I remember dreaming that I'd fallen down the stairs. Jerking myself awake, I shifted my position. I was barefoot and cold. I sat with my back against the wall, my body warmed by a small shaft of sunlight. I scolded myself for falling asleep, squirted the last of the grape juice into my mouth, then fell asleep again. This time, I dreamt I met the Easter Bunny face-to-face, that he spoke to me without moving his mouth and told me what I had suspected all along: we were too poor to receive live Easter gifts, too poor to feed them, unable to afford the necessary cage and the veterinary care that Easter pets required.

My mother jostled me awake. She demanded to know what I was doing sitting in the hallway at seven o'clock in the morning. After I'd explained my cockamamie scheme, she gave me a thorough tongue-lashing and hustled me inside. Two giant Easter baskets were on the kitchen table. She explained that the Easter Bunny was no fool, and this year had left our gifts in the front hallway.

They were magnificent baskets, wrapped in crinkly paper, each containing enough candy to last a week, and small toys to boot. It would be years before I realized they were more than my mother could afford, decades before I would come to understand the true meaning of Easter.

Easter 1996 was my mother's last on Earth. She spent the holiday in my home, with her grandchildren.

Since her passing I have had time to reflect on the material poverty of her life, her constant struggle to make ends meet, the small sacrifices and the significant efforts she made year after year to shield my sister and me from feeling too impoverished. She taught us to hold to our beliefs. She taught by example that true faith does not rest on logical proof or material evidence. She taught me that, sometimes, you've got to believe in what you can't see. I hope I can pass that lesson on to my children.

*Bob Thurber*

# Thumbs-Up Smiley Face

*Mirth is like a flash of lightning that breaks through a gloom of clouds and glitters for a moment; cheerfulness keeps up a kind of day-light in the mind and fills it with a steady and perpetual serenity.*

Joseph Addison

Long before "single parent" became a coined term, I was one. In retrospect, I didn't fully realize the overall impact that my husband's sudden death would have on our life. His passing happened shortly after our daughter, Kathy, had celebrated her ninth birthday. As any grieving person would do, from time to time, I silently questioned God's wisdom in having called my husband to himself at such an early age. Because there were no answers to my questions, I blindly chose to dedicate myself to the joys of raising a daughter, and immersed myself in my job at the nearby high school.

Being a bright-eyed, active kid, Kathy instinctively helped in many ways to "perk me up," doing her part to keep our home life from being too sad. She was relentless in her ongoing efforts to make me smile, no matter where we were or who was with us. She innocently discovered a surefire method of achieving her goal: when she detected that I was "down," she would simply take a pen, and on the rounded part of her thumb, inscribe a smiley face. Then she would proudly stick her thumbs-up smiley face directly in front of my eyes and as close to my nose as possible.

She was persistent in her efforts, amazing me by always having a pen available, and using her private signal to me everywhere and in any situation. I was the recipient of her thumbs-up smiley face while driving in the car, shopping at the grocery store, attending church services, trying to bravely celebrate holidays, visiting relatives, and on and on.

Her special signal always brought an immediate smile to my face, so much so that I began doing it for her as well. Of course, the first time I tried it on her, it evoked a loud, long laugh and a "You finally caught on, Mom!" look on her face.

I can't remember exactly how long this thumbs-up-smiley-face ritual continued. From time to time throughout the years, it still comes in handy, whenever Kathy or I seem to need it.

During her high school years and the ups and downs of getting to know the difference between boyfriends and just plain boys, the thumbs-up smiley face was used by both of us—when a boyfriend had told her he found a new girlfriend, I used it; and when certain boyfriends brought her home too late at night, she used it.

After she graduated from college, having obtained a dental hygiene degree but subsequently failing the comprehensive exam on her first try, the thumbs-up smiley face did its job.

When she asked that I escort her down the aisle on her wedding day, we both cried as she told me I had been both her father and mother for so long that no one else could do the job. And again, the thumbs-up smiley face worked its magic.

Now that she is married with children of her own, and valiantly facing the joys and dilemmas of parenthood, we continue to find occasions when the thumbs-up smiley face still strengthens the special bond between us.

*Patricia Buck*

# Looking for Love(s)

*Marriage is a great institution, but I'm not ready for an institution yet.*

Mae West

"It's all your fault," I screamed, throwing my hairbrush down on the chipped walnut laminate. Here I was—at what I'd been told was a "magic moment" in my life— about to go out on my first date. I was fifteen years old; the year was 1962. And my mother—my *mother*—was getting ready to go out on her "first date," too.

"You'll really like my friend Walter," my mother said in a soothing tone. Then, with more emphasis, "The fact that I'm divorced is not why this boy waited until now to ask you out. And it's certainly not Walter's fault that all your friends have been dating since the fall." Her tone softened again: "It's been longer than that for me, hon. I just want to have a good time again."

But I knew she was wrong. I knew everyone else in my class looked at me with a combination of pity and disgust. Besides, Mom didn't deserve to have a "good time." I was the one who was supposed to be having the time of my life.

I found myself nervously twisting a lock of my hair, and with trembling fingers, I quickly patted it back in place. I wondered how anyone could see the situation except as it was: My mother was so inadequate that my father had been forced to look elsewhere. And now she was desperately trying to find a "replacement." How utterly humiliating.

"When is your date picking you up?" asked my mother, in an attempt to get things smoothed over.

"Hopefully, before that man comes for you," I said, tossing back my head and refusing to look at her. I didn't want Dave to witness how low my mother had sunk, how shamelessly she could flaunt her singleness—her *different-ness* from all my friends' parents. It was most definitely her fault that no self-respecting boy would want to be seen with me.

Standing behind me at the full-length mirror and leaning to one side to peer past me at her own reflection, Mom asked, "Well, how do I look?"

"Old . . . fat . . . disgusting!!" I screeched, tears springing to my eyes. I rushed from the room and clambered up the stairs to the attic. I had to get away from her for a while. Then, just maybe, I wouldn't hate her quite so much. I fled to the refuge that had always helped me sort things out before: the trunk.

For years I'd come up to the attic to lose myself by going through the old clothes I found in the trunk. Often I tried them on. Mom had shown me the jacket she loved when she was not much older than I was. Looking at the jacket, I wondered why she had loved it so. I imagined her at age seventeen, huddled on the high-school bleachers nervously rubbing the edges of her bunny-fur bolero. I modeled a couple of old hats, but couldn't really get into the spirit. While digging out a pair of rusty old figure skates, I found that the bottom of the trunk could fold up.

Under it, I discovered a little compartment, and hidden inside it were some old crusty newspaper clippings and some letters.

"Dearest Marge," the first one began. "I can't believe how I miss you. I'm here in France, and, I'd never tell anyone but you, my squad actually got lost in the forest. It was so awful. God! I wish I was back there in Oblong with you, after the Friday night game. I love you so very much, and I just don't know if I can wait till we actually tie the knot. XOXO, Charlie." Attached was a clipping showing a picture of Mom, looking so young and slim—kind of like the old movie star Greta Garbo—and a man identified as Charles Somner. It was an announcement of their upcoming wedding!

But, that wasn't right. Charlie wasn't my father. My dad was *Dad*. My mother's husband was never a boyfriend who got killed in the war . . . was he? Mom had never whispered a word of this previous relationship to me. *What if she had married Charlie? Would I be here? Would I be me?* I wrapped myself in the bunny-fur bolero and began to cry again, just a little. Why did it all have to be so horribly difficult?

I sniffed, but widened my eyes, worried about making them red before my date, and started absently rubbing the bunny fur. Now that my mom and dad were divorced, I only had more questions, more problems. *What if Mom fell in love and married some third guy? Would I ever think of him as Dad? He couldn't be! Apparently she'd loved Charlie, the guy in the uniform, and I think she had loved my dad, too—once. But neither love had lasted. Could she, could any woman, ever truly love so many different men? What is it about love that makes you keep looking for it, over and over again?*

My thoughts were interrupted when the doorbell rang.

My mother went downstairs to answer it. I tore off the bolero, ran down from the attic and peered—secretively and ashamedly—from around the corner upstairs. "Oh, my God!" I whispered to myself. They were there. *Both of them were there.* Our "first dates" had arrived at the same time! What a horrible, mortifying coincidence!

As I hurriedly wiped my eyes and pinched my cheeks, I heard Dave say, "Mrs. Kersch, I just couldn't believe it. We were almost out of the house when I figured out that my dad had a date with my date's mother tonight! Incredible, huh?!"

*Walter was Dave's dad! My mother was going out with my date's father, and it was okay with Dave? He actually rode over here with his dad? His probably divorced dad!*

I took a breath so deep it hurt, then descended the stairs, shyly peered up at my first date and said, "Dave, I'd like you to meet my mom." Then I paused, slipped my arm around her waist and added, "She looks kinda like Greta Garbo, don't you think?"

I grew up quite a bit that night. And although my first date would not be my last, my first relationship—the imperfect bond I'd formed with my mother—would last forever.

*Kathleen Kersch Simandl*

# Life Lessons in a Can

*F*lops *are a part of life's menu, and I've never*
*been a girl to miss out on any of the courses.*
Rosalind Russell

It all started with the Spam pizza and my obsession with winning the "Cooking with Spam" contest at the Spokane Interstate Fair. First prize was a trip to the Mall of the Americas and a ten-thousand-dollar shopping spree. To me, a single mom working as a part-time teacher and freelance writer, ten thousand dollars represented almost my entire annual earnings. And for my three daughters and me, well, a vacation meant a hurried weekend trip to some out-of-the-way place to interview the subject of one of my feature articles. My girls were real troupers through it all. Admittedly, those trips taught them a lot about Washington State geography, journalism and the obstacles overcome by the everyday heroes I wrote about, but they hardly qualified as vacations.

So where others saw only a contest, I saw an opportunity to give my kids a real vacation—and a chance to spend money on something other than mortgage payments, utility bills and insurance premiums. I had a month to come up with the best Spam recipe ever.

With no time to waste, I headed to the store to buy Spam. I felt a small pang of guilt when the amount due flashed across the cash-register screen, but managed to convince myself that it was an investment, after all, and came home with enough to feed an army.

"Now, let's just brainstorm," I told Mindy, Lisa and Katie. "If it can be made with chicken, it can be made with Spam. If it can be made with beef, it can be made with Spam. If it can . . ."

"We get the idea," my daughters interrupted.

I pretended not to notice their raised eyebrows and rolling eyes and ignored the sideways glances they shot each other. As a mom, I knew that this situation presented the perfect opportunity for them to sharpen their creative problem-solving abilities. What's more, it would teach them the steps necessary to turn an idea into reality. From a purely practical standpoint, I figured they could learn a lot about cooking. Hindsight shows me now that I was doubly dangerous, driven by both a mother's instinct and the thought of that shopping spree. But all I felt then was an intense urge to forge ahead.

The cans of Spam had been stacked into a neat pyramid on the pantry shelf, representing the successful completion of Phase One: Operation Spam. Ideas pinged across my mind like popcorn in a popper. Baby, I was cooking.

Phase Two: The Pizza was unappreciated by my children and their friend, who took one look at the mountain of Spam and announced that she wouldn't be back again until the contest was over. If she hadn't been my boss's daughter, I might have given her a piece of my mind.

Undaunted by Phase Two falling flat, I forged ahead. Phase Three: Lasagna; Phase Four: Stew; Phase Five: Sweet-and-Sour Spam. But the girls, who seemed to have lost sight of the fact that I was doing all this for them, turned their noses up at every entree. And so it went, until finally we arrived at Phase Thirty. It was a creation that, in my eyes, did more to raise the pinnacle of human accomplishment than Mozart, Babe Ruth, Andrew Wyeth and Tennessee Williams combined. Phase Thirty was nothing less than Spam Cordon Bleu Casserole. It was more than food. It was art. And boy, was I ever proud.

Somehow, I just knew that the kids wouldn't be able to appreciate it, so I decided to expand my audience.

As soon as my sister-in-law answered her door, I knew she'd been warned, because her first question was: "Does it have Spam in it?" In that moment, I knew what it meant for a mother to be betrayed by her children.

*Fine,* I thought. *See if I ever fix her dinner after a busy day's work again.*

With that, I returned home, bent but far from broken. I held the winning recipe right there in my hand; of that I was sure. All that remained was to send it in. So I rummaged around in my desk for the entry form and started writing. But someplace between "name" and "address" my eyes caught sight of the entry deadline. It had passed two days earlier. A sick feeling washed over me. All the money I'd spent on Spam—wasted. All that time. And what had I taught the girls, anyway? Nothing except that, in searching for the forest, their mother had once again lost sight of the trees.

I put my creation, which by then had diminished in stature to a mere casserole, on the table and called the kids for dinner. Even in my defeated emotional state, I felt a tiny spark of pride when Lisa said, "This one actually smells pretty good." The spark grew to a flame when Mindy added, "Hey, this tastes great!" And it exploded into a roaring fire when little Katie, whose culinary preferences at that point were limited to cold hot dogs and peanut butter, asked for a second helping. I had hit the mother lode—sort of.

It seemed like a safe time to tell them about the deadline. I nearly cried when Lisa, in a sympathetic tone, reminded me that imagination and food go together like a hand and a glove, and that the world would never have any new recipes if everyone was afraid to experiment. It's a principle she exemplifies in her daily life. She's become an outstanding cook and finds immense pleasure in creating new recipes. Mindy, who responded that it's important to believe in yourself, did just that. She overcame her shyness, ran successfully for an Associated Student Body office in high school and took on the responsibilities of a residence-life job in college. I prefer to think that they learned at least part of it from what we've come to refer to as "our experiences with Spam."

But even if they didn't, there was one direct benefit: After the Spam was gone, I started relying, again, on our old standbys. And for a long time, it didn't matter what I put on the table—spaghetti, meat loaf, even hamburger gravy prompted no complaints, even from little Katie.

Sometimes, you gain as much from failure as you do from success.

*Sheryl Templeton*

"I hope you like tossed Lemon Meringue an'
chili-bean upside down pun'kin pudding."

# The Great Mate Hunt

*If love is the answer, could you rephrase the question?*

Lily Tomlin

"You know what?" my friend Sandra confessed to me. "I hate Valentine's Day. I absolutely hate it! If I see another lovey-dovey couple, I think I'm going to lose it!"

I knew what she meant. Valentine's Day can be a lonely time for a single parent. We are bombarded with signs of love and romance everywhere we go. Even in the toilet paper aisle of the grocery store, for goodness sake!

I used to let Valentine's Day turn my life into one giant pity party. I was overwhelmed with being a young single parent, being back in college and being several states away from other family members. Finally, after letting my annual Valentine's Day pity party linger for several months, I decided that the logical solution was to get married again. This is a typical decision for a single parent, but a potentially dangerous one because it leads to the "Great Mate Hunt."

When we were younger, my single-mom friends and I

were proficient Great Mate Hunters, skilled in all three phases of the hunt.

Phase One was "Ex-Spouse Bashing": We reminded ourselves of all the qualities that we would never again stand for in a mate. Couldn't a grown man, who was able to take apart a car, put his own dirty underwear in the hamper?

Phase Two was the "Ideal Mate List": After careful thought, we committed to paper the things we wanted in a mate. One of my friends had a list of fifty-five things she wanted in a mate. In addition to the usual character qualities and basic physical traits, she listed things like, "dimples—not too deep" and "sculpted abdominal muscles" and "must like my favorite song." The rest of us secretly scoffed at her naïveté—until she married a guy that had fifty-four of the fifty-five things on her list. As she walked down the aisle, the rest of us were busy revising our own lists. (In case you are wondering about the one thing on her list her Ideal Mate didn't have: he was only five feet, eleven inches tall, and she had listed someone who was six feet tall. She decided she could live without that extra inch!)

Phase Three was "The Hunt": Armed with a mental picture of our Ideal Mate and our lists, we went wherever we thought we might find, meet and capture an unsuspecting Ideal Mate. PTA meetings, Little League games and school activities were typical hunting grounds.

After her declaration of disdain for Valentine's Day, Sandra decided to scour the personal ads for Ideal Mate candidates. I read them a few times myself, but couldn't take them seriously. Most of the men were looking for a young Barbie doll. (Although I'm fairly confident that they did not look like Ken.) Most of them also mentioned liking to take long walks and having long talks and romantic dinners in front of a fireplace. What planet were these men from? In a moment of daring, Sandra set up a meeting with a self-described "handsome, blond outdoorsman." The "blond" part turned out to be an ill-fitting toupee that shifted every time he scratched his head.

Some of us refined our lists during the week and waited for Sunday. One hunting ground we all had in common was church. It seemed the logical place to hunt for the Ideal Mate. Especially at the singles' groups.

After enlisting my sister to watch my kids, I ventured out with Sandra to our very first singles' group meeting at our church. When we arrived, we noticed that there was a very small turnout. In fact, my friend and I were the only women there. We sat on one side of the room. Three men sat on the other side of the room. (I think that they were the models for the photographs of the geeky guys on greeting cards.) I don't remember what the meeting was about, but I do remember those guys eyeing us like they had never seen women before. As soon as the meeting was over, my friend and I hightailed it out the back door and vowed we would never go to another singles' meeting again.

But then we had a great idea. We would try the singles' groups at *other* churches and expand our hunting ground. We decided to try the singles' Sunday school class at a large church in a neighboring suburb. The class was huge! The mother lode! From the back of the room we scouted out some possible Ideal Mate candidates. I skillfully maneuvered for a seat across the aisle from one of them. Just as I got there, one of my earrings broke off, rolled across the floor and came to a stop right under the chair of the unsuspecting Ideal Mate candidate I had in my sights.

Never one to miss an opportunity, I smiled sweetly at him and told him that my earring was under his chair. All he did was move his legs so that I could get it myself. Still the optimist, I bent down to get it, looking up at him and flashing him what I thought was my most dazzling smile.

Unfortunately, I ended up flashing him more than a smile when two buttons popped off of my dress and went flying. I never went back there again.

The Great Mate Hunt can have its hilarious moments, but there is also a serious side. I watched some of my friends continue The Hunt and marry men that they knew were not a good fit for them, or for their children. But they had convinced themselves that they could not survive unless they were married.

After watching some of them suffer through unhealthy marriages, I made a decision to stay single and raise my children alone. Being married to someone who is not right for you can be worse than the loneliness you might experience as a single parent. I also saw what it did to the kids. I decided that if I were to get married again I would need a few signs, visions and an angelic visitation!

Now, having said that, wouldn't you expect that the next part of this story would be about the signs, the visions and the angelic visitation that heralded the appearance of my Ideal Mate? The perfect happy ending?

Actually, there is a happy ending. But not what you would expect. I did raise my children alone, and with God's help, they have grown up to be confident, happy, emotionally healthy, successful young adults. That's a very happy ending!

(But I must confess to you that, occasionally on Valentine's Day, in the privacy of my own home, I do take a peek at those personal ads! And, as long as I am confessing, I still have my list, which, by the way, needs updating . . . but that's another story.)

*Sara Henderson*

# Kool-Aid and Brown Sugar

*Joy has no cost.*

Marianne Williamson

I have been a single mother for most of my adult life. There have been times when my children and I endured hunger and devastating poverty. With empty cupboards and barely a dollar to our name, we had to be creative.

On one particularly hot summer day, the kids were complaining that they were thirsty and they didn't want water again. We were saving the last of our milk for the package of macaroni we had left in the cupboard. We had been drinking water and rationing what little milk we had left, but I wanted to give the kids a treat. It was only a day or two until our check would arrive, and I could buy more food. In the meantime, we had to make due. Managing to scrape together ninety cents, all in pennies, the kids and I walked to the grocery store to purchase a few packs of unsweetened Kool-Aid. We smiled eagerly at the young cashier as he rung up our purchase.

"Eighty-seven cents, please," he requested, bemused at

the site of my family, so excited about three little packages of Kool-Aid.

"We're having a party," my five-year-old informed the cashier as I handed him exactly eighty-seven pennies.

We headed home with our treat safely stored in my purse, my kids pulling on me to make me walk faster. Their excitement was contagious, and suddenly, I felt myself fantasizing about a tall glass of ice-cold Kool-Aid.

My son filled our favorite pitcher with tap water as I ripped open the Kool-Aid package. The kids gathered around me as I tipped the package over and let the contents spill into the water. The water turned blue, and the kids squealed.

"Could you get the sugar down from the shelf?" I asked my son cheerfully. "I'm sure we have one more cup."

"Um, Mom, no sugar up here," he replied.

"Are you sure?" I asked trying to remember when I could have used the last of it.

"Yes, I'm sure, Mom. All we have is brown sugar," he answered.

Avoiding my son's gaze, I turned away and swallowed my feeling of hopelessness.

Absorbing what my son had just said, a rather scary idea took root in my mind. "Give me the brown sugar."

"What?" he asked, not quite following my train of thought.

"Please hand me the brown sugar," I said again.

Looking at me as though I had gone completely mad, he reached up in the cupboard and handed me the box of brown sugar.

"You aren't going to use the brown sugar in the Kool-Aid, are you?" my son asked incredulously.

"Sure, why not? Brown sugar is sugar, only it's brown," I told him quite confidently, forcing myself to believe my own lie.

"I can't believe you are doing this!" my son protested vehemently.

"All right, here goes."

I squished the brown sugar into the measuring cup, then let it drop into the now-blue pitcher of water. Blue water splashed up and over the sides as the block of brown sugar sank to the bottom of the pitcher. Whistling a tune, I stirred the new concoction with vigor. We all watched in horror as the Kool-Aid went from a beautiful blue to a putrid bluish-brown.

The look in my son's eyes belied his previous faith in my intelligence.

"I'm sure it'll taste fine, it just looks nasty," I assured the children.

Smiling weakly, I brought the spoon up to my lips and tasted the ill-colored fluid. As my taste buds absorbed the illogical combination of unsweetened Kool-Aid powder and brown sugar, my face contorted involuntarily.

"Gross!" I exclaimed before I could stop myself.

My seven-year-old exclaimed, "Our Kool-Aid looks like poop!"

I started to correct my child on the inappropriate use of the word *poop*, when a chuckle erupted from my lips, and I started laughing. Suddenly, the kitchen was filled with the sounds of joy and laughter. We laughed until the tears flowed unchecked down our faces.

The children proclaimed it to be a tasty drink, and we made two more pitchers with the brown sugar: cherry (which was green) and another bluish-brown combination. We even froze some of the bizarre drink to make Kool-Aid Popsicles.

Today, as I look back on that day, it reminds me that, even in our lowest moments, we can always find joy.

*Donna M. Snow*

# The Fisherman

*Fishing is a lot like dating. . . . Somebody's try-*
*ing to do the catching while the other is trying to*
*get away.*

Anonymous

"Mommy, what're you doing?" Jake asked me, rocking a small tackle box by his side.

"Well, I thought I'd curl up with a book and read." I looked at my young son. "Why?"

"Can we go fishing?"

*Fishing? I'm a single mom! Worms, fish guts, empty, staring eyes—that is not in my job description.*

"I want to catch a fish, a big fish," he said, opening his arms wide.

"But Jake, I don't know how to fish," I answered.

"Me, neither," he said, plopping on the couch next to me. The small pole and string dangled by his leg.

"Sorry, but Grandpa forgot to teach me how to catch a fish," I apologized.

"Life's not fair," he whispered.

"Come on, you're only eight," I said. The guilt factor

multiplied in my stomach. "Want to play catch?"

"Nah, Grandpa forgot to teach you that, too."

"Huh?"

"You throw like a girl." He opened the tackle box, pulled out a red bobber and tossed it up and down.

"What do you mean I throw like a girl?" I asked.

"You always throw three feet away from my glove," he said dejectedly, slumping on the couch.

"And that's why you're the best shortstop at Little League. A ball can't get by you." I pointed to the trio of trophies on the mantel.

"But I've never caught a fish." He slid off the sofa, knelt on the carpet and held a colorful fly to the light.

"Grandpa said he'd take you fishing." Guilt twisted a tighter knot in my gut.

"Grandpa lives a hundred miles away." He unscrewed a jar of salmon eggs and played with the round balls.

"Hmm." A well-placed, tactical maneuver. *Boy, being a "dad" is hard.*

"Isn't today Saturday?" A plan was obviously formulating in his mind.

"Why?" I flipped another page of my book, not a word read. *Hmm? What is he up to?*

"Isn't there a singles' dance tonight?"

"I hate those dances, Jake." I feigned interest in my crinkled paperback.

"But there are guys there." He established his cause.

"That's right. Lots of guys looking for, well, not me." *I am not going to get reeled in.*

"Aw, Mom, all the guys love you." Flattery. The bait set.

"You're sweet, but no, I'm still not going."

"All you need is one who likes to fish." He dangled a treble hook and paused.

"What?" I stared at the metal claw.

"Please, Mommy." The sinker. "Go dancing and find me a fisherman."

"I don't have a sitter."

"I'll call Susie down the street." He jumped up from where he sat on the floor and ran to the kitchen phone.

"Jake!"

"Hurry up and get real pretty." Little orders flew from the kitchen. "And don't forget to stink a lot. Old guys like that."

"Wait," I glanced at the clock. It was half-past eight. The dance started at nine. "But, I . . ."

"Susie's on her way over." He pulled me from the comfort of the sofa. "You don't have much time."

"I don't want to go." My heels dragged against the carpet, his little hand in mine. I tripped and fell over the pint-size fishing rod. My ankle tangled in the line.

"Come on. All the good ones will get away."

*Let them go. My fishing license is expired. No more pond scum.*

I limped to the bedroom, slipped into a black halter dress and fluffed my strawberry tresses. A touch of makeup, an extra spray of musk, and I was off to snag the catch of the day.

A validation stamp on the back of my hand, fifteen dollars at the door, and I entered the dance. I purchased a drink ticket and stood in line at the bar.

"Hi, I'm Tim from Kensington." A Cheshire cat grin spread between the lower lobes of each ear.

"Hello." I inched ahead to the bar.

"Where do you live?" The script rolled off his tongue.

"East of the tunnel."

"Oh, you're geographically unacceptable." With that he turned and scampered away. I gave thanks.

The bartender gestured for the next customer. I ordered my drink and eased my way from the makeshift bar into the large room. Darkened lights created an ambience of what-we-can't-see-will-do-us-no-harm atmosphere. I nursed the cool mixture in my glass and surveyed the crowd. Great music.

As the evening wore on, I tallied the selection of men that had approached me to dance: one accountant, one engineer and one salesman. None of them appealing, none of them appropriate fishing buddies for Jake. The pond dry, the clock marked the eleventh hour. Time for decisive action. I angled to another corner and adjusted my gear. The lure tempted.

"Don't you run at Lake Chabot?" A question of substance floated my way.

"That's me." *Intriguing conversation.*

"I go there all the time. Do you want to dance?" He motioned toward the arena of swiveling and gyrating hips.

"You go to the lake?" *This has possibilities.* "Do you like to fish?" *A nibble.*

"I love to fish." He smiled. "The other day I caught a six-pound rainbow trout." *His story is animated. The man knows his sport.*

We twisted and turned into the early hours and exchanged phone numbers penciled on little napkin scraps. Later, I paid Susie and watched her walk home.

"You're back." Jake was stretched out on the sofa.

"Hey, sleepyhead."

"Did you have fun?" A yawn caught his words, and they tumbled out in slow motion.

"So-so." I replayed the evening in my head.

"Well?" He sat up slightly, bracing his weight on his elbow.

"Well what?" I reeked of stale tobacco.

"Did you find me a fisherman?" His eyelids were barely open.

"Yeah." I fingered Kevin's number in my hand.

"Thanks, Mommy." He curled back into sleep and hugged the waiting pole.

"You're welcome."

Mom, the fisher of men. What Grandpa forgot to teach, Grandma did not.

*Cynthia Borris*

# $\overline{9}$
# JOY AND GRATITUDE

*Occasionally in life, there are those moments of unutterable fulfillment which cannot be completely explained by those symbols called words. Their meanings can only be articulated by the inaudible language of the heart.*

Martin Luther King Jr.

# Mom Taught Me to Play Baseball

*Instruction does much, but encouragement does everything.*

Goethe

On June 1, 1995, I was standing on the pitcher's mound at Rosenblatt Stadium in Omaha, Nebraska, about to pitch the first game of the College World Series. I had completed my warm-up tosses, and I was ready to make the first pitch. It was a perfect Midwestern Saturday afternoon. The sky was a deep blue with a handful of clouds. Though it was humid, a light breeze kept it from being too hot. Twenty-five thousand fans were in the stands, three times more than had ever watched me pitch. The pregame crowd noise I was used to was louder here, more intense than anything I had ever experienced. I could feel the crowd's excitement and anticipation. The game was being televised nationally. Ten million people would be watching; I could feel the pressure. I paced around the back of the pitcher's mound, my mind racing, my mouth dry, my heart pounding. I was having a hard time catching my breath.

We were playing Cal State Fullerton, the number-one-ranked team in the country. In my three years at Stanford University, this was the first time we had advanced to the College World Series.

As I stood behind the mound doing my final stretches, I was trying to focus. Instead, I found myself caught up in the moment. I looked into the stands, something I rarely did from out on the mound. The crowd was an awesome and daunting sight. Right above our dugout was the Stanford cheering section, where all the family, friends and people associated with the university were sitting. In that sea of cardinal-red shirts, hats and signs, I saw my mom, Lois Dempsey Robbins.

*I wouldn't be here without her,* I thought. My mom taught me how to play baseball, sitting on our living-room floor, rolling a ball back and forth even before I could walk. When I was bigger, after the divorce from my dad, she'd take me onto the front lawn to play catch. She got me started in T-ball, and I'd been playing ever since. She was my biggest fan and my first coach. I gripped the ball in my left hand, sweat already dripping down both my arms. I thought about how quickly Mom had learned to fend for herself and her two kids, my sister Lori and me. Dad got sick after the divorce and had stopped paying child support. In the midst of this, she took the risk of starting her own business, something in which she had no experience, because she wanted the flexibility to be with her kids when we needed her. Years later, she told me, "I was not going to have some boss tell me when I could or could not see my kids." That's my mom: strong, determined and willing to do whatever it takes to be there for Lori and me.

The announcer's voice boomed in the background: "Now, batting for the Cal State Fullerton Titans, left fielder Tony Miranda." The game was about to begin, but my thoughts were still focused on the stands and on my mom.

I could count on one hand the number of my games that Mom had missed while I was growing up. In high school and college, she came to every local game and even some of the games on the road. It wasn't surprising to look up now and see her sitting proudly in the stands. She'd been doing that my entire career. She never flinched or wavered in her support of me. I could always feel her love and her commitment; I could always hear her voice cheering loudly as I ran off the field, "Way to go, Mike!" No matter what was going on in her life, she was there.

As Miranda stepped into the batter's box, I realized I was pitching in the College World Series because of the support Mom had given me throughout my life. She'd shown me what determination, loyalty and power meant. She'd demonstrated through her life everything that I needed to succeed in mine. I stepped up onto the pitching rubber and gathered my thoughts. I took the sign from my catcher, wound up and fired my first pitch, forever and gratefully my mother's son.

*Mike Robbins*

# My Birthday, Her Party

*To get the full value of joy, you must have some-
body to divide it with.*

Mark Twain

It was January 1999, and I was a single, successful and
totally bored thirty-eight-year-old woman. My life, while
fun and full of wonderful friends and family, seemed all
too much about me, and I longed to make a difference for
others in need. More than a year before, I had started the
foster-to-adoption process in the county where I lived. I'd
figured that the chances for a single parent to adopt a
child would be better if one had fostering-care experience
first. I had filled out the exhausting, twenty-plus-page
profile, went through the home-study process and began
to wait . . . and wait . . . and wait.

I had resigned myself that my goal of becoming a mom
to someone who needed one was never going to come
true and found myself telling a co-worker that I intended
to begin volunteering at a local senior center. Surely,
someone there could use my help and love.

The same morning I made this pronouncement to my

co-worker, the phone in my office rang. It was the county, and they had a ten-month-old baby girl who needed a foster home, and she needed it *immediately*. I went to the agency the following morning for our very first visit. What was to be a preliminary, getting-acquainted visit turned into a three-and-a-half-hour bonding session with a precocious, little dark-haired angel who was already walking. She walked into that room and straight into my arms, and never left.

It was obvious to everyone at the agency that this was a match made in heaven. With emotions whirling like a tornado, I put Jordan, God's little angel, in the car seat I had just installed in the back of my car, and began the journey of a lifetime: motherhood. From the car, I called my entire family and support system and asked them, one by one, to help me get together the necessary items for her immediate arrival since I had no time to go shopping. (Little did I know that, from that day forward, I would never *have* time for anything; I would have to *make* time.) They all answered with love and enthusiasm, and within twenty-four hours, her little diaper bag, which had only one shoe in it when it arrived with her, now contained thirteen pairs!

The next day was my thirty-ninth birthday, and my sister had asked me to bring the baby over for a quiet, family celebration. When I got to the house, I looked in the window and saw that it was filled with decorations, presents, family and friends. I was overwhelmed with emotion when I went inside and proceeded to celebrate *my* birthday, but it was really *Jordan's* party.

A few months later, on a beautiful summer day, God changed the life of two single moms in a beautiful way. It was the first visitation we were to have with Jordan's birth mother. I arrived early at the county office to get settled, only to walk through the front door and right into her.

There was no denying who she was: she and Jordan looked like they could be sisters. Both of us moms were apprehensive, but within a short time, we became two women who simply shared love for the same child. Since that time we have formed a unique friendship that is hard to explain and understand.

More than a year later, with a few bumps and dips in the road, Jordan became Jordan Smith, my daughter. We had another party, and this time it really was *hers!* I couldn't have been happier.

Every so often, my co-worker asks me if I have checked into volunteering at the senior center. My response: "I'm looking for volunteers to help *me!*"

*Gerilynn Smith*

# What's One More?

*Anything done for another is done for oneself.*

Pope Boniface VIII

Upon hearing about the impending birth of my third child, a neighbor told me, "If you have three kids, you might as well have ten!"

Since the birth of my third child, I've raised three daughters, virtually alone, as a single mother. Was that neighbor ever right!

My youngest daughter, Lisa, was a handful—never able to sit still, active, mischievous and determined to get her way. She's also the child who always had tons of friends over, inviting every kid in the neighborhood home to play. Our home was dubbed the "Kool-Aid House" because it was where everyone liked to congregate.

Her high-school years were no different. Scores of teen-agers constantly streamed through our doors. Sometimes, I would come home to find complete strangers in various parts of the house. One time, I walked through the front door to confront a tall, strapping young boy standing in the kitchen. I said, "Who are you?" He replied, "Well, who are you?!"

One late summer afternoon, just before the onset of the new school year, Lisa approached me in my office. Actually, Lisa never approaches; she "blows in" like a gust of wind.

"Mom, remember my friend Duane?" she asked breathlessly.

Exhausted, I replied, "No, Lisa, I don't remember your friend Duane." After all, with the myriad of kids always surrounding her, there was no way I could remember all of them.

Lisa proceeded to tell me that Duane needed a place to stay for the school year. Stopping her in midsentence, I said, "You're kidding, right?"

I was already dealing with a full household: her two older sisters, a new grandson born to my oldest daughter, and another young woman we had taken in. We were fresh out of bedrooms, and I was fresh out of patience.

She pressed on, and trying to ignore her pleadings, I told her to go home.

When I got home that evening, Lisa changed her methods and sat down quietly next to me at the kitchen table. "Mom, can I please just tell you about Duane?"

She proceeded to tell me that Duane was born in Detroit. As a toddler, when his mother was hospitalized for health problems, he had been sent to live with an uncle. His uncle soon couldn't handle the rambunctious boy, and Duane had been sent to live with his older half-brother, who was then attending Michigan State University. Growing up with his brother in cramped university housing, along with his brother's young bride and their own two children, and sleeping on the couch in the tiny living room eventually proved too much for all of them. The summer approaching his senior year, Duane found himself going from friend's house to friend's house and sometimes roaming the streets. A popular football player, the coach told him that, unless he found a permanent address for the school year, he couldn't play when school started.

I took one long look at Lisa after hearing this story, bending my head and shaking it in disbelief at what I was about to say. "Okay, Lisa. Tell Duane he can stay here for the school year. But, he'd better be a good kid or out he goes."

I had no idea who Duane was, but something told me I was supposed to say yes.

I fixed up a space for him in the basement and told Lisa to go get him. A few hours later, Lisa came in through the side door. I was doing dishes in the kitchen. "Mom, Duane is too embarrassed to come in. He's afraid you don't really want him here."

I thought for a minute and realized if we were going to integrate him into the family, I'd better start now.

I yelled, "Duane! Get your butt in here!"

In walked a gigantic, dark-skinned young man sheepishly carrying a paper bag filled with his possessions. He eyed me humbly, obviously at a loss for words.

Knowing that kids need to feel needed and included, I continued, "Duane, go put your things downstairs, and when you're done, come back up here to take out the trash, please."

Over the next few days, Duane slowly became accustomed to our chaotic family. He was fun-loving and personable, but I noticed he remained shy around me.

One day, while leaning over the kitchen sink, I heard someone rummaging around in the refrigerator. I turned to see Duane grabbing something to eat. I thought: *This is a good sign.* Anyone comfortable enough to open the refrigerator door in front of someone else must be feeling at home.

Duane closed the refrigerator, turned to me and said, "Mom?" *Another good sign.* "Can I have a sleepover on Friday night?"

Visions of a complete football team converging on my property with a keg of beer, toilet paper being strewn from tree to tree and the police knocking on the door in the wee hours of the morning flooded my brain. I nervously asked, "Duane, what exactly do you mean by a 'sleepover'?"

"Well, my friend and I are going to go to the movies Friday, and I was wondering if it would be all right if he spent the night afterward."

Relieved at not hosting a blowout of a party, I of course told him yes. The broadest grin washed over his face, as if he had just scored a touchdown; he turned around, beaming, and walked downstairs.

As I watched him walk away, it occurred to me that, in all his eighteen years, Duane had never had the privilege of growing up in a household where he had birthday parties, a neighborhood for playing or a room for friends to spend the night. Even though I always had to scrape to do things for my girls—and money was always, always tight—I somehow managed to buy tap shoes, send them to camp, take weekend vacations. Life had been full.

Duane's first sleepover proved to be one of many, and with Duane came a whole new group of young people showing up at my door. Furthermore, he became, literally and figuratively, a "big" brother to the girls and a playful uncle to my grandson, Tyler.

We managed to get Duane through a lot of senior-year activities: prom, spring break in Cancún, and most important, graduation. What a glorious day that was. His mother was able to attend, and we had a lovely party at the house for him.

Even though I've struggled as a single parent of three, I've never lost sight of my blessings. Having Duane in our family for eighteen months did more for us than we ever did for him. He was as much of a handful as Lisa, but brought me as much joy as if he were one of my own.

As my neighbor had told me long before, "If you have three, you might as well have ten." After all, with three, four or five—what's one more?

*Nancy Vogl*

# Sticky Notes

*Each day comes bearing its own gifts. Untie the ribbons.*

Ruth Ann Schabacker

Today, I received an e-mail from a friend of mine, sharing the good news that he had been promoted to vice president in a prestigious company. Now, I'm not certain what this means, but added to his retired government employee pension, I'm fairly sure it translates into pretty big bucks.

Was I pleased for him? I should have been. He puts in staggering hours at work and is extremely productive—an all-around great guy. Sometimes I wonder if his good wife remembers what he looks like.

But I wasn't pleased. In truth, I was just plain jealous! *Why him?* I thought. I'm pretty productive myself, but at my annual evaluation, I received a modest 4 percent raise and nothing resembling a promotion. I lay awake nights worrying about the hefty home-equity loan I had taken out to keep the roof over our heads. I pray that my college-age daughter doesn't overdraw her checking account again. I peek at the mileage on my 1993 Camry, and tell myself that 135,000 miles is nothing for a Toyota.

Instead of wishing my friend well, I was wallowing in self-pity—staring at the computer in an envious stupor.

Ah, but the Lord, indeed, moves in mysterious ways.

Something caught my eye. Two tattered sticky notes, attached to my computer. They've been there for a few years, so I don't really notice them anymore. But today, I saw them again, as if for the first time.

One is lime green, with the message: "Have a great day, Mom! I love you!" That one is from my daughter Helen. She was probably eleven or twelve when she wrote it. She's fifteen now, and besides being an excellent student, my little hospital candy striper is a beautiful and caring young woman. She still asks for a hug and still wants her "mommy" to tuck her in at night. Now, there's something money can't buy.

The second note is lemon yellow. This one is from my son, Stephen, now ten. Judging by the wobbly handwriting, I'm guessing this note is from when he was about six. It simply says: "I love you, Mom." He continues to echo that sentiment every day, in a long-standing ritual. When I drop him off at school, I always say, "I love you, Stevie." His reply is: "I love you. Angels around you and your car!"

I look around my office and see the homemade artwork and cluttered array of photos. I see a favorite picture of my oldest daughter, Annie, except in this picture she is an awesome little blonde creature of two, clutching her stuffed cat Ming, and leaning against her (wow . . . young!) mom. Ming hasn't changed much over the years, but Annie has. Despite the overdrawn checking account, she constantly amazes me with her self-motivation. I am convinced that Annie can do anything she sets her mind to, which includes making her crabby mother laugh whenever she most needs to. Annie is awesome.

With infinite gratitude, I realize that my friend can keep his vice president's title, and all the money that goes with it, with my best wishes for success.

I wouldn't trade my title for any other, and no one in the world will ever share it. I'm Annie, Helen and Stevie's mom. Priceless!

*Maureen Deutermann*

# Mommy and Santa

*I believe in looking reality straight in the eye, and denying it.*

Garrison Keillor

Winter had dug its heels in deep, leaving the city covered in its white residue. All the storefront windows were adorned with Christmas tress, Styrofoam snowmen, nativity scenes, blinking lights and other seasonal ornaments. Christmas was in the air and on the minds of everyone, especially young children.

As I walked the short mile home from school with my sister, looking at the snowflakes as they hit the ground, I thought about the topic of the day among my grade-school comrades. Each of them was ranting and raving about what they were going to get for Christmas. Apparently, everyone, except me, knew to take their Christmas wishes to their parents and plead for the things they desired. The general consensus was that their parents had agreed to get them what they wanted. That day the other kids had quickly educated me on the nonexistence of Santa Claus. Every present under the tree, no matter how big or small, was a direct result of Mom and Dad. I was shocked, but held up the façade that what they were saying was not news to me. But this realization explained why my Christmas mornings were always skimpier than theirs. All the other kids came from two-parent homes. Usually, two parents equaled two incomes; two incomes equaled more money; more money equaled more presents. Even with my fifth-grade education, I could do the math on that one.

In years past, when I asked my mother why our gifts were so few, she stated that our house was on the end of Santa's list, which meant that he was probably running out of toys by the time he reached our house. I remember wishing I lived closer to the North Pole. Maybe a shorter distance equaled more gifts. I had accepted this excuse for a long time, but now, thanks to the grade-school rumor mill, I knew the truth. It was a bitter pill to swallow.

When we got home, Lisa and I began making dinner. Spaghetti was the day's menu. Mom worked long hours and stayed for overtime whenever she could, trying to make ends meet. She had taught us at a very early age how to cook and clean and take care of the home. "It's just the three of us," she'd say. "We have to look out for each other. I'll do my part, and the two of you do yours. Together, we'll be all right."

"After dinner, I'm going to make my list for Santa," Lisa said.

My sister and I were only a year apart in age, but now there was a world of difference between us. I couldn't tell her what I had learned today. I knew she couldn't handle it, since I barely could.

"Well, don't ask for a lot 'cause Santa has to give gifts to a lot of kids, Lisa."

"I'll just ask for one of those big, walking-talking Lisa dolls. You know the one I mean; she's almost as tall as me, and she has my name. I've got to have her. I can dress her in my clothes and comb her hair and everything."

"I don't know if Santa will bring her, Lisa. She's kind of expensive."

"Santa doesn't care about price," Lisa told me. "Just whether you've been good or not. And I've been good."

With that, the front door opened, and Mom came in. We ran up to her, hugging her around her waist as she tried to put down her purse and bag. We always did that. We may have been short on material things, but we certainly weren't short on love. The Three Musketeers, that's what we were. Mom looked tired—she always did, but she also always made time for us. She ate her spaghetti while Lisa and I talked a mile a minute, trying to tell her the events of our day. We always talked fast; it was a habit we developed at an early age, trying to get all the details out before she fell asleep. This had happened midconversation on several occasions, so we kept the stories animated and fast to avoid its recurrence.

Lisa rambled on about how one of our friends had fallen while walking home from school. She didn't hurt herself, but she slid at least ten feet on the snow and ice. Her arms were stretched out in front of her and she looked just like Superman as she glided down the street. Mom laughed at Lisa's descriptive reenactment.

"Mommy, before I go to bed, I am going to make my list for Santa. Can you mail it for me tomorrow?" Lisa asked.

"Sure, but what are you going to ask for, honey?"

"I had a lot of things in mind, but Lori said if I keep it small, maybe Santa will bring it, so I'm only asking for one thing: the walking-talking Lisa doll."

"I told her it was expensive," I blurted out.

My mother's and my eyes met, and at that moment, she knew I had figured out the secret about Santa.

"Well, honey," Mom said to Lisa, "times are really tough

right now, so Santa may not be able to deliver the doll to you. Just in case Santa can't bring her, make sure you put some other things on your list. Write your list and I'll mail it in the morning."

Mom kissed us good night, and we all headed for bed.

Even at my young age, I wanted to cushion the inevitable disappointment my sister was going to experience, but I couldn't ruin it by telling her the truth about Santa. "You may not get that doll," I warned Lisa. "Sometimes, the best gifts go to houses with mommies *and* daddies," was all I could come up with.

"We don't need a daddy. We've got Mommy and Santa, and that's all we need," remarked Lisa confidently, as she scribbled out her Christmas list for Santa.

That weekend we were out at the local grocery store. Right inside the entrance was a big Christmas giveaway display, with a ten-foot red and white Christmas stocking filled with coloring books, jacks, jump ropes and everything else a little girl's heart could desire—and smack dab in the middle was the doll my sister wanted. Her eyes lit up as soon as she saw it.

"That's her, Mommy, that's her! That's the doll I want!" screamed Lisa.

"Wow, honey, she is very pretty indeed. And it looks like they are giving her away. Why don't we fill out some of these forms and see if we can win her?"

"I've already asked Santa for her, and I know he will bring her. But I guess we can fill these out, too . . . just in case," Lisa said.

My mom began filling out one form, then another and another. I could see the wheels of desperation turning in her head as she wrote her name, phone number and address, over and over again. I didn't ask why she filled out so many; I knew that she was trying to beat the odds.

"Wasn't she beautiful? Did you see all that long hair? I can't wait till Christmas Eve." Lisa was in a world of her own as we went down one aisle after another, selecting our items.

Mom was quiet that day and the days that followed. I could see the weight of the world on her shoulders, and as each day grew closer to Christmas Eve, I felt helplessly in the middle of Lisa's anticipation and Mom's anxiety.

We began preparing for Christmas by putting up our tree, hanging the stockings and the lights, and even singing along with the Christmas carols that accompanied the old *Frosty the Snowman* cartoon, which was one of our favorites. Finally, Christmas Eve arrived, and Lisa and I put out cookies and milk like we did every year. Mom was in an unusually festive mood. She had been smiling all day, and she even let us stay outside late (normally, we had to come in when the streetlights came on). That night, as the moon lit up the sky so brightly you could count each and every star, Mom came outside with us, and the three of us lay on our backs on the front lawn, spreading our arms and legs back and forth, until we had created three angels in the snow. Then we wrote our names under each one.

"There," Mom said. "Now Santa will know that we are home and waiting for him."

Lisa and I ran into the house and went straight to bed. Even if Lisa was high with expectation of what Christmas morning would bring, she still fell instantly asleep. I, on the other hand was restless, and sleep eluded me. A short time later, I could hear scurrying in the living room. I suspected, from what the rumor mill had told me, that it was my mom laying out our gifts under the tree. I wanted to sneak a peek, but I dared not. I pulled the covers over my head to muffle the sound, and soon I, too, fell fast asleep.

At 5:25 A.M., a pillow slap across my head awakened me.

"Come on, Lori, let's see what Santa left," Lisa tried to whisper, but to no avail. *Man, if it wasn't Christmas, I'd slap her good,* I thought. I rubbed my eyes to remove the sleep from them and had just enough time to put my feet in my slippers when Lisa yanked me off the bed. As we walked down the hall from our bedroom to the living room, I tried to adjust my eyes, and searched my brain for words to cushion the hurt that was coming for Lisa. But it was too early, and I couldn't think.

The living room was lit up with the blinking lights of the tree, but even in the semidarkness, we both saw her. Big and beautiful and wrapped with a bow. Among the other toys, she reigned supreme.

"I told you, Lori! I told you he'd bring her!" Lisa screamed.

I watched as Lisa tore away the wrapping and removed the doll from the box. I was so happy for her, I didn't pay much attention to my own gifts. As Lisa read the Christmas tag attached to the doll, I looked up to see that my mom was standing in the room, watching us, her eyes filled with joy. I assumed all her entries to the contest had paid off, but Mom never revealed that, one way or the other. The gift tag simply said: "Merry Christmas from Santa."

I looked my little sister in the eye and said, "I guess you were right, Lisa. We don't need a father, after all. All we need is Mommy and Santa."

*Lorraine Elzia*

# Choosing Single Motherhood

*Joy is the simplest form of gratitude.*

Karl Barth

The hairdresser had just finished cutting both my hair and my ten-year-old daughter's.

"Your hair is just alike: the same texture and color, the same red highlights," she noticed.

"I know," I replied with a grin. "It's amazing, since Anna is adopted."

Many people comment on how alike we look, but eight years ago, our lives were separate and very different.

I had been living alone in a high-rise studio in New Jersey, recently self-employed after losing my job at a bankrupt company in New York City. I had just received news that my college friend Leslee had been diagnosed with breast cancer, the disease that had killed her mother. I grieved for her, her husband and her two young sons. Her illness caused me to take a new, hard look at my own life, and I became determined to do those things that I had always planned to do "someday."

I spent a month painting in Italy. I sold my condo and

bought a real house, farther into New Jersey. I grew my home-based graphic design business.

One March afternoon, I tuned into Oprah, who was doing a show on finding fulfillment in life. Since my work had been feeling a bit stale, I thought maybe Oprah could show me how to spark up my career. At one definitive moment, Oprah commanded, "You've got to ask yourself why God put you on this planet."

And I answered, "To be someone's mother."

Over the years, I had never found Mr. Right or even Mr. Close! But not being a wife didn't bother me as much as not being a mother. So, at age forty-three, I decided that adoption was the way for me to become a mom. Although I was concerned about the pressures a single parent faces, and worried that my child wouldn't have a father in her life, my strong desire to nurture a child affirmed my commitment to adopt.

Being single and wanting a toddler girl, I was advised to adopt from Russia, where orphanages needed homes for many older children. I began the long paper trail that would hopefully lead to a daughter. One September day, I called my adoption agency just to check if they had received my final papers from the state, and they said yes, adding that I might receive news of a child that week. As predicted, not by stork but by FedEx, a file and photo arrived. The photo was a small black-and-white head shot of a three-year-old girl, with a buzz-cut thatch of hair, crossed eyes and an expressionless pout. I needed to decide if this child was to be my daughter.

It was a difficult picture to love. I drove with the new photo to my parents' house. Looking at the sad little girl, my mother said, "Oh, she's adorable. She just needs a mother to put a smile on her face."

Through my tears, I realized that this girl had my Eastern European cheeks and nose. I became more comfortable with the situation, but still needed some time to make a final decision. Driving home, I passed a garage sale and stopped for a look. I spotted an old-fashioned student desk. The wooden top was worn, marred with gouges and pencil marks, obviously well used and well loved. The homeowner proudly told me she had raised two merit scholars with that desk. Carrying the desk back to my car, I knew I had accepted my new daughter.

On a November evening, I was on a plane bound for Moscow to bring my daughter home. The adoption process in Russia went smoothly, although I spent five anxious days waiting for my new daughter to fly into Moscow from a town near the Ural Mountains. The wait was a long and emotional labor.

But finally, Anna and I were together. There was the wacky buzz cut, the crossed eyes, but also a big smile. She was all movement and curiosity, exploding with love and anger. She had spent two-and-a-half neglectful years in an impoverished birth home, then nine months in an orphanage. These traumas would come home with us as her emotional baggage. But we would work hard to overcome them.

Thirty-six hours later we were flying to America. Anna spent the entire nine-hour flight either running up and down the aisles with endless energy, or having wailing, flailing tantrums on the floor with equal energy. At one point, I sat with Anna on the floor of the back of the airplane sobbing to the flight attendants, "I'm too old for this!"

Sleepless and frayed, we got into the car I had hired to meet us at the airport. We settled into the backseat, and with Sinatra singing on the radio, Anna immediately fell asleep in my arms. We were going home.

On the February day that Anna turned four and a half, my friend Leslee lost her battle with breast cancer and died. That evening, when I picked Anna up at day care, I saw a thin sliver of moon in the cobalt sky and one bright star to its right. I felt Leslee looking down on us from heaven, and I thanked her for starting me on the journey that led to motherhood. I squeezed Anna's hand, she smiled up at me—her mother—and we went home.

*Mary Zisk*

# The Humbug Holidays

*Those who contemplate the beauty of the Earth find reserves of strength that will endure as long as life lasts.*

Pearl S. Buck

I was going through the motions, everything a good mom is supposed to do before Christmas. I lugged out the boxes of holiday decorations. I baked my every-year-the-same two kinds of cookies. I even bought a real Christmas tree, for a change. I was going through the motions, but my heart was bogged down with a dull ache. I wasn't looking forward to Christmas one bit. My divorce had been finalized the past April, and my husband was already remarried. My oldest daughter, Jeanne, was in Yugoslavia for the year as a foreign-exchange student and wouldn't be home for the holidays—the first time ever that all four of my children wouldn't be with me for Christmas. Plus, the annual New Year's Eve get-together at my folks' house in Illinois had been canceled.

I was tired and grumpy. My job writing radio commercials at Milwaukee's biggest radio station was getting more hectic every day. Nearly every business in town wanted to advertise during the holiday season, and that meant longer and longer hours at work. Then there was the real nemesis: holiday shopping, a chore I kept putting off. I was supposed to be planning and buying, not only for my annual neighborhood holiday party, but also for two of my children's birthdays—Andrew would be eight on December 27; Julia, seventeen on January 4. How would I get through it all when "bah humbug" was constantly on the tip of my tongue?

During the night of December 15, a snowstorm ripped through Wisconsin, dumping twelve inches of snow on the ground. Even though Milwaukee is usually prepared for the worst, this blizzard finished its onslaught just before rush-hour traffic, bringing the highways to a standstill. The next day, all the schools and most businesses were closed. Even the radio station where I worked, eighteen miles from my home, was urging early-morning risers to stay in bed because the roads were definitely not passable.

After viewing the picture-postcard scene outdoors, I grabbed Andrew, and forgetting my down-in-the-dumps attitude, said, "Come on, buddy, let's make a snowman." Andrew and I scooped up big handfuls of wet, perfectly packing snow and built a base fit for a kingpin. Andrew rolled a ball of snow for the next level into such a huge mass that I had to get down on my hands and knees to shove it toward our mighty base. When I hoisted Andrew's third boulder onto this Amazonian snowperson, I felt like Wonder Woman bench-pressing a hundred pounds.

As our snowman reached a solid seven feet tall, with the help of a stool, I carefully placed Andrew's bowling-ball-sized snow head on top.

"He needs a great face, Mom." While I smoothed the snow and pounded arms and a waistline into our giant snowman, Andrew ran inside and returned with a silly beach hat with built-in sunglasses for eyes and his Superman cape that we plastered on the front of the giant. Andrew and I stepped back to admire our noble snowman. Straight and tall. Ruler of the yard. When I took their picture, Andrew's head barely reached the snowman's middle.

It was warmer the next morning, and when I looked out the kitchen window, I noticed that Super Snowman seemed to be leaning forward a little. I hoped he wouldn't fall over before Andrew got home from school that day.

Late that afternoon when I returned home after a hectic, make-up-all-the-work-from-yesterday day at the radio station, I saw that our snowman hadn't fallen over, but he was leaning forward at a very precarious forty-five-degree angle. His posture reminded me of the way I felt: tired and crabby, with the weight of the world on my shoulders.

The next morning, Super Snowman was leaning so far forward as to seem physically impossible. I had to walk out into the yard to see him up close. *What on Earth is holding him up?* I wondered, absolutely amazed. The Superman cape, instead of being on his front, now dangled freely in the wind as old Frosty's bent chest, shoulders and head were almost parallel to the ground.

My own shoulders sagged beneath the weight of my own depression as I remembered that Christmas was almost here. A letter from Jeanne arrived saying that since Christmas wasn't a national holiday in Yugoslavia, she'd have to go to school on December 25. I missed Jeanne's smile, her wacky sense of humor and her contagious holiday spirit.

The fourth day after we built the snowman was Saturday the 19th, the day I'd promised to take Andrew to Chicago on the train. Andrew loved the adventures of his first train and taxi rides, the trip to the top of the world's tallest building, the visit to the Shedd Aquarium and the toy departments of every major store on State Street. But I was depressed by the fact that it rained all day, that the visibility at the top of the Sears Tower was zero and that the all-day adventure left me totally exhausted.

Late that night, after the two-hour train ride back to Milwaukee, Andrew and I arrived home only to be greeted by the snowman, who by this time, after a warm day of drizzling rain, was now totally bent over from its base and perfectly parallel to the ground . . . and yet still balanced six inches above the slushy snow.

*That's me out there,* I said to myself. *About to fall facedown into a snowbank.* But why didn't our snowman fall? Nothing, absolutely nothing, was supporting the weight of that seven-foot-tall giant. *Just like there isn't anything or anybody supporting me during this awful holiday season,* I blubbered mentally, wondering what had supported the snowman in such a precarious position. Was it God in his almighty power? A freak of nature? A combination of ice, wind, rain and snow that had bonded to the mighty Super Snowman? I had a feeling there was a lesson to be learned from watching his decline. Sure enough, the lesson came to me gradually during the next two weeks.

On Christmas Eve, at the children's insistence, we attended family services at our parish church and afterward dined on our traditional oyster stew. Then, Andrew brought out the Bible for the yearly reading of the Christmas story before we opened our gifts. Later, we attended a midnight candle service with friends at their church. Finally, a phone call from Jeanne in Yugoslavia brimmed with good news of an impromptu Christmas celebration her host mother had planned.

The next day, some friends offered to cohost my big neighborhood party, which turned out to be a smashing success. On December 27, Andrew was delighted with his three-person birthday party. The next weekend, my out-of-town family got together for a long New Year's Eve weekend at my house, filling our home with the madcap merriment of ten houseguests, all of whom pitched in to help. And when Julia simplified another dilemma by saying that all she wanted for her birthday was a watch and "lunch out with Mom," I smiled all day.

I learned that no matter how depressed, overwhelmed, saddened, lonely or stressed out we get, there's always someone or something to help us find or recapture our own inner strength, just like there was for the falling-down, stoop-shouldered Super Snowman. During his four-day life span, he showed me an amazing strength from within—a strength that came to me gradually, bit by bit, as each person in my life stepped up to boost my faith and my spirits to heavenly skies.

It was indeed a holiday season to cherish.

*Patricia Lorenz*

# Yet, We Were Happy

*H*appiness *is the meaning and the purpose of
life, the whole aim and end of human existence.*

Aristotle

Being the youngest of four kids in a single-parent home
often meant going without: without money, without time,
without the attention two parents can provide. Yet, we
were happy.

We didn't shop at Super-29, the fancy grocery store
with live lobsters clawing each other in aquariums, the
store with happy shopping music discreetly piped in
through the speakers, where clean-faced boys helped
carry out groceries to the vast parking lot. We shopped at
the discount warehouse on the edge of town, where groceries were stacked to the ceiling in bland cardboard
boxes. We bought generic foods in nondescript packaging
stamped "cereal" and "butter." The cashier would dramatically wave our food stamps in the air as we bagged our
own groceries and struggled to the car. Yet, at night, we
munched on popcorn and watched summer storms roll
in, knowing we had food to eat.

Our house never smelled of men's cologne in the morn-ing. Our bathroom sink never propped up shaving sup-plies. Our closet contained dresses and shoes, not suits and ties. Yet, we never had to defer our needs or our free-dom to a shadow occupying a recliner in the living room.

Our house wasn't like the other homes on the block. It wasn't the fanciest or the biggest house. We didn't have time to lovingly paint lawn gnomes to place on the porch. Our lawn didn't glow luscious green in the sun. Yet, our home was always clean because we worked together.

Our clothes were never brand name or brand new. They were hand-me-downs and garage-sale finds or dug out of plastic trash bags anonymously deposited on our back porch. Sometimes they were ill-fitting or torn. Yet, we had style; we were unique.

Girl Scouts and cheerleading camps were for those girls who had two parents. Their moms had time to sew patches on uniforms and bake cookies for fund-raisers. Their par-ents had money to pay for the monthly dues. Yet, we all had friends, kids like us, whose time was less structured.

We never had respect like the families who dressed every Sunday and walked into church like ducks in a row. Some kids told me my mom was going to hell because she was divorced, and that's where divorced people went after they died. Yet, when I looked at my mother's face and the love she had for her children, I knew she was sent from heaven and that, one day, she would return to it because she taught four children to love others unconditionally.

Yes, we had very little: very little money, very little time and very little support. Yet, we had so much. More than most. We had each other. We were happy.

*Toni Roberts*

# More Chicken Soup?

Many of the stories and poems you have read in this book were submitted by readers like you who had read earlier *Chicken Soup for the Soul* books. We publish at least five or six *Chicken Soup for the Soul* books every year. We invite you to contribute a story to one of these future volumes.

Stories may be up to twelve hundred words and must uplift or inspire. You may submit an original piece, something you have read or your favorite quotation on your refrigerator door.

To obtain a copy of our submission guidelines and a listing of upcoming *Chicken Soup* books, please write, fax or check our Web site.

Please send your submissions to:

**Chicken Soup for the Soul**
P.O. Box 30880, Santa Barbara, CA 93130
fax: 805-563-2945
Web site: *www.chickensoupforthesoul.com*

We will be sure that both you and the author are credited for your submission.

For information about speaking engagements, other books, audiotapes, workshops and training programs, please contact any of our authors directly.

# Supporting Others

In the spirit of supporting others, a portion of the proceeds from *Chicken Soup for the Single Parent's Soul* will be donated to the Orange County Rescue Mission and the Women's Resource Center of Grand Traverse, Michigan.

**The Orange County Rescue Mission** helps hungry and homeless families in Orange County, California, get back on their feet. The mission delivers hope by providing food, shelter, clothing, guidance, counseling, education, job training, parenting classes and health care. Its faith-focused mission is to minister the love of Jesus Christ to the least, the last and the lost.

**Orange County Rescue Mission**
P.O. Box 4007
Santa Ana, CA 92702
Street Address: 1421 Edinger, Ste. B
Tustin, CA 92780
Phone: 714-258-4450 • Fax: 714-258-4451
Toll Free: 888-946-HOPE (4673)

What began in 1975 as a grassroots effort to help women and to raise community awareness about domestic violence and sexual assault is today a full-service agency offering shelter, advocacy, education and counseling to hundreds of families. **The Women's Resource Center of Grand Traverse, Michigan**, provides comprehensive services that help women and families empower themselves and achieve an equitable, nonviolent environment.

**Women's Resource Center of Grand Traverse**
720 S. Elmwood, Suite #2
Traverse City, MI 49684
Phone: 231-941-1210 • Fax: 231-941-1734

# Who Is Jack Canfield?

Jack Canfield is one of America's leading experts in the development of human potential and personal effectiveness. He is both a dynamic, entertaining speaker and a highly sought-after trainer. Jack has a wonderful ability to inform and inspire audiences toward increased levels of self-esteem and peak performance.

He is the author and narrator of several bestselling audio- and videocassette programs, including *Self-Esteem and Peak Performance, How to Build High Self-Esteem, Self-Esteem in the Classroom* and *Chicken Soup for the Soul—Live.* He is regularly seen on television shows such as *Good Morning America, 20/20* and *NBC Nightly News.* Jack has co-authored numerous books, including the *Chicken Soup for the Soul* series, *Dare to Win* and *The Aladdin Factor* (all with Mark Victor Hansen), *100 Ways to Build Self-Concept in the Classroom* (with Harold C. Wells), *Heart at Work* (with Jacqueline Miller) and *The Power of Focus* (with Les Hewitt and Mark Victor Hansen).

Jack is a regularly featured speaker for professional associations, school districts, government agencies, churches, hospitals, sales organizations and corporations. His clients have included the American Dental Association, the American Management Association, AT&T, Campbell's Soup, Clairol, Domino's Pizza, GE, ITT, Hartford Insurance, Johnson & Johnson, the Million Dollar Roundtable, NCR, New England Telephone, Re/Max, Scott Paper, TRW and Virgin Records. Jack has taught on the faculty of Income Builders International, a school for entrepreneurs.

Jack conducts an annual seven-day Training of Trainers program in the areas of self-esteem and peak performance. It attracts entrepreneurs, educators, counselors, parenting trainers, corporate trainers, professional speakers, ministers and others interested in developing their speaking and seminar-leading skills.

For further information about Jack's books, tapes and training programs, or to schedule him for a presentation, please contact:

Self-Esteem Seminars
P.O. Box 30880
Santa Barbara, CA 93130
phone: 805-563-2935 • fax: 805-563-2945
Web site: *www.jackcanfield.com*

# Who Is Mark Victor Hansen?

In the area of human potential, no one is more respected than Mark Victor Hansen. For more than thirty years, Mark has focused solely on helping people from all walks of life reshape their personal vision of what's possible. His powerful messages of possibility, opportunity and action have created powerful change in thousands of organizations and millions of individuals worldwide.

He is a sought-after keynote speaker, bestselling author and marketing maven. Mark's credentials include a lifetime of entrepreneurial success and an extensive academic background. He is a prolific writer with many bestselling books such as *The One Minute Millionaire, The Power of Focus, The Aladdin Factor* and *Dare to Win*, in addition to the *Chicken Soup for the Soul* series. Mark has made a profound influence through his library of audios, videos and articles in the areas of big thinking, sales achievement, wealth building, publishing success, and personal and professional development.

Mark is the founder of the MEGA Seminar Series. MEGA Book Marketing University and Building Your MEGA Speaking Empire are annual conferences where Mark coaches and teaches new and aspiring authors, speakers and experts on building lucrative publishing and speaking careers. Other MEGA events include MEGA Marketing Magic and My MEGA Life.

He has appeared on television (*Oprah,* CNN and *The Today Show*), in print (*Time, U.S. News & World Report, USA Today, New York Times* and *Entrepreneur*) and on countless radio interviews, assuring our planet's people that "You can easily create the life you deserve."

As a philanthropist and humanitarian, Mark works tirelessly for organizations such as Habitat for Humanity, American Red Cross, March of Dimes, Childhelp USA and many others. He is the recipient of numerous awards that honor his entrepreneurial spirit, philanthropic heart and business acumen. He is a lifetime member of the Horatio Alger Association of Distinguished Americans, an organization that honored Mark with the prestigious Horatio Alger Award for his extraordinary life achievements.

Mark Victor Hansen is an enthusiastic crusader of what's possible and is driven to make the world a better place.

Mark Victor Hansen & Associates, Inc.
P.O. Box 7665
Newport Beach, CA 92658
phone: 949-764-2640
fax: 949-722-6912
Visit Mark online at: *www.markvictorhansen.com*

# Who Is Laurie Hartman?

Laurie Hartman is the director of licensing for Chicken Soup for the Soul Enterprises, Inc. In 1997 she helped launch the trademark licensing program for *Chicken Soup,* and has been overseeing its success ever since. Running a multimillion-dollar retail program with a wide variety of products ranging from "soup to nuts," Laurie most enjoys her hands-on role in product development and the relationships she has built over the years with many wonderful licensees. Laurie is most thankful for the opportunity to work with her mentor, Lois Sloane of SloaneVision Unlimited, Inc., *Chicken Soup's* licensing agency. "I'm proud to say that everything I know about licensing I've learned from Lois, a true giant of a professional in the industry and one of the most wonderful people I have ever known."

Laurie is the single parent of fifteen-year-old Connor, her true inspiration for this book. An aspiring entrepreneur, soon-to-be Eagle Scout and computer genius, Connor plans to one day own his own computer company based out of Japan. The boy thinks *big.*

A lifelong horsewoman, Laurie contributed a story about her horse, Rusty, to *Chicken Soup for the Preteen Soul.* Believing in the special bond and magic that comes with horse ownership, Laurie volunteers her time at a therapeutic riding academy for the physically and mentally challenged.

Laurie and Connor enjoy living in sunny Southern California with their cat, Harrison, who on many late nights was curled up in his chair in Laurie's home office while she worked on this book. You may e-mail Laurie at *Laurieh@chickensoupforthesoul.com.*

# Who Is Nancy Vogl?

As a single mother since 1983, Nancy has raised three daughters, Heidi, Monika and Lisa, to young adulthood. And as can be read in the story "The Family in My Heart," she has added a fourth daughter to her brood, her "adopted" daughter Michelle. All four girls are in college and working and thriving. Heidi blessed her with her beloved grandson Tyler, and Michelle with her delightful grandson Justin.

When the children were young, Nancy sold real estate in Lansing, Michigan. Fifteen years ago she left her real estate career behind to venture into the seminar and speaking business, producing events that have featured such renowned authors and speakers as Og Mandino, Wayne Dyer and Norman Vincent Peale. Eventually, she created Universal Speakers Bureau, booking celebrities, authors, sports and political figures, and professional speakers nationwide for corporations, associations and organizations.

A few years ago, Nancy relocated to beautiful Traverse City in northern Michigan, a resort community with miles of pristine shoreline, sand dunes, lush forests and vineyards, rolling hills and glorious lakes and bays. Nancy says, "It is a place that nurtures my soul and provides me with the serenity to write and create."

Nancy recently coauthored, along with her daughter Heidi, a children's illustrated book, *Am I a Color Too?* published by the award-winning children's publisher Illumination Arts, slated for release in 2005. Its simple and profound message on issues of diversity from a child's point of view is already garnering great praise!

In addition to a budding writing career and taking care of her speaking business, Nancy recently made room in her life (finally) for a special man. As Nancy tells it, "David Strange is the love of my life, my soul mate, and it was worth every minute of my fifty-two years waiting for him. He is the reward I've been given for all of the struggles (and triumphs) I experienced as a single mom."

David brings to Nancy's life six more children and four more grandchildren. Together they have ten children and six grandchildren and look forward to many more grandchildren down the road (and building a family compound on one of the many lakes in the Grand Traverse area for all to congregate).

You can reach Nancy via e-mail at *nancy@nancyvogl.com* or by writing to 526 W. 14th Street, #185, Traverse City, Michigan 49684.

# Contributors

Several of the stories in this book were taken from previously published sources, such as books, magazines and newspapers. These sources are acknowledged in the permissions section. If you would like to contact any of the contributors for information about their writing or would like to invite them to speak in your community, look for their contact information included in their biographies.

The remainder of the stories were submitted by readers of our previous *Chicken Soup for the Soul* books who responded to our requests for stories. We have also included information about them.

**Suzanne Aiken** is a life coach, writer and speaker known as the Obstacle Coach. Suzanne shows clients how to use stumbling blocks as stepping stones to create empowerment and choice. She lives in the Boston area with her children, Nicole, Amanda and David. She can be reached at *www.obstaclecoach.com*.

**Michelle Anzelone** is a displaced city girl trying to adjust to country life. In her playtime she can be found writing, gardening, dancing and amusing her friends and family with tales of her country exploits. She lives with her daughter, Alexandra, north of Pittsburgh, Pennsylvania. She can be reached at *MLAnzelone@aol.com*.

**Mary Lynn Archibald** is that rarest of creatures, a native Californian. She is a freelance writer and contributor to the *Santa Rosa Press Democrat, NorthBay Biz Magazine* and other publications. She has lectured in the fields of writing, art and interior design, and is currently working on a (she hopes) humorous nonfiction memoir. She is the proud mother of two enormously talented adult children, and lives in Healdsburg, California. She can be reached at *mlarchibald@mac.com*.

**T. J. Banks** is the author of *Souleiado* (Five Star, 2002) and a contributing editor to *Lajoie*. She has written for numerous anthologies, including *Soul Menders, Their Mysterious Ways, Until We Meet Again, The Simple Touch of Fate, Eternal Moments,* and *Touched from Above*. Her work has won awards from *Byline*, the Cat Writers' Association and *The Writing Self*. She lives with her daughter, Marissa, and their many animals in Connecticut.

**Jeff Barr** is a single father who has written four books and contributed to several others. His stories have appeared in *The Washington Post, The Detroit News* and several other magazines, newspapers and Web sites. He is an editor/writer for *Golfweek Magazine* in Orlando, Florida. He can be reached at *ashraebarr@aol.com*.

**Ellen Barron** is a single parent who was raised by a single parent herself. She lives in Austin, Texas, where she works as a paralegal. Ms. Barron lovingly dedicates her story to her mother, who encouraged her to write a story for *Chicken Soup*. She can be reached at *ellen_barron@netzero.com*.

**Kathy Bohannon** is a Georgia Press Award-winning author. She pens weekly columns for the *Savannah Morning News* and the *Times-Herald* in Newnan, Georgia. Kathy has written her first book, *Finding My Garden*, a compilation of humorous and inspirational stories. Kathy and her husband, John, have two adult children.

**Cynthia Borris** resides in northern California. Humor columnist for *Inside Livermore Valley* magazine, she is working on her next novel, *To Serve Duck*. For speaking engagements, visit her Web site at *www.cynthiaborris.com*.

**Sierra Sky Brocius** realized she wanted to write as soon as she could talk. Inspired by the small things in life, she enjoys cooking, photography, listening to records, producing her zine, *Constellations*, and volunteering in her daughter's classroom. Sierra eventually plans to write a novel. She can be reached at *constellaseven@yahoo.com*.

**Patricia S. Brucato** is the editorial director for *www.1-800-flowers.com* and lives with her fabulous son, TJ, in Long Island, New York. In her spare time, she is part of the Long Island Sweet Potato Queens and has a lifelong dream to play the banjo. She can be reached at *Patbruc@aol.com*.

**Marty Bucella** is a full-time freelance cartoonist/humorous illustrator whose work has been published over 100,000 times in magazines, newspapers, greeting cards, books, the Web and so on. To see more of Marty's work, visit his Web site at *members.aol.com/mjbtoons/index.html*.

**Patricia Buck** recently retired after thirty-plus years of working with boards of trustees in educational systems at the secondary and community college levels. She is the owner/creator of Tell Your Tale, which offers biographical writing services to those who wish to document their life stories in professionally bound books to be handed down to future generations. Pat is the proud grandmother of Parker and Blake (ages eleven and six), Kathy and Scott Parzych's two lively sons.

**Martha Campbell** is a graduate of Washington State University's Louis School of Fine Arts and a former writer/designer for Hallmark Cards. She has been a freelance cartoonist and book illustrator since 1973. She can be reached at P.O. Box 2538, Harrison, AR 72602, 870-741-5323, or by e-mail at *marthaf@alltel.net.*

**Bill Canty's** cartoons have appeared in many national magazines, including the *Saturday Evening Post, Good Housekeeping, Better Homes and Gardens, Woman's World, National Review, Medical Economics* and *Reader's Digest.* His syndicated feature, "All About Town" (*www.reuben.org/Canty*), appears in thirty newspapers. Bill can be reached at 908 Shorehaven Dr., Poinciana, FL 34759, and by e-mail at *wcanty@solivita.*

As the author of seven books, **C. Leslie Charles** is a model of success. Once a high school dropout, teen wife, mother and displaced home-maker, she had a tenth-grade education until age twenty-nine. Leslie enjoys reading, horseback riding, yoga, bird watching and beading. She can be reached through her Web site at *www.lesliecharles.com.*

**Terri Cheney** is a writer who publishes her own newsletter, *Penny Ann Poundwise.* She enjoys reading, writing, collecting and history. She is proud to report that her children are now adults and happily pursuing their own lives. E-mail her at *tea_cee1@yahoo.com.*

Born and raised in Queens, New York, **William Jelani Cobb, Ph.D.**, is the youngest of four children and the father of a wonderful daughter. He is also an Atlanta-based writer and professor of history at Spelman College. His work can be viewed at *www.jelanicobb.com.*

Forget **Heidi Cole**! Who you really should know about is the multital-ented superkid Tyler Cole, who is destined to follow in the footsteps of Michael Jordan or Bill Cosby. Watch out world, Tyler's a superstar ath-lete, funnyman and brilliant mathematician. His proud mother thanks him for being the inspiration for her story.

**Kathline Collins** received her bachelor of science in nursing from the University of Maryland in 1993. Four children call her "Mom." She enjoys hunting, fishing, camping and golfing with her husband, Jim. Running keeps her in shape. Writing keeps her sane. E-mail her at *kath-line@charter.net.*

**David Cooney**'s cartoons and illustrations appear in numerous *Chicken Soup for the Soul* books as well as magazines including *First for Women* and *Good Housekeeping.* David is a work-from-home dad, cartoonist, illustra-tor and photographer. David and his wife Marcia live in the small Pennsylvania town of Mifflinburg with their two children, Sarah and Andrew. David's Web site is *www.DavidCooney.com,* and he can be reached at *david@davidcooney.com.*

**Rob Daugherty** is a webmaster, lecturer, certified hypnotist, Reiki master and devoted father. His humor and insight have caused many to smile and look at life with a brighter perspective. At *LetusPonder.com*, Rob shares his adventures as he continually discovers new mystical, magical moments. He can be reached at *Rob@LetusPonder.com*.

**Ervin DeCastro** attended Loyola University, Chicago, from 1992 to 1996. He is an aspiring writer who enjoys baseball, softball, tennis, basketball and most types of challenges. He and his wife, Heather, were blessed with the birth of their first child in October 2004.

**Maureen Deutermann** is a nursing educator and lives with her three children in Virginia. She received her bachelor of science degree in nursing from Marquette University, Milwaukee, Wisconsin. She is currently working on a master's degree in nursing administration and aspires to write a book championing the nursing profession.

**C. J. Druschke** likes to spend time reading, writing, watching Cubs games and, most of all, hanging out with daughter, Hannah, at home in Chicago.

**Lorraine Michelle Elzia** is an aspiring writer from Austin, Texas, where she works as a paralegal. She has been married sixteen years and has two sons. Lorraine enjoys reading, writing and spending quality time with family and friends. Lorraine's goal is to inspire and motivate others with her writing.

**Joanna Emery** is the mother of three children and lives in Dundas, Ontario. She writes for children and has a special interest in history, unsolved mysteries and crop circles. Her Web site is *www.joannaemery.com*.

**Linda Ferris** is a registered nurse practicing in Michigan. Linda enjoys quilting, traveling and writing. She has published stories in the book *Heartwarms, Venice Golf Coast Magazine* and *Today's Christian Woman*. Her son Michael is a college student and now married. He and his wife Carrie are enjoying their first home. Linda can be reached at *lafrn10@aol.com*.

**Jeff Gemberling** works in the automotive industry in Lewisburg, Pennsylvania. Jeff enjoys spending his free time taking long walks, skipping stones and watching Noah and Autumn grow and become the people that God wants them to be. He plans to continue guiding and raising his family with God's blessing.

**J. D. Gidley** grew up in Savannah, Georgia, and left to pursue a life less humid. She's currently living in Seattle, Washington, where it rains all the time. Her short story, "Splendor," was published in *Inscriptions Magazine*. She can be reached at *jdgidley@hotmail.com*.

**Randy Glasbergen** is one of America's most widely and frequently published cartoonists. More than 25,000 of his cartoons have been published by *Funny Times, Reader's Digest, Guideposts for Teens, Campus Life, Group Magazine* and many others. His daily comic panel "The Better Half" is syndicated worldwide by King Features. He is also the author of three cartooning instruction books and several cartoon anthologies. To read a cartoon a day, please visit Randy's Web site, *www.glasbergen.com*.

When not creating at her keyboard or sneaking toasty snacks, **Toni Hall** is part of the Church Volunteer Network, an organization that shows people from various churches how to get out into the communities where they are needed. She can be reached at *tonihall2003@yahoo.com*.

**Susan Hamilton** received her bachelor of arts from Susquehanna University. She is a freelance writer and an advocate for single parents. She has taught classes and organized outreaches for single parents at her church. She has been published by Focus on the Family's *Single Parent* magazine, and is the proud mother of two children.

A single parent for six years, with four small children, **Rosemary Heise** worked while attending college and teaching. With the children now grown, she has retired from a satisfying career in special education. With grandchildren nearby, Rosemary and her husband garden, read, write and enjoy the neighboring wildlife in central Illinois.

**Sara Henderson** holds a master's degree in educational leadership from Bethel College in St. Paul, Minnesota. She has taught kindergarten and second grade, and is currently the elementary principal at Maranatha Christian Academy in Minneapolis, Minnesota.

**Dorothy Hill** has previously been published in *Chicken Soup for the Christian Woman's Soul, Nudges from God* and *Angels on Earth*. While she is no longer a foster parent, she still teaches high-school social studies part-time and works with children at her church. She can be reached at *missisip@dixie-net.com*.

**Hazel Holmes** writes, hikes and gardens in northeastern Pennsylvania. She shares her writing experiences with the world on her Web site, *www.writingwhore.com*.

With a multinational communications background, **Patty M. Kearns** holds awards in human diversity, community relations and health-care advertising. Creator of the Archangel Series stress-relief programs, her CDs and seminars offer support for hospice, cancer survival, pain management and unemployment. Her spirit-building book for exhausted caregivers will soon be published. She can be reached at *pmkcommunica@hotmail.com*.

**Wendy Keller** is the founder of Keller Media, Inc. She has been responsible for the successful placement of more than 450 rights deals worldwide. The company sells book ideas to publishers, books speakers into engagements and trains people to excel at both. Wendy herself inspires audiences by presenting programs on overcoming life's hardships. Her Web sites are *www.KellerMedia.com, www.LifePresent.org* and *www.HealFromDivorce.com*.

**Carol A. Kopacz** is still "porch stooping" with neighbors and her frisky pal, Sweetie, a fifteen-year-old Lhasa apso. Her daughter rejoins her on occasion, although she's "all grown-up" and has a porch of her own.

**Michelle Lawson** lives in Lansing, Michigan, where she is studying to be an elementary-school teacher. The sound of her son Justin's laughter is what makes her most happy. She believes in children, hugs and the Boys and Girls Clubs of America. She can be reached at *misschelle1978@yahoo.com*.

**Patricia J. Lesesne** received her bachelor's degree, cum laude, from Harvard University, her master's in teaching from Tufts University. She teaches history at a high school in South Florida. Patricia works to secure equal educational opportunities for inner-city students. She enjoys spending time with friends and family. She can be reached at *patricia_lesesne@yahoo.com*.

**Patricia Lorenz,** a single parent of four since 1985, had kids in college for seventeen years in a row, and is now enjoying her empty nest and her seven grandchildren. She's the author of five books, has stories in twenty *Chicken Soup for the Soul* books and can be reached for speaking opportunities at *patricialorenz@juno.com* or by visiting *www.patricialorenz.com*.

**Stephen J. Lyons** is the author of *Landscape of the Heart,* a single father's memoir, and *A View from the Inland Empire.* He writes essays, articles, poems and book reviews from central Illinois, where he also teaches guitar.

The father of three beautiful children, **Steven H. Manchester** is the published author of *The Unexpected Storm: The Gulf War Legacy, A Father's Love, Jacob Evans* and *At the Stroke of Midnight,* as well as several books under the pseudonym Steven Herberts. Three of his screenplays have also been produced as films.

**Donn Marshall's** wife, Shelley, was killed on duty at the Pentagon on September 11. He currently directs a charity he established, the Shelly A. Marshall Foundation, to touch others with her spirit (for more information, visit *www.shellysfoundation.org*). Donn and his children, Drake and Chandler, live in Shepherdstown, West Virginia.

**Victoria McGee** has a background in education, counseling and acting, which she blends together in writing and producing educational videos. She is the author of *Just Look at Yourself*, a self-esteem curriculum for pre-teen girls. Victoria enjoys spending time with her family and exploring the spiritual journey.

After studying writing for publication, **Jim McLaughlin** was president of Ina Collbirth Poetry Circle and California Writer's Club, Peninsula Branch. His writings appeared in many publications and his four poetry books. While working as Belmont city clerk for twenty years, he was president and newsletter editor for his neighborhood and the City Clerk Association.

**Ed Mickus** is an aeronautical engineer living in a suburb of Atlanta, Georgia. As a single dad his life revolves around his daughter, Jordyn, who by all accounts is handling the duality of her split family very well. Both parents are focused on Jordyn and strive to supply her with many life experiences, including the unconditional love of a mommy and daddy. Anyone wanting information about Chinese adoptions may e-mail Ed at *ed.mickus@lmco.com*.

**Victoria Moran** (*www.victoriamoran.com*) has written ten books including *Younger by the Day* (HarperSanFrancisco, 2004), and the bestselling *Creating a Charmed Life* (HarperSanFrancisco, 1999). An international speaker, she has appeared twice on *Oprah*. Victoria has remarried; her daughter, now twenty-one, is a working actor.

**Dorothy M. Neddermeyer, Ph.D.**, is the author of *If I'd Only Known . . . Sexual Abuse in or out of the Family: A Guide to Prevention*, a speaker and seminar leader with over twenty years' experience in personal and professional development. She is noted for her pioneering work in physical and sexual abuse prevention and recovery. She can be reached at *dorothyneddermeyer@gen-assist.com* or *www.gen-assist.com*.

**Karen J. Olson** is a writer and columnist from Eau Claire, Wisconsin. She graduated from the University of Wisconsin-Eau Claire with enough knowledge in psychology and sociology to make her wildly successful at Trivial Pursuit and freelance writing. She loves reading, bicycling and chatting on the telephone. She writes magazine and newspaper features as well as a number of columns. She especially likes writing humor and inspirational pieces. You may reach her at *kjolson@charter.net*.

**Richard Parker** is a graduate of the Culinary Institute of America and an executive chef at Truffaut's. He resides in Michigan with his wife and two dogs.

**Christine E. Penny** lives in a small town in Ontario, Canada. She enjoys the outdoors and spending time with her only son, Daniel. She believes that he is her greatest accomplishment.

**Linda H. Puckett,** as a single parent, began working on her master's degree in gifted education, which she received in 1985 from Southern Illinois University. She writes, paints and works with her husband on their Kentucky tree farm. She can be reached at *lhpuckett@hotmail.com*.

**Brandi N. Rainey** is the single mother of two little girls in northern Florida. She is known in various online poetry communities as LyrikalShe. A collection of her poems is due to be published soon. She can be reached at *lyrikalshe@yahoo.com*.

**Mike Robbins** is an inspirational speaker, author and coach who empowers people to be successful. Prior to establishing his speaking/coaching business, Mike played baseball at Stanford University (class of 1996) and with the Kansas City Royals. Injuries prematurely ended Mike's playing career in 1999.

**Toni Roberts** is a humor columnist/comedian living in central Kansas. Sign up for her weekly column at *www.toniroberts.com*.

After nearly twenty years as an advertising copywriter, **Jane Robertson** now writes both fiction and nonfiction for the pleasure of it. Since she and her husband, Tom, see about seventy-five movies a year, she has also reviewed films for *www.crosshome.com*. She can be reached at *janerobe@yahoo.com*.

**Joseph Salazar** is a thirteen-year-old seventh-grade student at Andrews Middle School. He is also autistic. He loves to write and hopes to one day be a writer. He can be reached at *jogie1990@yahoo.com*.

**Barbara Schiller** has been a pioneer and internationally recognized consultant in single-parent family ministry for eighteen years and a psychotherapist for three. She is the founder of Single Parent Family

Resources and former columnist for *Christian Parenting Today* magazine. She is also the author of *Just Me & the Kids*, a support group curriculum for single-parent families: *www.singleparentfamilyresources.com*.

**J. W. Schnarr** lives in Calgary, Alberta. As well as having numerous online publishing and photography credits, his work has appeared in the *Calgary Sun, Circle Magazine* and the *Local Art Scene*. He is currently the story developer for Deadline Interactive.

**Joseph Seldner** runs a medium-sized movie and television production company that has produced, among others, the HBO movie *61\**. He is a Pulitzer Prize–nominated journalist, and his work has appeared in the *New York Times, Los Angeles Magazine* and many others. He has an MBA from Yale and degrees in psychology and journalism from Columbia. Most of all, he is the proud father of Daniel and Laura. He can be reached at *joeseld@earthlink.net*.

**Michael Shawn** was born and raised in Kailua, Hawaii, and after spending time in Seattle, Phoenix, Los Angeles and Boston, he has returned home. He is an aspiring author and would appreciate all comments and criticisms. He can be reached at *kimmchl@aol.com*.

In her prior life, **Kathleen Kersch Simandl** was a teacher in the rural schools of Wisconsin. Now she is retired and living in Mexico, where she sometimes takes time off to enjoy the sunshine. Usually you will find Kathy hunched over the computer—basking in digital photography and writing.

**Wanda Simpson** grew up in Cleveland, Ohio. She holds a bachelor's degree in history and is currently working as an information technology professional in Holland, Michigan. Her first love is writing. She is working on a screenplay based on material touched upon in "About the Doubt." She can be reached at *wlsimpson56@yahoo.com*.

**Gerilynn Smith** studied criminal law and ended up in the educational area of the medical field. She enjoys helping out at her daughter's school when time permits. She likes to work in the garden, travel, go to sporting events (especially her daughter's), beach bonfires with family and friends, and to enjoy each day that God gives her.

**Sande Smith** received a bachelor of arts in Portuguese and Brazilian studies from Brown University. In her search for inner riches, she's found that joy is key: So, she dances every weekend, and writes about amazing women who are creating a world in which all of us are cherished. She can be reached at *sande@globalfundforwomen.org*.

**Donna M. Snow** resides in San José, California, with her six children, who are ages seven to nineteen years old. Her oldest child, her son, now takes every opportunity to tease her about her apparent lack of knowledge in the baking department. Ms. Snow runs a highly successful Web development business and writes whenever she has the time. She can be reached at *donna@snowwrite.com*.

**Barbara Stanley** is an award-winning journalist and the owner of *www.bluestarbase.org*, where she writes political and fictional articles and commentary on today's world scene. She lives in upstate New York and enjoys the country life. She can be reached at *barbara@bluestarbase.org*.

**John Steelman** is currently the district court administrator of the Fourth Judicial District of Kansas. Prior to this job, John was the chief court services officer in the Fourth Judicial District, where he developed one of the first divorce mediation programs in the state of Kansas, after several years of performing child custody investigations for the court. He received his bachelor of science in psychology from Ottawa University in 1978 and his master's in education/counseling from the University of Kansas in 1980.

**Barbara Stephens-Rich** is a United Methodist minister who holds degrees from McDaniel College (B.A. summa cum laude, 1973) and Boston University (M.Div. cum laude, 1976). Barbara currently serves as the director of religion and education at the Lakeside Association, Lakeside, Ohio. Her greatest joy is parenting her two children.

**Carmel Sullivan-Boss** is the founder of Co-Abode, an innovative non-profit organization that connects and supports single mothers and their children. She has been a successful artist/painter and progressive child-centered educator. Her interests include personal development, film, art and travel. She can be reached at *carmel@co-abode.com*.

**Sheryl Templeton** graduated cum laude from Whitworth College and teaches kindergarten at a tiny rural school in northeastern Washington. Sheryl loves rural America and enjoys gardening, writing and oil painting. She can be reached at *sheryltempleton@msn.com*.

Born in Yugoslavia, **Mother Teresa** taught geography at St. Mary's High School in Calcutta from 1928 to 1948 before becoming especially interested in the poorest of poor and starting her own order, the Missionaries of Charity, in 1950. She won many awards, including the Nobel Peace Prize.

**Bob Thurber** grew up in Rhode Island and now lives a charmed life in southeastern Massachusetts. He can be reached at *www.bobthurber.net.*

**Tanya J. Tyler** is a writer and editor in the advertising creative services department of the *Herald-Leader* newspaper in Lexington, Kentucky. She is also working on her master of divinity degree at Lexington Theological Seminary. She can be reached at *Revicet928@aol.com.*

**Jennifer Clark Vihel** is the 2001 winner of the *Chicken Soup for the Writer's Soul* nationwide short-story contest, winning with the short story, "Vamps, Vampires, Elvis and Me." She writes inspirational nonfiction and novels, including the women's fiction, *Trinidad Head*, from a cabin on a creek in Bayside, California.

**George Walther** is an acclaimed speaker and member of the Speakers Hall of Fame. He's authored several books on communication, sales and service topics. After gaining custody of his young daughter, he chose to "demote" his career priority and focus on being a dedicated parent. He can be reached at *george@georgewalther.com.*

**Susan Carver Williams** is a personal historian living in Durham, North Carolina, and founder of Artful Words. She specializes in creating unforgettable memoirs of a lifetime or a special time—including weddings, births and final years—as well as histories through recipes. She can be reached at *susan@artfulwords.com* or *www.artfulwords.com.*

Now a screenwriter, **Marvin J. Wolf** is the author of a dozen books and hundreds of magazine articles. His stories have appeared in several previous *Chicken Soup for the Soul* books, including *A Christmas Treasury for Kids* and *Chicken Soup for the Writer's Soul.* Samples of his writing, and of his award-winning photography, may be viewed at *www.marvwolf.com.*

**Trina Wray** is a twenty-six-year-old child-day-care provider living in Mission, British Columbia, Canada. She is actively pursuing a career in writing and editing, and enjoys hiking, swimming, reading and taking care of her children, both biological and nonbiological. Trina has been a single mother for five years and her daughter will be six in October 2004. She can be reached at *t_wray@shaw.ca.*

**Bob Zahn** has had thousands of his cartoons and several of his humor books published.

**Mary Zisk** in the author/illustrator of the children's picture book *The Best Single Mom in the World: How I Was Adopted*. Professionally a graphic designer, Mary lives in New Jersey with daughter Anna, a poodle, a cockatiel, a guinea pig and fish. Visit her Web site, *www.maryzisk.com.*

**Richard Zmuda** kept a diary as a newly single father during the first year after his young wife passed away from breast cancer. This essay and numerous others, were compiled into a humorous, heartfelt book entitled *A Father's Notes*. He can be reached at *towardcure@aol.com*.

# More Great Books

**#1 New York Times**
BESTSELLING AUTHORS
Jack Canfield
Mark Victor Hansen
Nancy Autio
Patty Aubey
LeAnn Thieman

**Chicken Soup for the Father & Daughter Soul**

Stories to Celebrate the Love
Between Dads & Daughters
Throughout the Years

Code #2521 • Paperback • $12.95

**#1 New York Times**
BESTSELLING AUTHORS
Jack Canfield
Mark Victor Hansen
Dorothy Firman
Julie Firman
Frances Firman Salorio

**Chicken Soup for the Mother & Daughter Soul**

With Stories By:
Joan Borysenko
Jacquelyn Mitchard
Eda LeShan
Laura Lagana
Patricia Lorenz

Stories to Warm the
Heart and Honor
the Relationship

Code #088X • Paperback • $12.95